THE CONFLATION

politics and politrics beyond the ecstasy

Volume 1

NILANTHA ILANGAMUWA

FOR PABASARA

It is not easy to make a commitment while trusting someone whom you have never met in person and make a decision to leave all the materialistic world you have known since you were born with the desire to share the life of the physical unknown. You who made that unbelievable decision, to struggle for peace and calm with comprehensive tolerance, are better people this account of conflation is dedicated to.

CONTENTS

ACKNOWLEDGMENTS

THIS book would have been a day dream if I did not receive gentle feedback and support from readers since I started my work as a journalist when I was 20 years old. Over a decade my life has been determined with an incalculable speed. Though modern technology needs fewer machines to count our own desires it cannot count the real time in the universe that we pass through.

This book contained interviews that I conducted over the last few years as a journalist with various people who have their own causes and reasons to make their lives meaningful. Most of them talked freely and expressed themselves with the facts that they felt important. Some of those expressions were fantasy while some of them were based on the illusion in which they were engaged.

It was no surprise that many "specialists" or "experts" on the subject believed that the LTTE would never be totally defeated, and never achieve the state of Tamil Eelam. But one senior member of the TMVP, which is break-away faction of the LTTE under Col. Karana Amman, who was later lucky enough to deserve a ministerial post in the ruling party, told this writer several times that the total defeat of the LTTE would be possible when the government started fighting against the LTTE in the Eastern Province of Sri Lanka. It was a myth and the result of an exaggeration by the media that many people believed that the LTTE would never be defeated or wiped out, he said while laughing. "This is non-other than a psychological warfare," he added while recounting his experiences with the LTTE for over 10 years.

The undeniable truth is that, people who live on the ground and experience reality know are about the facts than those who engaged at a distance and articulate their theories to fulfill their emptiness. But unfortunately those who are on the ground rarely come forward to share their views. It is then that society needs to stir itself and search for the truth. I have no better way to express this than to quote the serge words of Edward Abbey, *"Society is like a stew. If you don't stir it up every once in a while then a layer of scum floats to the top.* " But, the country which lost hundreds of thousands of lives for the cause of freedom did not evaluate the real cost. And there is hardly any research or factual analysis which is able to tell the story that we are forced to ignore by the 'power'.

Attempts to publish a few voices from the various fields will not fulfill that large vacuum but it may be a small contribution to participate in the debate. This is time for Sri Lanka to get rid of its political vulgarism and politricks. This is the time for Sri Lanka to restore a system which is based on justice and freedom of all citizens.

There are numerous friends and colleagues who helped in publishing this book and it is not possible to name them all. However, I must mention a few. My appreciation goes to Stewart Sloan, a colleague and a friend of mine, who gave his tremendous help in editing and sharing his views on many issues that I had to focus on. Also, I had the good fortune to have, Ryan Anderson and Eric Bailey offer their generous comments and assistance in editing, also my friends, Ron Jacobs for writing a preface to the book and Laksiri Fernando for writing the epilogue.

This book would not have been possible if I did not have the help of Pabasara. She who helped me to put my previous works together and encouraged me to work hard while enduring many burdens, misfortunes and hesitations on our journey. Therefore I thank all of you for being part of my success in volume one of this publication.

Nilantha Ilangamuwa
March 31, 2014
Hong Kong SAR

PREFACE

by RON JACOBS

THERE are those who fear any truth but their own. When these people are in power or aligned with those in power, they monopolize truth itself. If left unchallenged, the truth these people claim becomes universal; no matter how much of it are lies. This is why journalism is supposed to exist; to challenge the powerful and those who pay their bills.

George Orwell, who was one of the first to understand the nature of modern propaganda, is quoted as writing:

"Journalism is printing what someone else does not want printed: everything else is public relations."

If we take Orwell's dictum as genuine truth, then in today's mainstream publishing world, where so many media outlets are owned by so few financial interests, there really are no journalists. Instead, there are thousands of shills—for governments and corporate power. Real journalists—those who "print what someone else does not want printed"— are only found in media that has little or no corporate and government sponsorship. Unfortunately, this media usually has considerably less circulation, as well. There is more than one way to censor information. When one means of censorship is overcome, modern authorities have another to put in its place.

Any journalist who desires to be a true journalist and not merely a pen (or laptop) sold to the highest bidder faces a challenge. They must make a living yet be true to their desire (indeed, their need) to discover the truth behind the official lies and obfuscations. Nilantha Ilangamuwa knows this fact quite well. His life in Sri Lanka was cut short because he challenged the official line on the Tamil people's struggle for self-determination and was witness to the brutal elimination of the Sinhalese youth by security forces in the South. For reasons of his own safety he exiled himself from his native country. The authorities held and interrogated him in the (in)famous interrogation centre known as the Fourth Floor, trying to get him to confess to non-existent links with foreign intelligence agencies. After his exile, Sri Lankan readers in Sri Lanka were denied access to the *Sri Lanka Guardian*, the online newspaper Ilangawuma publishes. There is more than one way to censor information.

The *Conflation* is a collection of interviews conducted by Nilantha Ilangawuma over the past decade, with an interview of the author as its beginning. Most of the interviews discuss the situation in Sri Lanka, while the last few broaden their prism to include the rest of the world, specifically the nations of the west now engaged in their worldwide "War on Terror," an exercise which has meant the end of previously stated principles relating to human rights and the rights of nations and peoples. The ultimate implications of these discussions are yet to be realized. However, the fact of their existence provides us with a hope that journalism will not fail in its true task as elucidated by Mr. Orwell.

[RON JACOBS is the author of All the Sinners, Saints, a novel. He is also the author of The Way the Wind Blew: a History of the Weather Underground and Short Order Frame Up and The Co-Conspirator's Tale. Jacobs' essay on Big Bill Broonzy is featured in CounterPunch's collection on music, art and sex, Serpents in the Garden. His third novel All the Sinners Saints is a companion to the previous two and is due out in April 2013. He is a contributor to Hopeless: Barack Obama and the Politics of Illusion, published by AK Press.]

INTRODUCTION

THE leach needs blood for its survival. The mosquito needs blood for its successful reproduction. The bird needs feathers to in order to fly. An infant needs tears for its protection. The man needs thoughts for his progress. Governing is the formulation of thoughts that were developed during certain periods with the physical experiences of mankind. Everything is interconnected. Everything has its own formula to deal with the subject. As we were taught in high school, man is a political animal, Aristotle observed: realisation of this very fundamental truth can be experienced from the very beginning of your engagement with society. Everybody likes to talk politics, everything on politics is an undeniable idea that we can observe throughout life. But politics, as the subject, has its own frames to articulate the theory than the politricks as the trick that mankind got into the trap to put tyrants in power.

The recent political evolution in Sri Lanka can be understood as one in which one monster defeats another monster to get rid of his personal difficulties. Once he accomplishes his game against his counterpart, eventually, the monster enters other parts of society to eliminate the other layers, to establish "absolutism" and the total elimination of dissent. Autocracies do not need to see the functioning social system. Perhaps its main object is to eliminate the functioning system to strengthen an ego-centric power, which is exactly what has happened to the country. The 18th amendment to the constitution only took this further.

Thus, the 'leaders' of the people can survive only by making people powerless and denying them control over their lives, thanks to the incompetence and brutality of the state. These developments are not accidents or mistakes (*Rajan Hoole , Tamils in Sri Lanka: A nation in limbo*), but were done deliberately. It was a major strategy used by the monster to control and put the entire society in limbo.

To conduct such felonious activities, effective methods had and have to be propagated. To create trust in an autocratic system, one has to destroy the trust in the existing system. That is why we are seeing a huge propaganda machinery conducted by the government while disabling access to the voluntarily funded dissent of media outlets. But few people are able to understand and are daring enough to question how public taxes have been used to brainwash us to further a political agenda. The autocratic juggernaut and its rabid insecure supporters has, on the other hand, the task of buying 'curtains' so multitudes can be influenced in order to change something as common as common sense. This is the real motive behind the actresses/actors, sportsmen, certain sections of the academia and others engaging with President Mahinda Rajapaksa— not though social service or politics but by expanding their personal wealth by appearing on stages of cheap political missions. And in this way they were able control sections of society having a disproportionately influential power for social change.

This idea has been used effectively in many places all over the world. The regimes have urged certain individuals who have the power to change public belief to join in their consolidation of autocracy, so then the regime can make the country into a blind nation, not just a blindfolded one. I can do no better than quote the sage words of Noam Chomsky, "...State propaganda, when supported by the educated classes and when no deviation is permitted from it, can have a big effect. It was a lesson learned by Hitler and many others, and it has". (*Noam Chomsky - Media Control - The Spectacular Achievements of Propaganda*)

In this situation, as Chomsky informs us, "An alternative conception of democracy is that the public must be barred from managing of their own affairs and the means of information must be kept narrowly and rigidly controlled. That may sound like an odd conception of democracy, but it's important to understand that it is the prevailing conception. In fact, it has long been, not just in operation, but even in theory." (Ibid)

Here again we can recall a character named Arthur Abdel Simpson in Eric Ambler's novel Dirty Story, regarding the advice he received as a child from his father, "Although I was only seven when my father was killed. I still remember him very well and some of the things he used to say… One of the first things he taught me was, 'Never tell a lie when you can bullshit your way through'". ('*On Bullshit*', *by Harry G. Frankfurt, p. 48*). The present regime is not only going to tell a lie but will continue to bullshit its way through. This social phenomenon is instantly recognizable when one carefully considers the false fictional stories surrounding the recent attack on the Secretary of the Judicial Service Commission that have been spread by the regime.

> *The power of a community depends not only upon its numbers and its economic resources and its technical capacity, but also upon its beliefs. (Bertrand Russell – Power – P. 99)*

The problem is not rising from outside but rather from within themselves. As long as the world about them does not change, the regime will remain content with their way of life and indeed, feel superior to other people around them as they can ignore them. The trouble is that the world is changing as it happened in the past. This ironically points to the need that we all have to understand, not only what the regime is doing, but also what other organizations are doing as well. However, the present regime is still able to manage the ground situation in the country while continuing their vulgarism as political ideology. Under these circumstances, the regime is still lucky to enjoy their ultimate power.

As long as the opposition parties engage in tickling politics that makes fun for them, the norm of freedom will never be born due to dissimilar power. But the people who are suffering most from this uncertain power would continue to manifest the tensions of life and the nudity of social control. These People represent the insight of the politicians. The current regime is thus seeing itself through this insight, the people, without the clothes of civilization acceptable to outsiders. From time to time, the people come out in their natural form and become visible to the wider world and that is when the regime stands stripped of its clothes.

Keeping a weaker opposition or opposition with multiple internal conflicts or rifts is an important factor for the absolute power to systematically assassinate the social order and introduce disorder to the system. And then, as Slavoj Žižek described, we enter the situation where the regime only "imagines that it believes in itself". In Žižek's words, "The formula of a regime which only imagines that it believes in itself" nicely captures the cancellation of the performative power ("Symbolic Efficiency") of the ruling ideology: it no longer effectively functions as the fundamental structure of the social bond." (*quoted: First As Tragedy Then As Farce --Slavoj Žižek*) This is exactly what Sri Lanka , like others countries in the subcontinent, is facing.

Society's direction has been changed into what we are imaging, and our imagination has always been limited by experiences. Power can create new experiences to limit your exploration and it can put entire society in the cage. Nevertheless, the regime can continually enjoy their rule as long as they are able to break/close the tunnel that updates the people about the dynamics of power. In this situation, the regime is always speaking directly as an emotional vampire and it continues to mobilize a horror mythology. It fuels emotional destruction rather than constructing the wall of common ideologies. It gives birth to intolerance while making cultural diversity of ethnicity, the point of social repression. Depression and hopelessness will be a constant social phenomenon and many people will believe that there is no alternative if we lose the present.

President Mahinda Rajapaksa has created his whole political argument with this principle and has taken the country into his control. What he is carefully engaging in is to control the possibilities of the rise of an alternative force that can tackle the trap. That is why the President is still on the loggia of power even after facing tremendous challenges from the international community and the people who live outside the country. In these circumstances the conditional release of the former Army General Sarath Fonseka was a tactic that the President applied to whitewash his nudity of bad governance. What we cannot forget is that cattle can eat grass as long as its keeper has the reins. In other words, present opposition in the Country is not another version of the quails' story where the quails gave a good lesson for the farmer who tries to hunt them. Today, the opposition in Sri Lanka is the symbol of dissension, which could be possibly changed by an accidental event. Fonseka's first political appearance was an accident, but his second induction created challenges.

On June 17, 2012, it was reported by Colombo-based newspapers that General Fonseka has hardly created a common political front with some politicians while key members of major parties are opposed to joining him. In this situation he will be another different version of old leftist activist -- like a sheep without skin. This is not the first time in political history in Sri Lanka when a rein has used power against its opponents. The sad reality of our country is that political rein works in favour of the power, thus it has destroyed many possibilities of check and balances. If this had not succeeded, the entire society might have changed in 1982 when many opponents were cracked down to assassinate the new dawn of politics by the absolute power. At that time it was the cynical manipulation of power by former President JR Jayawardene that created a priceless loss to our society. None of us seem to have the capability to project that the same incident in different face will be repeated because sincere ignorance and conscientious stupidity are major factors within opposition.

However, nobody can reject the claim by some analysts that the Sarath Fonseka phenomenon is the logical outcome of this process of politicisation of the military. He is not the sole cause but only a significant consequence of this long process. At the same time what we cannot ignore is that as Niccolò Machiavelli noted in his prime work, *The Prince*, "...prince who, relying entirely on their promises, has neglected other precautions, is ruined; because friendships that are obtained by payments, and not by greatness or nobility of mind, may indeed be earned, but they are not secured, and in time of need cannot be relied upon". (*quoted: The Prince - Niccolò Machiavelli*).

Before creating a new front of common opposition, Sri Lanka needs today the courageous rehabilitation of the idea of a pre-emptive strike, "war on terrorism", the most abused words (concept) in the past decade of internal politics. It has expanded absolute power which was introduced through the 18th Amendment to the 1978 Constitution, has created its own justification to infringe freedom and has instigated nepotism. Fonseka's dream to wipe out "rampant corruption and nepotism" prevalent in the country, abolish the executive presidency and restore an independent judiciary will be unreachable without first rehabilitating our ideological wrongness. Then our beliefs will change and fanatical creed will replace rational hopes where new political direction could open.

ABBREVIATIONS

APRC: All Party Representative Committee
AFP: Australian Federal Police
BMICH: The Bandaranaike Memorial International
        Conference Hall
CIA: Central Intelligence Agency
CFA: Cease-Fire Agreement
CWC: Ceylon Workers' Congress
GSP: Generalised Scheme of Preferences
GOSL: Government of Sri Lanka
ICC-International Criminal Court
IPKF: Indian Peace Keeping Force
ISI –Inter Service Intelligence
IDP: Internal Displaced People
JHU: Jathika Hela Urumaya
LTTE: Liberation Tigers of Tamil Eelam
JVP: Janatha Vimukthi Peramuna
NATO: The North Atlantic Treaty Organization
PTA: Prevention of Terrorism Act
R&AW: Research and Analysis Wing
SLMC: Sri Lanka Muslim Congress
SLFP: Sri Lanka Freedom Party
SLG : Sri Lanka Guardian
SLAF : Sri Lanka Air Force
TMVP: Tamil Makkal Vuduthalai Pulighal
TNA: Tamil National Alliance
UGC: University Grand Commission
UN- United Nations
UNP: United National Party
UNCAT: United Nations Committee Against Torture
VOA: Voice Of America

1
PUBLIC AWAKING AGAINST INJUSTICE

"Mahinda is not a Mahatma. He is only extending the established historical hate agenda of the nation much more boisterously. Due to his narrow minded attitude we are unable to praise our real heroes. In the past, we did not have the courage to come forward against injustice and when few did come forward they were killed. It will take time for the people to realise the situation they are in as a result of failing in good governance. Mahinda's foolishness will not be tolerated forever and the people will respond in kind and it is not too far away."
-Nilantha Ilangamuwa

THE following interview was conducted by the Salem News with the author of this book. It was widely re-published by several media.

Nilantha Ilangamuwa is an ambitious young journalist purged by the government for his conviction to uphold freedom of speech and independence of media in the island nation.

He was taunted by the agents of the government and its secret service for fearlessly managing the *Sri Lanka Guardian* that is continuing to expose several sensitive news that is causing major irritation to the government.

The very first point in the nine points mission statement of the *Sri Lanka Guardian* says it all: 'Adhere to the journalistic values of honesty, courage, fairness, balance, independence, credibility and diversity, giving no priority to commercial or political considerations over professional ones'. With that strong commitment, the *Sri Lanka Guardian* is fearlessly striving even after being officially banned by the President Mahinda Rajapaksa's government.

In his first-ever interview with the media, Nilantha Ilangamuwa, the editor and founder of the *Sri Lanka Guardian*, a well-known online newspaper on Sri Lanka, visualized the regime that is governing Sri Lanka.

He says the government will have to find its way out of its hypocritical politics and he feels that there would be an awakening of masses against the very foundation of bad governance embedded in the habitual political life of lies and crony vulgarism. He claims that these are the despicable core values of the government to stay in power.

In this interview, he talks about his profession, experience and his understanding of inherent problems in the country.

Question (Q): What made you to go into media?

Answer (A); Well, several reasons influenced me to become a journalist. I was born in the central hill country, where one could see more of the darkness of the country, than in other parts.

Most of the people in the village do farming and this was what my parents were doing. As a child during the late 80's, I witnessed the bloody JVP riots during which many youths were assaulted, killed and their possessions looted. I still remember going with my parents and friends to see half burnt dead bodies lying here and there on the roads in our village.

Some of our neighbors were also killed in the riots. I would say most of those victims were innocent civilians who did not have any political engagement at all. Many in fear, sought refuge and came to our house too. Our house was located further away from the main road.

They came to us for their protection and spent days and nights at our house in the dark. The whole village was shocked by the massacre. All that the villagers wanted was peaceful life. But the politicians and their henchmen played their dirty role with the lives of the innocent people– it was back then, but unfortunately this campaign is even continuing now in a subtle way. You can call it a systematic state terrorism that is consuming the lives of the people.

Almost everyone in our village was fed-up with the way politicians were conducting themselves.

I left the village for higher education, during which period, I acquired good understanding of the ethnic crisis progressing in the country.

As the president of the student union, with the guidance of my school headmaster, I organized an event to interact with the inmates of a rehabilitation camp for the LTTE suspects based in Bindunuwawa and Bandarawela, where hundreds of us and the LTTE suspects spent a whole day together.

It was first time in our school history that we had this kind of experience. We all gained a lot from it and the LTTE suspects and some of LTTE cadres who had surrendered to the Army prepared foods for the students, performed dramas and played cricket with us. I recall, a former LTTE rebel Chandrasekaran. I was the commentator of the day's events.

It was for the very first time in my life, I spoke to a LTTE rebel, who seemed to have had a very good understanding of the problem that we all were facing. He talked fluently in Sinhala and told me that the rehabilitation process would not work unless the government is in a position to solve problems associated with the essential needs of the ordinary masses.

'I don't think, this rehabilitation process will work' even the army colonel (as he referred to him who was of in-charge of the camp) had said. Chandrasekaran said ' 'Sir' is a very good hearted man with good understanding of intricacies of the problem'.

'I joined the LTTE at my own will and fought with the only objective to get parity of states with the majority. It is true that we ordinary people whether Sinhalese, Tamil or Muslims, don't have any problems with each other, but these politicians are using us for their own benefits. When I am released from this camp, I will go home and spend some time peacefully and then will join the LTTE' he said.

He made these comments whilst we were having our meal together. His views and the other LTTE suspect's friendly attitude inspired us, and most of the students talked about them very positively.

Few years later, we heard the news that there was a massacre at the Bindunuwawa detention camp in which more than 20 LTTE suspects were slaughtered by the Sinhalese extremists motivated by the racist politicians.

This was the time when I started to work as a journalist. I still remember one report headlined 'human flesh for Lions' in the media. Sadly, this is the pathetic side of our beautiful country where these extremists dictate the lives of our people.

These two core incidents influenced me very much in addition to my personal interest to be a journalist – for example the urge to write, the will to know and to be known and to be heard by other people in my society; a desire to influence the good in my society and the thirst for knowledge, etc. were some of the personal reasons that guided me to become a journalist.

However, my family members were unhappy from the beginning that I was leaning towards journalism. My mother said to me: 'being a journalist you will do nothing to help the society but it is an unnecessary risk to your life. At crucial times there will be no one to help you and they will point the finger at you'.

However, I always dreamt to be an independent writer with good command of the languages. This gave me the innermost strength to become a professional journalist.

As human beings, we may be unable to find people who are one hundred percent perfect and mistakes are always possible. It's true that journalism in reality is not the journalism that we learnt in the university. It is far from it. But there are some dedicated persons in the world who genuinely seek to expresses their true hearts into words to share their real experiences. Assassinated Sunday Leader editor Lasantha Wickramatunge is one of them. His inspiring extraordinary article from his grave was published three days after he was assassinated by the government goons in Colombo. The letter said it all about the status of Sri Lanka.

Q: Let us know the Newspapers that you have served before becoming an independent web-publisher.

A: I started writing when I was 18 years old. A year after I came out of school, I published the Monthly Magazine called *Siwdesa*. I was one of the main contributors to the Magazine and my mentor was Sandun Gunasinghe, who is the son of late Dayasena Gunasinghe, who was the founder and chief editor of *Divaina*, a weekly edition. Let me talk a bit about this.

Sandun had deep understanding of journalism, but later he was away from the field due to some personal reasons and the bitter experiences he had experienced in his work. During that time, he shared his father's experiences with me and told me about how colleagues of the same paper had indulged in foul play.

Once he told me about an editorial written by his father, that was critical of the President J R Jayawardhane's unethical politics. One of the deputy editors, translated that editorial into English and gave it to President JRJ who could not read Sinhala.

A close ally of the President visited him with the article and the translation and told him that the writer is against the President and that he must do something immediately to deal with the write up. The trouble makers are the pathetic predators in this profession. It was one of main reasons that influenced the late Gunasighe to say goodbye to that paper and start the magazine Siwdesa where I started my journalism. Late Gunasinghe was a real hero of Sri Lankan journalism, even though not many today talk about his service.

It is very common in our culture that people with acclaim are not appreciated whilst the corrupts thrive are mushrooming all over. Late Gunasinghe never accepted any benefits from the state to mitigate his writings. He was a born an independent and lived as an independent and died with self-esteem too. I recall that his house was half constructed, when he and his family were facing troubles. At that time high level ministers offered him large sums, but he never accepted them.

After my work at *Siwdesa*, I moved to *Divaina*, which is a sister paper of the Island published by the Upali Newspapers Group. I worked there for few years and contributed a lot, but suddenly there was an internal conflict in management. One group that had extreme views, tried to kick the editor out. I too got caught in the debacle and was accused as an agent of foreign intelligence agencies helping the separatists.

But I never supported the separatists or separatism. I was one of those who strongly criticized the LTTE's violent attacks on civilians. I was never against Tamil people that was what some writers misinterpreted.

I know many writers who wrote what the politicians wanted them to project. I still remember one of the deputy editors of the newspaper who was always proud of the maverick Minister Marvyn Silva saying that, "every month I receive essential stuffs from the Minister'.

However, after Divaina, I worked with Mawbima, (which was later banned by the Government) and the Sunday Standard. The Sunday Standard was the first paper where I started my journalism in English. Hanna Ibrahim was my first editor, and she gave me all the encouragement to develop my skills. My entering into English medium brought troubles with some of my colleagues who wrote bad things about me and expressed strong criticisms.

Q: Please provide us the names of the websites you have run and why some of them were abandoned.

A: Before I started the *Sri Lanka Guardian*, I used to write for few web sites. In August 2007, I started the *Sri Lanka Guardian* as a result of the banning of our existing newspapers by the Government saying that we are helping the LTTE. As far as I know, we never helped the LTTE, but there were articles that were from Tamil people. Back then, we had the slogan – 'Our Journalism is not only for the South but even beyond that of Omanthei check point.' Omanthei was the border post for the government and the Tamil Tigers.

The reason why the *Sri Lanka Guardian* was banned was simple. It was because the government thinks that the *Sri Lanka Guardian* and few other websites can cause harm to the public opinion about the government. It is true that we were criticising the Government and its allies because in a democracy we have the fundamental right to do so.

We are not subjects of an autocratic King, but are citizens of the country contributing to the advancement of our people who pay taxes out of their hard earned income.

The government seems to believe that these websites that are character assassinating the ministers and their leaders and the officialdom that provides unaccountable service to the masters.

What is wrong in the character assassination when the very same eccentrics in the government who point their fingers at us publicly character assassinate themselves. Whether these men have good "character" to promote is another matter. If they are really concerned, they must first abandon the state run newspapers before they attack the websites as they are the ones originating the news about these dubious characters.

Banning the websites like ours is simply a paranoia that is pervading the massive intelligence service of the government.

Q: What are the core values or principles of the SLG? Who are your contributors?

A: Well, as I told you earlier, the *Sri Lanka Guardian* was started in August 2007 after the newspapers I worked for were banned by the government. There was threat on other papers too, not to recruit those journalists who had worked for the banned newspaper company that I worked for. I had no choice and started the *Sri Lanka Guardian*, with a group of friends, most of them were based outside Sri Lanka. I personally invited some well-known writers and analysts to contribute to our website. Our basic principle is to open the gate for voiceless people and facilitate the freedom to express their views, feelings and thoughts without any fear. *Sri Lanka Guardian* is an open forum and accommodates diverse views even if they offend the government, groups or individuals so long as they are just, fair and truthful.

Today, the *Sri Lanka Guardian* has many contributors from several countries and there is no need to mention all by their names.

Q: You are an exiled journalist. What made you to leave the country? Will you or can you return to Sri Lanka now or in the future.

A: The intelligence service attached to the Military of Defense started to follow me for a while. They arrested and interrogated me in the notorious fourth floor cell in Colombo for over 6-7 hours. Following that, an order was given by a top military man to take necessary action against me.

Without proper reasons and based on gossips, the government took this decision against me. The gossip was that a government pampered the gutter media based in Helsinki run by a notorious money launderer who accused me of links with the Indian Intelligence Service- Research and Analysis Wing (R&AW). According to the news, I am a R&AW agent because I published articles of former high profile R&AW officials in the *Sri Lanka Guardian*. This was the cause for the intelligence to take action against me.

I didn't and don't have any agenda as accused by the government. If at all, it is the nefarious Helsinki gutter editor who had an agenda. He meets the President when the President visits the West and the government provide him with five star facilities to engage with him and to receive advise. This controversial man was part of the jumbo team of campaigners of Sri Lanka at the UNHCR session in Geneva.

These types of association with the unscrupulous persons are rotting Sri Lanka. They are been used to prop up charges against individuals and I am a victim of this degrading conduct. These are done at a heavy cost to the victims, whist ensuring the reprehensible agent's safes are always loaded with laundered funds to provide the government with their despicable service.

I still remember, as an independent reporter when I went to Jaffna to report on the ongoing war. This irritated a top military official who became suspicious of my presence. Later, I came to know that they kept a distance from me because they had received calls from Colombo warning of my involvement with the R&AW.

When I reached Muhamalai, where hundreds of soldiers were killed by the Tamil Tigers once, one of the commanding officers who got to know me realized that I did not have any links as others had claimed. But the campaign of caricaturing me as a R&AW agent extended further and many other writers followed the scandal generated by the Helsinki opportunist.

My safety in Sri Lanka became precarious and there was ample evidence that the Government will target me. It was the main reason why I left the country with the help of Mr. Basil Fernando of the Asian Human Rights Commission. If I'm an agent of the RAW, then why should the AHRC help me?

If I had remained in Sri Lanka, by now I would been six feet below the ground or my body destroyed without any trace of evidence. If not for Mr. Basil Fernando my fate would have been in the hand of the government's death squad.

The day that the government pampered Helsinki website started to attack me by saying that I am an agent of the RAW, I phoned the Defense Secretary Gotabhaya Rajapaksa and I asked for his advice and assistance.

I was surprised when he said, 'Nothing will happen if you make a complaint to the police. Only thing you must do is to attack them back. It must be tit for tat response'. I was astonished to hear his comment. If this had happened in a responsible democracy, the response would have been to protect me. Gothabaya holding a green card of the USA should have shown maturity in his handling of my call.

The current situation is precarious for the exiled journalists to return to Sri Lanka. The government does not like any form of opposition. Killing the chicken to scare the monkey is a proverb that projects the government's attitude.

The President's policy is clearly– 'if you're not with us you're a traitor of the Nation'. This speaks volume of the mindset of the government. The very basis of trust needed for good governance has been torpedoed in Sri Lanka. There is worry that the autocratic rule will go further to reflect regimes like that of Stalin's Russia, Pol Pot's Cambodia and Bokassa of Africa.

Q: Why did GoSL ban the *Sri Lanka Guardian*? Are you affected by this decision?

A: The *Sri Lanka Guardian* was banned because of its outspoken stand and as a result of government sympathetic dubious and intolerant worms in the media like the one operating from Helsinki dictating terms. Soon after the ban, we published an editorial quoting an Assyrian proverb: 'I need not fear my enemies because the most they can do is attack me. I need not fear my friends because the most they can do is to betray me. But I have much to fear from people who are indifferent.'

The response on the ban is mixed. The readership from outside Sri Lanka has grown whilst readers in Sri Lanka has been denied access. Even the dedicated readers from Sri Lanka are accessing *Sri Lanka Guardian* via proxy web links. What we published is reproduced in many websites that are not affected by the ban. According to statistics more than five hundred thousand people were accessing our site a month before the ban and after the ban readership went down dramatically and we are seeing steady increase now but not of the scale experienced before.

Going further, to the obsessed government, the *Sri Lanka Guardian* is guilty of publishing articles upholding the fundamental democratic value of freedom of speech. The *Sri Lanka Guardian* is the voice of the oppressed and an outspoken media on issues that the state wishes to suppress. It gives opportunities to wide range of views, including that of the opposing. This is what the government wants us to compromise and become a poodle media like those surviving under its control.

The legal idiom: 'You are innocent until proved guilty' has no meaning in Sri Lanka, as one is made guilty and punished before charges are even framed. We were fascinated to read the news of the government, that the banned web media should contact the Information Ministry to have a chat to remove the ban. The *Sri Lanka Guardian* will not enter into any pleas when sword of the Damocles is held on its head.

Q: GoSL says it wants some discipline in the media. Why can't you abide by this?

A: What Sri Lanka needs is media freedom where news is reported freely and responsibly and opinions expressed without fear. In order to maintain accountable media there must be mechanisms to deal with complaints and a responsible legal system to deal with claims. The control of media from the biased politicians must be shifted to an independent authority and judiciary too must be made independent from the politicians to make fair decisions.

When the government agenda is motivated to control the media to reflect only its voice, the voice of the *Sri Lanka Guardian* has become a thorn in the flesh to face heavy sanctions.

Q: Have you applied for registration with the GoSL? If not why?

A: No, we have not applied and may not apply under present circumstances. The banning of some media is an agenda to silence the independent web media.

The government's approach on this is pathetic. It rushed and introduced the ban following local and international pressures from its supporters. To this date, we have not received any official notification of the ban. They banned the websites based on a pending law. What this pending law is? It is clearly, a bull in the china shop situation- destroying the very foundation of democracy for selfish reasons.

Our registration with the domain company binds us and we follow the publication laws. You can't open even free email service without registration or signing an agreement.

Q: What is your readership prior to the ban and now?

A: Until last October, we had more than five hundred thousand readers per month, which works out to be over twenty thousand per day. But at the end of November last year following the ban, around three hundred thousand access were registered. But it is progressively increasing.

Q: Is SLG reaching Sri Lanka? If not, do you have alternative strategies?

A: The readers cannot access the *Sri Lanka Guardian* in Sri Lanka after the ban. But they can access through proxy websites. We are however maintaining free email service for our readers through which they can receive all the updates of the SLG daily. We are also using social networks and micro blogging sites to reach Sri Lanka. In the future, we are planning to technically expand our website to reach Sri Lanka in a much bigger scale.

Q: There is a claim that you have link with the TMVP, the de facto faction of the LTTE which was led by Karuna Amman, who is a Minister in the present government. What do you have to say on this?

A. As a journalist, I have contacts not only with TMVP but also with wide range of links. Without contacts how can you manage a news-site? I was the first journalist to interview Karuna after the formation of the TMVP and after he came to Colombo, following his imprisonment in London.

I met him several times at his office in Narahenpita, Colombo. He also called me frequently. We had many discussions, but nothing beyond journalism and all the time I spoke to him about the national issues.

At one point he was in deadly conflict with Pillayan as a result of the Helsinki money laundering journalist's campaign, who fermented a wedge between both. I have written to TMVP officials about recruitment of child soldiers by the group, and about poverty in the eastern province.

With Karuna joining the government, his intentions too changed. He joined hands with the government intelligence service and caused problems for me personally and the SLG.

Q: What do you wish to say to the GoSL?

A: The Sinhala saying 'don't try to play your fiddle to a deaf elephant' is my advice to the Sri Lanka government. In my life, I voted only once and it was during 2005 presidential election. We were inspired to vote for President Rajapaksa, even though knowing about his very many worrying problems in his political career including that of the murder in Beliatta and exclusively patronising his southern base Hambanthota. Many people have good thoughts about the President. Perhaps they still believe he will restore rule of law in the country.

War against the LTTE was an important factor. I was always saying people from all walks of life must be stakeholders in the effort. But at the end, the President and his family members took advantage of the war effort and used it to undermine the peoples' rights. Both Tamil and Sinhalese as well as Muslims, became easy pawn to the power hungry Rajapaksa & Co., and Mahinda is trying to portray him as the greatest leader Sri Lanka had by defeating the Tamils like the historical Dutugemunu.

What we have to realize is that terrorism is the product of failures of the state. The Government killed the terrorism three years ago, but the deep rooted disease is still festering.

Medication for the disease is not just devolution or giving police some power or dealing with the land power to selected institutions but it must be restoring rule of law for the entire country and devolving powers without any hidden agendas.

For that, the President must prove he is honest and sincere and will go beyond his vote bank to become a statesman. You can't solve long term problems by ducking and diving. Good governance practices must progressively come into the administration of the government.

To achieve this, constitutional changes must be brought in to ensure defined, independent, responsible and accountable divisions of powers between executive, legislative and judicial mechanisms and devolvement of powers for the people to participate in their affairs, thus facilitating a short to long term plan to address the grievances of the minorities. Anti-minority sentiments in the state bureaucracy must be weaned out and broadminded officialdom must play its due role to create better governance in the country.

Further, state interference in the freedom of speech must be brought to end together with the closure of impunity enjoyed by the state and its agents that is undermining the people's right to live and liberty.

I had a long conversation with Lal Wickramatunge (the brother of assassinated Lasantha Wickramatunga of the Sunday Leader) about a report published by the *Sri Lanka Guardian*. He told me that his dead father's ashes that was brought from abroad, was mishandled and thrown away by the officials at the Colombo airport.

This country belongs to all of us but what the President seems to be thinking that it only belongs to his family and friends. In order to give an image that he is the peoples man, he portrays himself down to earth in front of the people.

Q: What do you wish to say to the people in Sri Lanka and the world at large about your predicament and also about your wishes?

A: Mahinda is not a Mahatma. He is only extending the established historical hate agenda of the nation much more boisterously. Due to his narrow minded attitude we are unable to praise our real heroes. In the past, we did not have the courage to come forward against injustice and when few did come forward they were killed. It will take time for the people to realise the situation they are in as a result of failing in good governance. Mahinda's foolishness will not be tolerated forever and the people will respond in kind and it is not too far away.

President Rajapaksa is an extension of the old breed of hate politics. He is thinking that the world is still in the 70s and 80s. If he continue to extend his hegemonic heroic policies, only the time will make him a discredited villain.

People are now coming forward and seeking justice. How far Mahinda & Co., will tolerate this changing trend when they are getting cornered in many fronts is a real worry and if it escalates further, his regime may unleash spate of calculated violence against the people like what happened in 1915 (Gampola) , 1956 (Galoya), 1958, 1977 and 1983.

Intolerance to injustice could be an alternative though. That could be the creation of a real opposition. Such an opposition will lead to balance of power. Balance of power could lead to the creation of principles for good governance. Good governance will help change the present state of social disorder to social order. This may lead to the creation of the basic institutions that today do not exist in the country. But, the present regime is deliberately engaged in sabotaging every possibility of such a dream becoming true. The government of Sri Lanka is engaged in the systematic elimination of everything and everyone who is intolerant to injustice.

See what has happened to this President. His own commissions of inquiries, promises to provide justice and his rantings to find a durable political resolution acceptable to all the people have been proved a façade. He was able to use his authoritative card of defeating the LTTE all these while. But finally got caught on the implementation of LLRC report. His manipulations did not work internationally and the matter has now reached the UN forum.

International awareness of his deceptive practices is the reflection of the frustration that is prevailing in Sri Lanka which the President is trying to undermine by the traditional emotive and hate mongering politics.

The LLRC must be the starter to bring about good governance in Sri Lanka. Mahinda will be made to implement it and if he fails, Sri Lanka will continue to face pressures from the international community. In the event of not responding to the UNHRC resolution, Sri Lanka will enter into the next phase when the UN effort will impose an international inquiry. If this too is undermined, the matter will certainly reach the Security Council. Sri Lanka cannot take comfort that China and Russia will help preventing a Security Council resolution. Sudan is a good example when friendly Russia and China abstained on the vote against the resolution.

If Sri Lanka antagonizes India to prop up China, it will put Sri Lanka into greater peril. If India decides to take decisive steps against Sri Lanka to exert its regional authority, China will find it hard to interactively support Mahinda. The situation will become worse when India is backed by the West and it has the clout to influence Russia.

Sri Lanka is starting to face the indirect sanctions as a result of aids not filtering through from the West and due to US sanctions against Iran. If Sri Lanka attempts to undermine the carrot and stick policy of the international community and play deceptive games to enjoy the carrots only, it is expected to face serious consequences in the international field.

Mahinda has made the biggest mistake by exposing his siblings and relatives in the partnership business of administering Sri Lanka in a scale unprecedented in the history of Sri Lanka. This could lead to serious consequences when his family members collectively participate in the failures and the end result could be of any ones guess.

Finally, I can only tell my brethrens back home that unless they wide open their eyes and respond to the country's leadership beyond the parochial prejudices, the Mahinda administration will only lead them to peril.

April 04, 2012

2
TAMILS ARE A VANISHING COMMUNITY

We Tamils as a people have a right to live under a culture we choose. The very presence of Tamils in Sri Lanka living as Tamils is being ideologically challenged by the JVP and JHU. The fighting and the attendant safety issues raised increase this challenge as people leave - leave the North-East and leave Sri Lanka.

- Ratnajeevan Hoole

PROFESSOR S. Ratnajeevan H. Hoole, former Vice Chancellor, University of Jaffna, who was forced to flee Sri Lanka because of death threats by the LTTE, in a no-holds-barred interview, gives his view on political developments in the country, refugee influx in the East, LTTE activities in the Jaffna University, literacy rate in Jaffna and his position as the VC. This interview was conducted in 2007 when the country was facing the final war between the security forces and the Tamil Tiger guerrillas.

Question(Q): What do you think about the current political developments in the Country?

Answer (A) : I am very sad at the developments and only hope that good sense will prevail. There is no military solution. As long as there are Tamil people in Sri Lanka and they are not treated as equal citizens, there will be no solution. So long as Tamils are denied their due place, young hot-blooded youth will always feel inclined to join militant movements.

Q: The Government says the East will be liberated within a few weeks. What do you think?

A: Liberated from what? The history of the East has always been being under somebody's cruel boot. I am personally aware of eastern Tamil students who had under-age brothers hiding in their rooms at Peradeniya to escape LTTE forced recruitment. I have had students who were in a company of other students of whom some were killed by the STF and they had escaped only because they were able to beg the soldiers for their lives in Sinhalese. Today by all accounts Col. Karuna who troubled Eastern Tamils with LTTE power is continuing the same, this time in the name of the eastern people with government backing. Strange, isn't it, that those who appoint themselves our representatives invariably seem to be acting against our very interests? In times of war, the cruelty of man towards man is the natural order and I do not believe the army's winning would represent any liberation. The large numbers of refugees are an indication of the continuing misery and the callousness of authorities to that misery.

If the army wins as you seem to predict, it would be short term. Soldiers are tense in war time and will be cruel to the citizens they control. It can only mean greater Tamil militancy and even greater misery for us Tamils.

Q: Many organisations have blamed the government for creating a large number of refugees in the East. They even say that it's a big humanitarian crisis in the Country. What are your remarks?

A: Bull's eye! I fully agree. The Tamils or the Sinhalese cannot prosper while putting down the other. A catastrophe for the Batticaloa Tamil is as much a catastrophe for the Jaffna Tamil and the Sinhalese and indeed the whole country.

Q: What is the Eastern peoples' challenge?

A: You are right in saying peoples. Yes the East has peoples.

Tamils who assert their right as a people cannot deny the rights of Muslims as a people and perhaps even the rights of Eastern Tamils to peoplehood if that is what they wish.

In some ways the rights of the Eastern people to have their distinct ways have been challenged as they were subjected to greater forced recruitment and had to bear the greater brunt of military onslaughts by the state and child recruitment. I believe that most of the TELO cadre massacred in Jaffna as the IPKF left were from the East. As the government colonized the East and Tamil villages were depopulated through massacres by the STF, it is the East that suffered in ways the North had never seen or imagined. However, the Eastern peoples' challenge is a common challenge to all Tamils. The strongest reason for Federalism is that we Tamils need an area where we can live in safety, free of the massacres by the army we have seen in the East. The permanent merger of the North-East is so emotive because it is our guarantee of safety in numbers, especially the safety of eastern Tamils. Anything by Tamil groups like denial of freedoms, internecine murders and child-recruitment that makes Tamils feel unsafe in the North-East weakens this argument.

We Tamils as a people have a right to live under a culture we choose. The very presence of Tamils in Sri Lanka living as Tamils is being ideologically challenged by the JVP and JHU. The fighting and the attendant safety issues raised increase this challenge as people leave - leave the North-East and leave Sri Lanka. Remember that at the time of independence we 'Tamil speaking peoples' were close to 27% of the population. The fissures with the Muslims were a major debacle. Jaffna Tamil callousness as our plantation brethren were disfranchised resulted in further reduction in Tamil numbers as many of them were repatriated. Today with many of us having fled to India, Canada, and Europe, our total Tamil numbers combining so called Ceylon and Indian Tamils are down to about 11.2% -- the bulk of these outside the North- East and in the estates. No one talks about this. For the government it is embarrassing. For us Tamils the real numbers would mean fewer seats in Parliament and lower university quotas. So we all pretend that Tamils are at the level of the last census in 1981. This prevents Tamils from recognizing the real problem of our being a vanishing community. A few more years of this war, we Tamils may not exist in Sri Lanka as a people. That is our greatest challenge. And any war that leads to that is not liberation.

Q: The Vice Chancellor of Eastern University was kidnapped a few months ago. But it is not known what happened to him. What are your remarks?

A: His kidnapping is a measure of the sickness that has overcome Tamil society. It is deplored unequivocally. Having said that I am also duty bound to say that such kidnapping is nothing new at Eastern University. Previously VC Santhanam and Acting VC Thangarajah were kidnapped. VC Mookiah was surrounded by the student union which demanded his resignation and he fled to the South with only the clothes he had on and resigned. All three are from outside Jaffna. Eastern Deans have also been kidnapped (Ramakrishna, Balasugumar). At a university where Ph.D-holding staff are rare, easterners Dr. K. Kobindarajah and Dr. Thriuchelvan were threatened (the latter by a shot to the thigh) and are abroad now still defending their positions as the Council has given notice of termination. Why are those Tamil newspapers and NGOs that were silent on these atrocities against scholars then, now having a correct but mysteriously sudden interest in a kidnapping in the East? Is it because Col. Karuna is the prime suspect in Prof. Raveendranath's case while the other atrocities were by the LTTE? Let us do all we can to secure Prof. Raveendranath's safety but be equally conscientious when people we may like or fear do the same thing to people who are not from Jaffna. I too felt a burdensome loneliness when I was under pressure to quit Jaffna. Tamil newspapers had news releases (by anonymous organizations claiming to speak in the name of the people of Jaffna) given to them to print. The editor of a major newspaper told me that he had no choice but to print these and could help only by printing replies. (As an afterthought he rhetorically asked me, "But who is there to reply?") He added that there are reporters less than 25 years in age who are sent to him to employ and that he cannot pull out what they write, but again could only print replies. I suppose the Free Media Movement would say that they did not know of this situation to protest against the pressures suffered by Tamil newspapers as they freely do against government pressure.

Q: University of Jaffna was a huge base of Tamil military movements' propaganda during the past. Could you explain that history?

A: The university is a non-political academic institution that is supposed to advance learning. But we academics have failed to uphold this academic tradition. It is sad that this politicization seems to come from the very top. As reported in Tamil Net on July 5, 2006 with colour photos, Prof. Kumaravadivel, the man handpicked by the UGC to cover my duties as VC, celebrated Black Tigers Day at the university, joined by high LTTE officials. He led the occasion by lighting the traditional oil lamp. I suppose the VC's entertainment budget was used for the tea that followed. A previous Vice Chancellor had a stainless steel monument for fallen Tigers built right in the middle of the campus. I hope government funds were not used for it.

Jaffna degrees have been issued to several people who never sat the exams. After exposure of the scandal, the university has not moved to withdraw the degrees. The newspapers that originally raked it up also suddenly fell silent. The UGC too has been silent despite the press. This makes clear the affiliation of those who graduated thus from Jaffna.

I think the TULF, a party to which I have emotional and family ties, must accept some responsibility for this politicization of the young. Frustrated by lack of advancement of Tamil rights through Parliament, the party embarked on so called protest boycotts demanding schools and shops to shut down as often demanded. When some expressed doubts, the party used the youth as goon-squads to enforce its will and lost control as our youth, drunk with new power, got radicalized.

Q: Whom have you identified as the agents of terrorism?

A: Terrorism in Sri Lanka has come from the state, the JVP and the LTTE. The state as legitimate authority has the largest onus to do things right. It is sad that a minister in this government, Champika Ranawaka, can remain a minister after publicly saying "If [terrorists] can't be dealt [with] with existing laws, we know how to do it. If we can't suppress those bastards with the law, we need to use any other ways." What moral authority then has a government to condemn those who resort to terrorism while a respectable minister threatens terrorism? However the state has fulfilled its role creditably with respect to rehabilitating the JVP and obviating some of the causes of its radicalism. I know from my university days that colleagues who had joined the JVP were treated with a generosity never shown to the LTTE. I remember sitting exams with JVP friends who had been given books in prison and brought to the exam hall to sit with me and are engineers today. A person from the second insurrection after release from jail graduated and even became my rather youthful boss at Peradeniya and simultaneously the Chairman of a state corporation. Others are even MPs and until recently Ministers.

On the other hand, Bindunuwewa with its shameful impunity and a judiciary sympathetic to those who murdered youthful persons under rehabilitation is what Tamils remember of LTTE rehabilitation. We Tamils and Sinhalese are obviously not equal children of the state.

Q: Are you satisfied about government politics in the North and East?

A: Things are far better than they were up to 1994. But political wisdom seems to be in short supply again today - especially the wisdom that terrorism is not fought through wars but through addressing the causes that make normally good people resort to terrorism because there seems to be no other way. The government must have the wisdom to implement the language laws in the North-East, and establish a federal system there minimally with powers over land, education, police and taxation and punish soldiers who terrorize the public. With some firm international guarantees over the behavior of the other side, I believe the country would quickly be transformed into a place that all of us would love to live in, and call our own. The BC pact was acceptable to Tamils at that time but seems too little today in the light of all that we have been through. Thus as we delay, all the feasible options become more and more extreme to Sinhalese and less and less enough to Tamils. The UNP-PA pact must be revived if something is to be done quickly.

Q: Could you recollect your experiences at University of Jaffna working as a Vice Chancellor?

A: I am glad you asked. I was appointed VC/Jaffna effective March 12 by the President. University of Peradeniya accordingly released me to Jaffna. I functioned from Colombo, issued instructions as VC and represented the university in official capacity. There is record of all this at the UGC.

Because of threats to my life the UGC gave me leave to go abroad. It is noteworthy that the UGC giving me leave was necessarily recognition of my being VC. If not, it would have been only up to Peradeniya to consider my leave.

Since my departure, events have taken an unfortunate turn. I have not been paid my salary since March 12, 2006, not even for the period of my approved leave. The UGC does not reply or even acknowledge receipt of my several letters. I have emailed the Chairman with copies to the Secretary. I have faxed letters to the Chairman's fax and to the Secretary's fax. All to no avail! Prof. Parameshwaran, the most senior academic at the university and former Dean of Medicine agreed to cover my duties provided the UGC also asked. The UGC did. He faxed the UGC in the morning of one day saying that he had begun work at the VC's office. After "a visit" by some persons, he faxed the UGC the same day in the afternoon saying that he is unable to cover my duties. After Prof. Kumaravadivel was allowed by these visitors to function, Prof. Parameshwaran wrote a justly angry letter to the UGC and others pointing out the situation where such a person is allowed to cover my duties. Prof. Kuamaravidivel who now covers my duties at the request of the UGC has signed letters placing my seal "Vice Chancellor, University of Jaffna".

It is relevant that there can be no Acting VC either, since it would mean that there is no VC. It creates the problem of salaries for 2 persons as VC when there is financial provision for only one person to be paid as VC. The UGC seems to have thought that it is all right to hand over the university and drop me quietly so that they can be seen to be maintaining order.

As far as I know the law, only the President can remove me from the post of VC. He may well do so but I have not been informed of such precipitous action by him. Until the President removes me, there can be no other VC or even Acting VC for University of Jaffna, .unless I vacate office or my 3-year term ends If the UGC wants me to step aside in the interests of the university I will do so. But then it must tell me so. Ignoring me is certainly not the gentlemanly way to deal with a VC and former Commission Member.

Q: How are the LTTE activities in the University?

A: I have been out now for a year to comment. But I understand that a Jaffna Council Member, to the great chagrin of the UGC Chairman, had asserted at an official meeting with the UGC that Sri Lankan laws do not apply there. I would urge the LTTE to allow the university to be independent. It is in the Tamil interest to develop the university and we cannot expect the Sri Lankan government to be whole-hearted about pouring money into a university where the government has little say.

Q: Do you justify any university students being involved with politics?

A: As adults all university students are entitled to engage in politics. But our politics must be confined to the legal. The real problem was brought about by the Sri Lankan political system being non-responsive to the parliamentary politics of Tamil moderates. When moderates could show no progress on behalf of the Tamils who had elected them, there was frustration and young people took to street politics and then to guns. What you see at the university is a response to frustration with the ineffectiveness of civilized methods. It is a sign of the failure of the Sri Lankan polity.

Q: Many students of University of Jaffna have been killed by unidentified gunman during the past. It's a catastrophe for future of students. What are your remarks?

A: I agree it is a catastrophe. That is why all parties must leave the university alone and depoliticise it.

Q: Who is this shadow killer?

A: There is no one shadow killer. My information is that the Army, the LTTE and several Tamil victims of the LTTE now working with the army are engaged in tit-for-tat killings.

Q: Could you tell us about your opinion about PTA [Prevention Terrorism Act]?

A: The PTA has no place in a civilized society. Putting criminals behind bars is far less important to a civilized society than avoiding the inimical transformation of a society that comes with putting innocent people behind bars, killing and torturing innocent people, etc. When we as a people accept the PTA, we make savages of ourselves and diminish our civilization.

Q: Could you summarize the Indian position on the problem of Sri Lanka?

A: I cannot speak for India. But what I gather is that India tried to help us, Tamils and Sinhalese alike, and sort out our problems at a time when we were killing each other. But we turned our guns on India and humiliated India. Through this involvement, we even ruined India's carefully cultivated image as a society committed to high principle. Indians now do not trust us and I do not blame them. They do not want to be involved because of this lack of trustworthy partners. Those whom they do trust, have no power to be of any use. But it is time for India to forget this hurt and take on her responsibilities as a great power in the region.

When there is a huge war on India's border, and refugees pour into India, Indian fishermen are shot at and Indian soil is used for gun-running, India has a humanitarian responsibility and duty to assert herself and indeed a right to act in the interests of her own security.

Q: Some sources said India is unhappy about the defence pact between the government and USA. What do you think?

A: I think US interests are far greater in India than in Sri Lanka. It is difficult for Sri Lankans to accept this but it is very true. Today the US and India are firm partners on many fronts. I therefore seriously doubt that there was no quiet nod from or consultation with India before the US signed this pact with Sri Lanka.

Q: What do you think about the next step of the LTTE and their leadership?

A: If I had the power to tell the LTTE what to do, I would not have had to flee Sri Lanka. But if I were to advise them, I would say this. The war has to stop. Negotiate with the Sri Lankan state and get control of the North-East so that it is a preserve of Tamil culture. As I said earlier, a few more years of this fighting, there would be no Tamils left to even dream about an area of Sri Lanka where Tamils can live their culture in safety. Possible LTTE military gains pale into insignificance in relation to the imperatives of population statistics. Come to any negotiated position quickly to take control of Tamil areas. Ensure that Tamils do find it pleasant to live in the North-East and have no reason to flee. Come to an understanding with the Muslims.

Q: Please explain the current literacy rate in the North?

A: I think thanks to government policy and the war, literacy is down and the UGC's categorization of Jaffna as a backward district would be justified. Vavuniya's cut-off mark for university admissions was higher than Jaffna's 2 years ago. This year Jaffna is a little higher - a sign of the so called peace dividend. With the current situation I am sure Jaffna will go down again. As for schools, my wife undertook a massive survey on behalf of Save the Children. Schools in the North- East and Kandy and Moneragala were studied. Her findings were published by Save the Children. Her findings in summary: Schools in the Tamil districts of Kilinocchi and Mannar have few access roads. Some schools in Mannar and Kilinochchi have no buildings. The NE has the smallest percentage of teachers and resources in the good category. When it comes to teachers in Kilinochchi, 67% are not trained (as opposed to 23% on average), And 50% of English teachers are voluntary (as opposed to regular teachers elsewhere).

The schools in the North-East are largely without a playground. The textbook position is the worst. While all schools are supposed to receive free textbooks, the North-East does not get them and when they do they are not on time.

The ranking of schools says it all. The North-East Schools have most schools in the lower ranks. The Kandy and Monaragala schools have most of their schools scoring for human resources in the highest category 70-80 whereas North East Schools are mainly in the 60-70 range and this only because of the voluntary teachers. (Gampaha schools were the model). But in allocated physical resources, Kandy is up around 80% while Kilinochchi is down to 35%. Unless something is done soon and the war is stopped, we Tamils will soon become the coolies of Sri Lanka.

Q: What are your plans?

A: I would love to return and contribute. But I can do that only if things are safe for me. And interviews like this do not help!

23 March, 2007

3
WE CAN FULFILL OUR POTENTIAL

I was arbitrarily instructed to relinquish my post, without even being given the standard three months to do so. I was given just one month. It was very embarrassing to me because even our adversaries asked me "is this the reward your Government gives you for your efforts and performance?" while our good friends and allies said "you should be given a high honor by your Government for having so successfully defended your country". I was embarrassed not for myself but for the opinion that was being formed of the Government of my country.

- Dayan Jayathillake

"THERE was a major effort by some Western European states to secure a UN mandate from the Human Rights Council, for a War Crimes inquiry. These elements first tried to get a UN mandate under the guise of a humanitarian ceasefire and protection of civilians, to abort our final operations against the LTTE," Dr. Dayan Jayathillake said in an interview with the writer in Colombo recently.

Question (Q) :You have wide range of experience starting with your role in the North-East Provincial Council when the 13th Amendment was implemented. Has the Provincial devolution politically empowered the people of Sri Lanka and has it contributed towards genuine socio-economic progress in the country.

Answer (A) : The Provincial Council system showed its potential with the performance of the Wayamba or North-West Council under the Chief Ministership of Gamini Jayawickrema Perera. Under his provincial leadership and during the Premadasa presidency, the Wayamba experienced a developmental mini-miracle, which shows that with the right local leadership the PC system can work wonders for a province and its people. In the North-East it did not work for two reasons: the LTTE was engaged in full scale war and obstructed the functioning of the Council, and the adventurist Vardharajaperumal administration of the NEPC was not willing to function within the 13th amendment, absurdly hoping that it could use the leverage of the IPKF presence to outflank the Tigers on the Tamil nationalist flank. The latter tendency was the very reason that I resigned from my Ministership in the NEPC, one year before Perumal's lunatic UDI.

Q: Power sharing in the Eastern Province appears to be a sham exercise. Whilst the government is having the controlling interest in the day to administration, the elected members are frustrated that they are unable to exercise their powers. The government sources are saying that the elected members are unsuitable for good governance therefore they have taken charge of the situations. Is this what we expect from the devolution?

A: Let's face the facts. The main weakness of the Eastern PC is the split between two very capable and courageous Tamil political personalities, "Karuna" and "Pillaiyan". This politically weakens the Tamils of the East and is open to manipulation by some elements. If these two personalities do not overcome this split, they will find that at the General election next year, the Tiger proxy, the TNA will raise its head even in some areas of the East.

Q:The 13th Amendment is over twenty years old now. It is proved that it has not achieved the desired objectives. How best the Provincial power sharing can be strengthened? Do you think foreign intervention like the Indian involvement in the 1987 is needed for this change? Also in your opinion what is the best power sharing arrangement Sri Lanka could adopt to resolve the conflict?

A: The 13th amendment is over twenty years old on the statute books, but it has not been in practice for even a year in peacetime in either the North or the East, so how can anyone say that it has not achieved its desired objectives? It has to be tried out for a decent length of time for anyone to conclude that the experiment has not succeeded. Provincial power sharing can be strengthened by first putting it into practice under conditions of peace and normalcy. Foreign intervention or involvement can only delegitimize any national institution. What is needed is the broadest international consensus in favor of the full and expeditious implementation of the 13th amendment, which after all, is part of our very Constitution and is something we have solemnly promised. Such an international consensus is different from intervention or involvement.

Q: The President has not clearly spelt out his position regarding a political resolution to the conflict. The APRC proposal is now in his hands and no one knows what he has done with it. Is he maintaining secrecy to let the rabbit out of his hat at an opportune moment?

A: I do not know the answer to that question but I do know that one hundred days have passed since our historic military victory and we have not yet followed it up with a political component which is necessary to reinforce that victory, and while we have lost time, the TNA which contested the 2004 elections claiming that the Tigers were the sole representatives of the Tamils, have made a comeback in the North. If our political process continues to delay or be inadequate, what is to prevent the Tamil voters from either boycotting in large numbers or opting for the TNA at the forthcoming parliamentary elections? If we had moved fast enough to implement the 13th amendment, which does not require any fresh mandate from the people, the Tamil moderates such as the EPDP and PLOT would have been stronger in the North than they are now, while the TNA would not be on the comeback trail, as it is today.

Q. The IDP situation is an eyesore for the government. The government is managing the situation without the full support of the INGO's and in a transparent manner with the engagement of the opposition parties and the media. This is not a helpful situation isn't it?

A: While the latest report signed by a group of expatriate Tamil personalities who visited the IDP camps (carried in DBS Jeyaraj's Transcurrents) shows that the situation is not quite as bad as depicted in some sections of the Western media, we must ask ourselves whether we are doing the very best we can on this issue. How we would all have behaved had these been a quarter million Sinhalese of all ages behind barbed wire and armed guards, rather than a quarter million Tamils. The IDP issue is being looked after by an 18 person Task Force which is headed by a Sinhalese and initially had only Sinhalese members, though two Tamils were added later, at mid-level. Would we have put up with a situation in which a quarter million Sinhalese were behind the wire while their issue was being handled by a Task Force which was composed almost exclusively of Tamils? At least we should have the Social Services Minister, who is a Northern Tamil, as the co-chair of the IDP Task Force.

Q. There is war crimes cry against Sri Lanka. Sri Lanka too is preventing any access to find out the truth about its war efforts. Do you think Sri Lanka will be taken before the War Crimes Tribunal?

A: There was a major effort by some Western European states to secure a UN mandate from the Human Rights Council, for a War Crimes inquiry. These elements first tried to get a UN mandate under the guise of a humanitarian ceasefire and protection of civilians, to abort our final operations against the LTTE. They made this effort in Geneva from March 2009 onwards, up to May 14th, which was the date they were pushing for the Special session of the Human Rights Council. We fought hard and prevented that. Then they tried to punish us for destroying the LTTE leadership by pushing for a War Crimes inquiry at the UN HRC special session. We beat that by a dramatic margin, 29 to 12. Thus we not only prevented them from getting a UN mandate which they would have taken to New York as well as other places such as the international courts, we actually gave them a negative mandate; a mandate against that, by preemptively putting forward our own resolution and securing a handsome majority for it. I am pleased and proud of the role I was able to play in this, as the point-man, the man on the spot, in the trenches of our international frontline. As for whether there will be a renewed effort on this War Crimes issue and whether it will be successful or not depends entirely on the success of our foreign policy and diplomacy. Crucial to this is knowing who we are, where we belong , who our friends and foes are, building the broadest coalitions, keeping our neighbors -- especially India-- on side by fulfilling our commitments, winning over world opinion, and not losing what Professor Emeritus of International Law at Princeton, Richard Falk terms the 'legitimacy war'.

Q. Do you think South African type Truth and Reconciliation Commission will be a vital process to heal the deep wounds people have. Will it materialize in Sri Lanka? If this is not appropriate what could be done to heal the deep wounds?

A: A South African type Truth and Reconciliation Commission is a method of Transitional Justice. In South Africa there was a negotiated transition from minority rule to democratic majority rule. In Sri Lanka the principle of democratic majority rule was opposed from 1939 by the Tamil nationalists, and our war was to reunite the country by defeating the separatist military drive of a minority. It has nothing in common with the South African situation. Furthermore, Truth and Reconciliation Commissions and forms of transitional justice take place when there is a stalemated situation leading to a negotiated settlement of a civil war or violent conflict, and NOT when one side decisively defeats the other in all out warfare. The endgame at Mullivaiyakkal was hardly a negotiated transition at a roundtable conference! So this method is ridiculously unsuitable for Sri Lanka. Each society finds its own ways of catharsis and social accountability; of remembering, forgetting, healing, reconciling and moving on. So too will Sri Lanka. Methods that can be used are raising issues in Parliament, the media and the courts, and perhaps above all, through the arts.

Q. What was the real reason for your removal from the UN post? Is it because of your write up about the 13th amendment?

A: I do not know. It is odd if it were about the 13th amendment because Deputy Foreign Minister Hussein Bhailla, whom I have considerable respect for, confirmed in parliament the other day in response to a question by the JVP, that the President had on January 27th 2009, expressed to the Indian leadership, his intention to implement the 13th amendment without delay and to move further than the 13th amendment. We also know that the joint Indo-Lanka statement of May 21st 2009 and the joint statement of the Govt of Sri Lanka and the UN Secretary General of May 23rd 2009, contains a commitment to implement the 13th amendment. The latter statement refers to the President's "firm resolve" to do so. Therefore, if I were sacked for this reason it is strange because I was only articulating and defending in the English language, the declared position of the Sri Lankan Government at its highest levels. I was arbitrarily instructed to relinquish my post, without even being given the standard three months to do so. I was given just one month. It was very embarrassing to me because even our adversaries asked me "is this the reward your Government gives you for your efforts and performance?" while our good friends and allies said "you should be given a high honor by your Government for having so successfully defended your country". I was embarrassed not for myself but for the opinion that was being formed of the Government of my country.

Q. What is your vision for Sri Lanka? What advise you can give to each of the communities in Sri Lanka?

A: To the Sinhalese I would say we have achieved a great military victory of which we can be proud as a people. Our military-men have proved themselves contemporary Asia's Masters of War. We must now be wise and prudent. We must not win the war and lose the peace. The USSR that Hitler's best divisions could not defeat, and which broke the backbone of the Nazi army, fell without a shot being fired. That can happen if we lose the "legitimacy war", the war to secure the moral high ground. There is no longer an enemy army to keep pointing to. The world is watching us without a Prabhakaran standing in between. Most countries of the world

34

supported us to finish off Prabhakaran and the Tigers; not the Tamils. They will not stand with us if it seems we are bullying or oppressing the Tamil minority. We are no longer the underdogs; the Tamils are, especially the IDPs. We are being judged by how humanely we treat them. Our decision makers have a choice: are we going be like President Putin or President Bush? President Putin, a tough leader, smashed the Chechen separatist terrorist army, but quickly followed it up with a political process and wide local autonomy for Chechnya, which Moscow has stabilized through a local ally native to the area; not by large scale Russian military occupation, still less efforts at "Russification". George Bush however won the war in Iraq but created a quagmire by not following it up with a successful political project. If we try to hold down the Tamils, they will pull us down too, and we shall both lose. We cannot force the Tamils to abandon their 70 years long effort to find some autonomous political space at the periphery. The wisest thing is to speedily implement the 13th amendment, before the island presents a picture of two utterly alienated communities, dead-locking each other.

As for the Tamils, my advice is to learn the lessons of triple, successive historic failures: federalist agitation, secessionist war, efforts at international intervention. None of these worked. A major war, a Thirty Years War has been decisively lost and there is no going home again to the old slogans. These slogans such as "internal self-determination" and "federalism" can be uttered but they will be ignored, while "facts are created on the ground", altering existential realities. Far more prudent to seek the full implementation of the 13th amendment for which there is regional and international acceptance as well as a commitment by the President. Anything beyond that will lead to an endlessly repetitious reinvention of the wheel.

To the Muslims and Christians I would say, you can play a bridging role. The Muslims speak Tamil, while the Catholic and Protestant Christians span both Sinhala and Tamil communities.

To everyone I'd say "we have lost so much time; so many decades. Asia has taken off and we can catch up. We can fulfill our potential, or we can stagnate. We have come out of a long tunnel;

let us not enter another one. Let us learn the lessons of the past. We have to share this small island on which we do not live alone. We have to coexist. We have to learn to respect each other's distinct identities and give each other space. We cannot force togetherness or integration but if we cooperate and then unite, we can create wonders. Let us join Asia and the global mainstream. Let us not deadlock each other and isolate ourselves instead...

August 29, 2009

4
CASTE ORIGINS OF
SRI LANKA'S AUTHORITARIANISM

When you demolish something all you do is go back to how things were. Sri Lanka has returned to her feudal foundations. In the psyche and the minds of the elite who were educated outside, their inner minds, their inner psychosis, their inner psychological and social foundations were not changed. There is a whole process, like in the natural process, also in the psychological and social process of the evolution of thoughts, or ways which are part of a ruling. The ways of power in the country have always been authoritarian. It was the absolute power of the king and a few land owners and in the feudal pyramid.

- Basil Fernando

BASIL Fernando needs no introduction. He is a pioneer of Human Rights and a well-known poet and jurist. Here is a series of interview that we had in few occasions on the caste system in Asia.

Question (Q): Today authoritarianism in Sri Lanka is a common topic which is very much discussed. You have written extensively on authoritarianism in Sri Lanka, particularly since the 1978 Constitution. Could you try to explain why a Sri Lanka which began its independence period as a democracy shifted to an authoritarian system?

Answer (A): Recently, I was explaining to an American student about Sri Lanka's special history. I was showing him a book which documented 200 years of history of the Supreme Court of Sri Lanka. He asked me this question: obviously Sri Lanka has had a very long history of trying to introduce institutions of the judiciary into the country based on a common law system. However, it has now shifted to an authoritarian model. How did that happen?

He was wondering as to whether Sri Lanka have a sufficient amount of competent, well-trained judges. Or whether this happened because of a lack of human resources to run these organisations. Of course that is not the case.

For over 200 years Sri Lanka has had well trained lawyers. People initially went to the United Kingdom and were qualified in the British universities. There were British judges in the country for a long time and other training, including that of law graduates, started with the institutions like the Faculty of Law which started in the University of Ceylon, and then other institutions were created like the Law College of Sri Lanka.

Looking into the long record of new law reports we see judgements written by judges in Sri Lanka on criminal law matters, civil law matters and also constitutional and administrative law matters, and all this indicates that there is a competency of judges in Sri Lanka. There are many persons from the legal profession and sometimes the judicial profession also who have initially started their practices in Sri Lanka and then gone into important institutions outside like the United Nations and even the International Court of Justice, and taught in international universities and played their parts in many ways and in many capacities.

So from the point of view of the basic training of lawyers in the past, and the education profession, it is not the explanation about the manner in which Sri Lanka abandoned the conception of the rule of law and professionalism in a very fundamental way and now serious erosion has entered into the very practice of the independence of the judiciary in the country.

Also it is important to note the subjugation of the judiciary to the executive which is controlled by one man. The absolute power concept has replaced the idea of rule by any kind of checks and balances. So the reason does not lie in the absence of competence. We have to look to other sources to see how in the course of 30 years a whole tradition came down.

Q: So, how is it possible to bring down a 200 year tradition with some many competent persons within such a short time?

A: That is the very issue that needs to be discussed. First of all the people that did away with the system came from this section of people who had their training on the judicial system. The Jayewardene's were involved in the law business. Although J.R. Jayewardene tried to create the impression at one time that his father was a judge this has now been challenged. Anyway, his father was a senior lawyer at the time and his brother was a Queen's Counsel and a leading lawyer at the time playing a very important role as the President of the Bar Association. Many prominent personalities supported him and his party. Even the chief justice he appointed from outside the judiciary was a prominent QC, Mr. Neville Samarakoon.

Even before J.R. Jayewardene, the first attacks on the judiciary came from the coalition government which ruled from 1970 to 1977, when there also prominent lawyers were in the government. For example Colvin R. de Silva is known as one of the best criminal lawyers produced in the country and had quite a great reputation. There were others like Felix Dias Bandaranaike who was also a senior lawyer who came from a family involved in the legal profession for a long time.

So the dismantling process of the separation of power concept, attacks on the checks and balances and the attempts to replace the independence of the judiciary all came from the so-called legal elite of the country.

Q: Then how could that happen? How could they be involved in attacking the foundation in which they themselves had their education and social status?

A: Once again this is all about knowledge. They knew the system very well. They knew of all the loopholes and the ways to undermine the system in much the same way an engineer might know how to demolish a building.

Someone who knows the structure of a building and the construction industry could be part of modern terrorism. For example there are talks about the 9/11 attack in the United States and how those huge buildings could have been brought down by such an attack.

The reason lies with the fact that some knew exactly where to attack in order that the buildings collapsed.

In the same manner, the Jayewardene brothers in particular, knew all the weak points of the system which was prevailing in Sri Lanka and in designing the 1978 Constitution they used this knowledge in order to undermine the very system of constitutional governance through a constitutional process.

Jayewardene made himself the first executive president of Sri Lanka with all the powers vested in him as the head of state by adopting a constitution through the formal process of passing a new constitution with the required majorities.

Furthermore, inbuilt into the new constitution were certain clauses which would virtually undermine the power of the cabinet by transferring its power into the hands of the president. It also undermined the parliament, virtually subjugating it to a place where it only had rubber stamping functions. It became a parliament that could not undermine the power of the president except by way of an almost practically impossible process of impeachment.

Above all, Jayewardene knew where to attack the judicial process.

With the capacity of a powerful president to direct the process of the selection of judges, purely by no other means than the choice of the president himself, is not just formality. By a process of controlling the budgets they knew that they could undermine the earlier construction of the constitution that had been in place.

This was what was done by the 1978 Constitution. Particularly by creating the position that put the president above the law.

It is a very funny way of using the constitution because usually the idea of constitution in a liberal democracy is to create the idea of the supremacy of the law over all the branches of the government, including the executive.

However, this particular constitution was made for the purpose of changing the system which accepted the supremacy of the law and replacing it with one by which the president was more powerful than the law.

That was the ultimate aim and the construction was done in such a way so as to achieve this.

Q: We do not need to go into the details of the Constitution itself in this discussion because that has been done elsewhere. However, the question is as to how, despite of over 200 years of judicial history was it possible to displace such a system and what was it replaced with?

A: This really brings us the more important question about constitution making in Sri Lanka,

Particularly in the way in which the Soulbury Constitution was made, which was a law drafted by the British by a British constitutional expert Ivor Jennings, and whose operation was directed by the Colonial Office of the United Kingdom, must be examined.

What was needed was to make a constitution that was really a part of dealing with the problems of democracy as against the feudal foundations of a society.

In today's democracies like France, the United Kingdom and many others, there is a period in which there was a deliberate demolition of the feudal foundations of a state and a building of the democratic foundations of the state. No such internal political process took place in Sri Lanka. things were introduced into the country with the idea that when the new institutions were established and had been running for a long time the people would be accustomed to these new institutions and the belief that the memory of the old system would pass away. And the new system would be the ground on which the whole edifice of the social and political life of the country was built. It is this fundamental belief that was flawed. The house was built on sand whereas the inner foundation was not prepared and with a little bit of wind, in a political sense, the whole edifice could break. The social process of democratisation of a feudal society into a democratic society cannot be done purely by the introduction of institutions without an internal process. And that is what we see from the example of Sri Lanka.

Externally the processes of adult franchise was introduced, representation was introduced, the parliament was built, the laws were introduced in almost every area of life. In criminal law, there were criminal procedures and constitutional law. However, the building did not last and with a few clever tricks it was possible to bring it down.

Q: What did we get back?

A: When you demolish something all you do is go back to how things were. Sri Lanka has returned to her feudal foundations. In the psyche and the minds of the elite who were educated outside, their inner minds, their inner psychosis, their inner psychological and social foundations were not changed. There is a whole process, like in the natural process, also in the psychological and social process of the evolution of thoughts, or ways which are part of a ruling. The ways of power in the country have always been authoritarian. It was the absolute power of the king and a few land owners and in the feudal pyramid. The king stood at the top and this feudal pyramid was cemented by the social organisation of caste. These are the two factors that need to be understood in Sri Lanka, the concepts of monarchy and the concept of caste. These are the things on which the power and the social control of the country have been kept over centuries. Now we have returned to this caste foundation. Instead of the monarchy we have a modern terminology, but essentially it is a power pyramid in which there is absolute in the hands of the executive president and there is nothing to control or check that power. In fact, there is the psychological and social foundations of caste and the psychology that was built through caste systems of intimidation and fear that supports this whole system.

So, what we have returned to is our origins, we have returned to our year zero. Our year zero is that zero that begins with absolute power and ends with absolute power systems. That is what we have at the moment. There is the façade of institutions but without power they are a force that has no real power today to deal with the questions of governance. The president is above the law; therefore, the courts are below him. Therefore without equal power in an abstract constitutional sense it is not possible to challenge another power. In the power dynamics, the courts, even if they do not want to despite of who the personality might be, do not have the power, the real actual power, to demonstrate a genuine independence of the judiciary that is possible within a liberal democracy with a foundation that gives considerable power to the judiciary.

When the judiciary is powerless there is very little that the individuals can do. Individuals do not matter very much in this and that is also the case of every other institution. So, we are back to the caste foundations, absolute power foundations and our feudal foundations. And it is in this area that any serious student today of politics in Sri Lanka should try to understand if we have to make some sense out of the present situation. Before we deal with solutions we have to understand the problem.

> *When these basic concepts of equality before the law are absent, the next thing to happen is that the punishment meted out to different groups varies. Therefore there is disproportionate punishment of the weak and the poor and those who don't belong to the privileged. This not only inherent in caste but is conceived to be a virtue.*
>
> *- Basil Fernando*

Q: We talked about the linkage between the collapse of the rule of law, democracy and human rights violations in Sri Lanka and also the relationship to the issue of caste. Can you elaborate on this aspect?

A: In a caste based society there is no concept of the equality of the law. What this means is that there is no acceptance of laws common to and binding on all persons on an equal basis.

Without this there is also no basis for representation which is the basis for representative government. In fact, there is no room for inter-communication between various groups in society. In caste, instead of inter-communication what you have is very strict separation; something even more than the separation in apartheid.

Once you have no basis for inter-communication then there is no room to recognise freedom of speech, communication and media.

When these basic concepts of equality before the law are absent, the next thing to happen is that the punishment meted out to different groups varies. Therefore there is disproportionate punishment of the weak and the poor and those who don't belong to the privileged. This not only inherent in caste but is conceived to be a virtue.

In caste society the hierarchy is an ideal. If things are organised hierarchically in caste society the belief is that things will work well is way.

The top of the pyramid should have everything; the bottom of the pyramid should have nothing.

That is what caste is and it is what democracy is not. That is why we are giving up even the limited extent of democracy introduced with the independence and returning to authoritarianism.

Q: People will argue that there is no equality anywhere. Even in the developed world like the United States there is a tremendous gap between the rich and the poor. This is common throughout the world. So what is so very different in the caste society context and these other experiences?

A: The question of equality, in economics or social equality and the concept of equality before law are two very different concepts.

Equality before law means that despite of being rich or poor, powerful or otherwise the laws of the country apply to all in a similar way.

For example if there is a crime called murder which is called into law, a murder committed by a poor man and one committed by a rich man should not be different. It also applies to any other law, for example corruption. Let us say there is a crime called bribery. Whether an officer of lower rank obtains bribes or when the higher ranking officers or even persons holding political office obtain a bribe under the rule of law there is no difference.

The same law applies to all. Both officers need to be punished by the state. And the state must have the political will to punish both for similar types of crimes.

Of course the rule of law is not only about crime but everything else. For example, suppose you must declare your income. In fact, everyone, irrespective of rank has to declare their income according to the methods prescribed by the law.

It someone does not comply the law should also have the means and the methods of prescribing similar punishment to both.

No one should be able to enter court and say that he is the holder of a certain office and therefore he cannot be brought to court. That is the minimum of the rule of law, even if it is the king himself; the king cannot say to the court, "Your court is not for me. You cannot ask me to appear and to answer questions. You cannot even ask me to reply to charges when they are laid down properly according to the law".

The idea that anyone is above the law is completely alien to the idea that everyone is equal before the law. We cannot say that everyone is equal before the law except the king.

In a caste based society the principle is different. In India the Brahmins are the top caste. They were above any of the rules. The rules only applied to those of lower caste according to their rank. If a high ranking person demands the produce of the villagers, the working farmers, they have no choice but to give it.

If a Brahmin demands a daughter of even a second ranking caste member, like the traders or warrior caste they have to hand her over.

Rape was not a crime in a similar way to any Brahmin. It can of course be a crime of unforgivable nature if by any chance a lower caste, a *Sudra* for example who did physical labour or an untouchable Dalit, were to rape a Brahmin girl not only the rapist but his entire family and his clan could be wiped out, their houses burned and by that everyone would be taught a lesson.

So that very concept of crime was relative; relative to the position held in the caste hierarchy. In the context of the rule of law irrespective of your economic, social or political position the way you are treated before the law is the same.

The same crime, the same punishment by the same process of law and the courts has the power to do that. No such court system could exist within a caste society. Thus the concept of the administration of justice as required by a rule of law system never arose in societies as long as the system which prevailed in the past was the caste system.

Even when colonial powers introduced it, it did not take root, in such countries.

Therefore before the colonial powers introduced the courts systems that developed later, in Sri Lanka we do not have the experience of justice in the true sense with which we talk about justice today.

For example the word 'yukkitiya' does not have the same meaning with regard to a landlord or a 'radalaya', an ordinary peasant. It is even worse if they belong to a lower caste, the fisher folk for example, or a washer man, there is no common idea of justice.

In caste society, inequality is inbuilt into any kind of punishment or justice. Privilege is justified and protected by the whole system.

Any kind of advantage is gained only be way of some kind of patronage of the people at the top. Being servile to the top, showing every kind of deference to the top, respecting the people at the top, meaning doing whatever they wish is the normal law of caste and that is the kind of situation we are returning to in every respect within our social context also.

So the difference between democratic society and a caste based society is not about some kind of absolute equality which is not even an ideal. The ideal is equality before the law, the same laws, the same kind of treatment for non-observance of the law by the same kind of courts with the powers of those courts to ultimately monitor the observance of the law and having the same respect for the rights of everyone.

There must be rights for everybody, not just for some people and duties only for other people in caste society; duties for everybody other than those small privileged groups. The top group has the privileges the rest of society has only the duties and if they don't carry them out they can be punished as harshly as possible by those who have no concept of common right and wrong.

> *The absence of remorse on the part of the Sri Lankan regime at the time, as well as on the part of a significant section of the intellectual classes, for those who were slain in times of repression particularly through forced disappearances, is a useful reflection of the value system within a once caste-based society, and the continuing effect of that mentality on society.*
> *- Basil Fernando*

In the last discussion, we examined the inequalities which are inherent in the caste system.

Q: How does caste affect the social aspects of Sri Lankan society?

A: Caste systems idealize inequality, which creates and justifies cruelty in the treatment of the weak. Cruelty is not an accident when the caste system exists. In democratic societies, there are instances in which cruelties occur. However, the ideal of democracy espouses the prevention of cruelty and the maintenance of a humane society which respects every person.

This is not so with the caste system; the caste system idealizes a ruler who is capable of being harsh and cruel. If the ruler is not able to be harsh and cruel, then the ruler is seen as weak. Therefore, a mentality that is ingrained in the caste system allows rulers and those who engage in security to be harsh on others, without there being any problems of conscience.

Q: Could you clarify how cruelty is within the very ideals of a caste-based society?

A: Let's discuss it with an example. We know the famous Indian legend of Sambukar. Sambukar was a low caste person. He was supposed to do menial work, including physical labour, and was to refrain from making attempts to engage in learning or any kind of intellectual effort. But secretly, Sambukar aspired to be well-read and learned. With that aim, he studied the various Shastras, and Vedas, the books for Brahmins. In doing so, he transgressed one of the fundamental rules of caste society. But he did it in secret, and over time, he mastered the art of the yogis. He was able to do what any yogi could do in terms of breathing exercises. It was a habit among the Brahmins who engaged in yoga to develop various postures that they could hold for a long time. Sambukar developed the art of staying like an owl in a tree for a long time as well as other methods of yogis. During this time, the son of a senior Brahmin died. Brahmins believe that everything in their lives happens according to various rules and theories in their books. The senior Brahmin interpreted the death of his son as being due to transgressions in the order of the caste society. With that in his mind, he took his son to the house of Rama, their leader, and complained that the son of a Brahmin could not die if there had not been a societal transgression. He told the Rama that he should find out what had happened and immediately put an end to it. Angery Rama got into his legendary vehicle with his powerful weapon given by the gods, and immediately travelled around to find out what has happened. He went everywhere but he could not find anything that had gone wrong, or anyone other than a genuine Brahmin to have entered the Brahmin area. So he tried a trick which has been developed by Brahmins to find out who a Brahmin is and who is not: he asked for their genealogy. When he came to Sambuka, Sambuka humbly said, "I do not have any Brahmin genealogy." He explained that he belonged to a low caste, but by his own effort has learned the shastras and had achieved what he had achieved. The story goes that Rama was so furious that he took out his weapon and slew Sambuka right there. In response, the gods rejoiced and came down from the heavens to thank Rama for saving their system. The Brahmin son was revived, and everywhere, Rama was praised by the Brahmins.

This story illustrates the core of expectations of a ruler within the caste hierarchy: he must defend the rules with all possible ruthlessness. Rama does not ask any questions of Sambukar, nor does he see any sympathy for a downtrodden man who, in modern terms, was socially mobile, and was able to attain learning against all odds. And indeed, the rule within the caste system involves zero sympathy for those of low caste, and a ruthless defensiveness of the social order. Now, in Sri Lankan society, we have also seen a great deal of ruthless violence when citizens express any kind of dissent. Take the south, for example. The Sinhala Armed Forces were used to ruthlessly suppress the JVP in the late 1980's when over 30,000 people were forcibly disappeared. Is this not a reflection of a similar attitude?

The absence of remorse on the part of the Sri Lankan regime at the time, as well as on the part of a significant section of the intellectual classes, for those who were slain in times of repression particularly through forced disappearances, is a useful reflection of the value system within a once caste-based society, and the continuing effect of that mentality on society.

Extensive research with foreign researchers as well as through government-appointed commissions into forced disappearances have demonstrated that the majority of those killed were poor and belong to what is known as the lower caste. The earlier research into this by Francois Houtard, a Belgian socialist, clearly established that the majority of the rebels who were killed belonged to the lower caste.

This is the whole issue of an absence of sympathy for people of a lower caste within the Sri Lankan hierarchical social system. Among the disappearances was the death of Richard D Soiza. This death provoked the Sri Lankan middle class. But all such killings should have provoked similar reactions. However, that reaction was not extended to others who were made to disappear and were exposed to enormous cruelties. It is the same in the north and the east for a longer period. There, the fact of ethnicity and the fact of caste were combined. With a simple excuse of dealing with ruthless terrorism in a ruthless way, the issue of large-scale cruelties perpetrated on a large population has been ignored.

This mental attitude is not about the suppression of terrorism, but has been bequeathed from centuries of caste oppression, caste system and the hierarchical values that have been established within a caste system. Today, repression has become a way of life within Sri Lanka. The law is not enforced at all in these matters.

Q: Has there not been any kind of significant enforcement of law relating to the victims of disappearances in the south, north and east

A: It can be said, categorically, no. Let's take the example of habeas corpus actions. This is an enormously important remedy in any rule of law society or liberal democracy, and Sri Lanka does call itself a rule of law society and a liberal democracy. There is a study which has not been published into over 900 *Habeas Corpus* applications that have been filed in the appeal courts of Sri Lanka in recent decades. There isn't a single case that could be called a success. Under various kinds of small pretexts, the cases have been dismissed and the excuses given by the establishment have been accepted. The courts have also found various legal excuses which allow them to not deal with the fundamental issue of the liberty of the individual. The liberty of the individual is at the core of the remedy known as the habeas corpus action. With the disappearances of people, the habeas corpus action has also disappeared from Sri Lankan law.

The virtual disappearance of the capacity of the courts to defend the individual liberty of citizens, which is the reason for the existence of the courts, is now becoming extremely visible. And now, the ideals of caste society are replacing the ideals of a rule of law and democratic society.

In caste-based societies, one of the methods used to discourage attempts to seek justice is the mockery of tragedies and ridiculing of victims. A caste-based society is a heartless society at all times. It cannot deal with people who complain against the wrongs that have taken place within the society. Instead of dealing with their complaints, the caste system has devised a number of methods to deter victims from complaining, such as ridiculing those who suffer from tragedies and ignoring protests using unscrupulous methods to denigrate those who persist in complaint-making.

Thousands of examples can be given for illustrating this aspect of a caste-based society. We will take two well-known instances from recent times. One is the manner in which Manorani Saravanamuttu, popularly known as the mother of Richard De Soyza, was treated after the disappearance of her son. The other is the more recent case of treatment of Sandhya Eknaligoda, the wife of the disappeared Prageeth Eknaligoda.

A number of disappearances in the south during this period were officially recognized to be about 30,000 people.

The abduction and disappearance of Richard De Soyza and the later re-appearance of his dead body on Koralawella Beach was one of the most shocking events for Sri Lankans, particularly middle class Sri Lankans in the 1990s. Following his abduction, his mother, a medical doctor, got herself involved with other mothers of disappeared persons and formed The Mothers Front of Sri Lanka. Ms. Saravanamuttu demanded an enquiry into the abduction of her son and identified Ronie Gunasinghe to be the leader of the team of people who took her son from her house. Ronie Gunasinghe was attached to the security unit of then-president Premadasa. She identified him after seeing him on TV. As she demanded enquiries into her son's death and actively participated in the work against disappearances with other mothers, she came under attack from many quarters. Her own words about the circumstances she faced are quoted below.

51

"It is the most devastating experience to have a child pulled out of your arms. My boy 'disappeared' and 48 hours later, his mutilated body was found. Since then I have received numerous threats, anonymous letters, telephone terror and I am also certain that my telephone is tapped. I want to pursue my son's case. Many friends and colleagues have asked me to stop, 'the one who seeks the battle should not complain about the wounds,' but I know there are tens of thousands of relatives who have been affected by the violence. I will never advise the women I work with to forget, I will tell them that they must speak. 20,000 - 30,000 did not join, out of fear of reprisals to other relatives."

The extent to which Ms. Saravanamuttu was pursued by the Ranasinghe - Premadasa regime and those who supported him is well known. There were even attempts to file lawsuits against her on the basis of the complaints she made against officers who she suspected to have abducted her son. As the attacks mounted from every angle, she had less and less friends and it is well known that by the time she died in February 2001, she lived a highly isolated life, thoroughly disappointed by the inhumanity of a society which did not protest against such gruesome inhumanities as forced disappearances.

When the abduction and disappearance of Richard De Soyza became a scandal against the government at the time, the government began a campaign to ridicule the personality of Richard De Soyza. The emerging leader of the United National Party at the time, Ranil Wickramasinghe, tried to portray the abduction and disappearance as something to do with the sexual orientation of Richard De Soyza. He went on to publicize some letters that were alleged to be related to Richard De Soyza for this purpose. A malicious campaign was carried out against the personality of Richard De Soyza in order to discourage those who demanded enquiries into his abduction and disappearance. It took many years for the inquiries to be conducted, and even today, the whole case has not been resolved in any manner that could be deemed satisfactory.

Reflecting on the situation of the mothers who face disappearances, the words spoken by Ms. Saravanamuttu are worth being quoted again.

"Whether they know why they are doing it, I do not know. Whether they have been told today is the night for so and so. They probably do not question why we are doing this. What has this fellow done to us that we should go and take him, and kill him? That I do not know. But they come. They come with their eyes that are empty of everything. They come with their guns. They come with the assurance that they will not fail in their missions. They come and knock at doors. Ring bells and they look at you, and frighten you, and threaten you. If I had thought for one moment that they had come to take my son I would have died there at the door…it's the women who bear the brunt, and it's the women who are the strong ones, because when you lose a child, you lose yourself." (quoted from a video interview by Nimal Mendis)

Nearly twenty years after the disappearance of Richard De Soyza, another disappearance caught the attention of Sri Lankan society. This was the abduction and disappearance of Prageeth Eknaligoda on January 24th 2009. Following the abduction and demand for inquiries that were made which have become increasingly embarrassing once again a similar pattern of attack on the disappeared person himself and those who are calling for inquiries began to surface. The pattern of behaviour was exactly the same as the manner in which Manorani Saravanamuttu was treated during her tragedy.

Media people who are well known to be associated with the presidential secretariat and security apparatus started attacking the personality of Prageet Eknaligoda. There were attempts to suggest that he was not actually a journalist and attacks on his financial situation, attempt to portray him as a pauper and unscrupulous person who was trying to achieve asylum in another country. It took efforts on the part of his friends to expose the fact that these claims were baseless. Indeed, the attack on Mr. Eknaligoda's personality did not come from fact, but was fabricated in the name of a cultural tradition which discourages protest by engaging in severe slander campaigns against victims of a tragedy.

This attack was extended to Sandhya Eknaligoda, in the same way that the attack against Richard De Soyza was extended to his mother, Manorani Saravanamuttu. Newspaper articles portraying her as a person who is fabricating stories and engaged in some kind of drama to get attention was published in newspapers such as The Island. To this date, there have been no apologies for this unscrupulous slandering of family members who have been subjected to one of the worst treatments of society through the forced disappearance of a loved one.

Q: Beneath all this is a mentality that has been shaped by a caste-based society that knows no remorse regarding even the worst tragedies that occur. In all societies, the causing of disappearances is known to be one of the most heinous of all crimes. This recognition does not exist in Sri Lanka.

A: In the last four decades, as many as 50,000 or more people have been forcibly disappeared in Sri Lanka. These disappearances have involved abductions, followed by interrogations, assassinations and secret burials. This whole process continues to be part of the ethos of Sri Lanka. There has not been a strong enough protest crying out against this heinous crime from the government or the society at large.

Old mentalities bred through centuries of caste-based systems where victims are denigrated as people of no importance is a fundamental part of the Sri Lankan psychological framework. This behaviour of mocking tragedies and ridiculing victims is reproduced over and over again in the country. The country's justice system has been unable to deal with this problem. Thousands of people have gone to courts either by making habeas corpus applications or other petitions to courts, but have not been able to receive adequate justice which would revert the process of absolute indifference that the state and society shows against the most brutal forms of violence which prevail in Sri Lanka.

In the midst of such a cultural tradition, talk of lessons learned and attempts at reconciliation remain nothing but another example of highly organized denial. The whole attempt at commissions is nothing but a process of mocking those who ask for justice. By arranging farcical commissions and inquiries, those who make complaints are brought to greater mockery and humiliation and a message is passed to the whole nation that there is nothing that can be done against injustice but to stomach all insults and injustices and all forms of protest, since they would bear no results. Such is the way centuries of caste practices have been reproduced in Sri Lanka.

That basis of social organization of Sri Lanka, at least by Polonnaruwa Period was the 'caste system' is recognizing as a historical fact. However what has not been revealed is the manner in which such social organization on the basis of caste, was established. The analysis of history in terms of caste has not yet been done. However analyzing from this point of view can throw light on many of the problem still persisting on contemporary Sri Lankan society.

There may be many reasons for undermining caste analysis. One of the most important reasons is the romanticized view of nationalism, that in its many varieties. The Sinhala nationalist narrative and Tamil nationalist narrative want to present romanticized views of their history as well as their problems. Bringing the internal conflict within each ethnic group in terms of caste would undermine much of the pain of nationalism that is made of its deferent varieties. This is perhaps one of the very reasons why more attempt made to understand the inner dynamics within societies in terms of its own internal problems in which caste place a very important role within the Sri Lankan society.

Dr. S. Rathnajeevan H. Hoole in a very quiet incisive analysis in a paper entitle 'Caste as a Hate Crime: Reassessing Arumuka Navalar and Vellala Dominance in Sri Lanka' which he wrote with E. Elilini Hoole, speaks of 'Sudra''s origin on the entire Tamil community. Today Tamils claims to belong to various castes among which 'Vellala' are the dominant caste. More and more people have made claims to belong to this caste in an attempt to claim some kind of respectability within the community. Amusingly according to the Dutch records, numbers of persons belong to Vellala were 30% of the populations while at present this has increased into 50% of the populations, showing clearly various kinds of migrations into this caste. But who are Vellala. Is it a variety of Brahmin caste, which came from India as stated by early historians during Portuguese and Dutch times the Vellalas were themselves Sudras. Is that so, how did Sudras become Vellalas?

Certainly Vellalas are not originate from the Brahmin caste. The Brahmins were forbidden by the 'rules of Manu' to travel by ship and to go abroad. These rules were strictly upheld. Therefore the early migrations from India could not have been from the Brahmins.

A very strict rule within the caste system is that Brahmin could marry only within their own caste and therefore the question of some migrant Brahmins coming and getting married in Sri Lanka and creating more Brahmin was also not possible. In the natural cause of things, the people who migrated early leave their lands when their once who face greater difficulties in their societies and then from this point of view it was the Sudra caste which could have been the early migrants which settle in the Tamil areas of Sri Lanka.

Q: Caste Among the Sinhalese

A: This same premise could be valid in terms of the Sinhalese. The early migrants from India to Sri Lanka, who settle in Sinhala Speaking areas and who latter created the Sinhala civilization would have been Sudras. The creation of the myth attributing a princely status, to the mythical person who is supposed to be the originator of the race is quite understandable. In order to give some respectability to the entire race this person has to be from a princely family or even as a 'Sinhabahu' legend goes, from a lion. While such attempts to give some respectability to race is understandable. However,the fact that it was originally the Sudras that would have migrated to Sri Lanka, is very much more pausible. Therefore, Sinhala speaking people who settled in Sinhala areas were also Sudras. Sudras gradually may also have married into the 'Vadda' community and therefore combinations of Sudra and Vedda communities would constitute the beginnings of the Sinhalese. Clearly any kind of claims that the origination from the Brahmin has to be excluded.

Anyway, in Indian status ladder famers are sudras. Therefore ,Govigamas like the Tamil Vellalas are of Sudra origin. Vijaya of

Mahawama, if there was such a person would have been a Sudra. Therefore Sinhala Kings like the Tamil ones too, were persons who originated from the Sudras .

Two questions that arise are, what kind of society did the Sudras created at the beginning and At what kind of relationship there was among themselves? The next question is how does Sudra settlements gradually developed the caste habits which belong to the Indian caste traditions without there been migrations from the same Indian castes to Sri Lanka? How does the social aspect of caste system and hierarchical structure, enter into Sri Lankan society?

Q: Re-establishment of Caste system in India

A: In the Indian society after there was a serious setback of the caste system due to the influence of 'Jainism' and 'Buddhism' in India, there was once again a revival of caste system after few centuries. The revival of caste system and the wiping of the Buddhism happened more or less at the same time in India. There is some knowledge about the manner in which this revival of caste system and the wiping out of Buddhism took place in India. That was done by vigorous social movements which were given a religious coloring, engaging in a systematic repression and persecution of the Buddhists . This was accompanied by a forceful replacement of the caste system, over a long period of time with the support of the rulers of the time. After the 'Asokan' period which supported Buddhism, new dynasty established itself, which was totally opposed to Buddhism and which replaced Buddhism with the Brahmin religion together with the reestablishment of the caste system.

There were village to village reorganization of caste, by Barahmins, who were well instructed on the work of the reorganization and thus virtually an enormous social experiment took place by way reorganizing the society on the basis of caste.

Indian experiment brought to Sri Lanka

By the end of the 'Anuradhapura' period with the invasion of

'Kalinga Maga', there was a period of social reorganization in Sri Lanka. The similar type of social experiment which was carried out in India of reorganizing villages on the basis of the caste principles would have taken place during this time. This reorganization was also connected with the development with the system of monarchy with absolute powers. Thus the development of the monarchy and the development of caste principle during this time transformed Sri Lanka into social organization which was based on caste. Thus the Sudra communities settled at the beginning was transformed into caste based new hierarchy through social transformation which took place latter. However the original populations which settled in the country were Sudras and therefore it was a transformation of Sudra society into caste system with new claims made by various groups for high states.

Thus, despite of false claims for new identities' all Sri Lankans share common identity of being *Sudras*.

June 7, 2010

5
SRI LANKAN GOVERNMENT IS BARKING UP THE WRONG TREE

Q: Can Government of Sri Lanka ever annihilate the LTTE? If so how long would it take?
A: Never.
Q: Can the LTTE win Eelam?
A: No.

— *Answered by Ashok Kumar Mehta*

"MANY governments in the past have lived with an illusion like a current government in Sri Lanka; Maj. General (Rtd) Ashok Kumar Mehta spoke his mind clearly on Sri Lanka's crisis nightmare in an interview with the writer. Ashok K. Mehta was a former Major general of the Indian Army, and a radio and television commentator, and a columnist on defence and security issues. He was founder-member of the Defence Planning Staff in the Ministry of Defence, India.

Q: What do you think of the new political and military developments in Sri Lanka between Government of Sri Lanka and Liberation Tigers of Tamil Eelam?

A: There are two aspects, military and political. On the military side, the government has changed tack and shifted the focus from the ethnic conflict to counter terrorism. By doing so, they have derived considerable international cooperation and understanding. The liberation of the East is a big feather in the military cap but this does not mean that the LTTE has been completely cleared from the East. There are known to be at least 200 armed Tigers in hiding and an equal number of sleepers. In addition there are the various Tamil paramilitary groups like Karuna and Pillaiyan and Tamil political groups chiefly EPDP. These are bound to come into conflict with one another in the future. Therefore the main task for the Army and STF will be in managing the East.

Colombo has been sanitised and made safer but this has consumed at least one Infantry Brigade and some Special Forces. The occupation of the East and security tasks in the Colombo region are bound to affect the troop strength available for operations in the North. The recent attacks on Anuradhapura and Yala demonstrate that the LTTE has both reach and resilience which go beyond the North East. On the political side, the devolution package remains an elusive as it has always been in the past. Despite the APRC with some 50-plus meetings the end product will lack a southern consensus as the TNA, JVP and UNP are formally out of it.

Q: We met for the first time at the International Counter Terrorism Conference at BMICH, Colombo a few days ago. That day you have spoken on what the Government of Sri Lanka can do to counter terrorism in Sri Lanka. Also you welcomed recent operations won by Government troops against the LTTE. Does the Anuradhapura airbase incident change all that and your views? Can you critique GoSL's Counter Terrorism operations?

A: The Sri Lankan Security Forces are fighting a conventional war while the LTTE is using a mix of guerilla war, conventional tactics and terrorism. But it has to be noted that the bulk of the targets they have attacked are military ones. The objective of the SLSF is both the capture of territory and attrition - weakening the LTTE. The aim is to separate the LTTE from their support base of 400,000 local Tamils. The Air Force is supporting the Army and Navy in their operations against LTTE. In addition, the security forces have launched productive intelligence operations and the results are manifest in the targeted assassination of SP Tamilselvan and the success story scripted by the Sri Lankan Navy over the last ten months. It has virtually crippled the logistics lifeline of the Tigers which will require at least 12 months to restore.

The LTTE is trying to make inroads into Jaffna and the daily attacks against FDLs are designed to infiltrate their cadres into Jaffna.

Q: Is there a military solution to the current problem? In the light of Anuradhapura, is GoSL even capable of a military solution even if it were feasible?

A: Categorically no. But the Sri Lankan Government thinks there is. Many governments in the past have lived with this illusion. And paid dearly for it. The intention to liberate the North as was done in the East is bound to fail due to various reasons; notably there is no Karuna group to support the military; no one knows the Wanni region as it has never been under SLSF control. Further, the LTTE has very strong defences and an elaborate network of barriers and minefields. A protracted war can result in a humanitarian disaster especially if air and naval bombardments are combined with ground assaults. So the Sri Lankan government must rethink its offensive plans. Rather than open a new front it should consolidate its gains in the East and carry out focused development. The attack on Anuradhapura should caution the establishment.

Q: Some say there is no difference between LTTE bombs in Colombo on the one hand and the massacre of Tamils civilians in periodic riots from 1956 and government shelling of civilians on the other. Please comment on the origin of Terrorism in Sri Lanka. What are the recent influential factors leading to the buildup terrorism in Sri Lanka?

A: I think all human beings have the gift, from God, of forgetting. A lot of forgetting has to be done by both sides in Sri Lanka. The LTTE calls itself a left-leaning people's army. Please explain to me how the rights of the oppressed, no matter what their race, are served when you blow up trains and put bombs in public places where the working classes congregate. I don't think anything is served by repeatedly raking up issues of whether LTTE terrorism came up first or state terrorism. Sri Lanka is a polytechnic society. It needs a polytechnic polity. Both sides must demonstrate the ability to share power.

Q: As far as Tamil civilian deaths during military operations are concerned, do you see any substantive difference between Sri Lankan Army or Air Force operations and IPKF operations?

A: The IPKF did not use its air force in the manner the Sri Lankan Air Force is employed. Only armed helicopters were selectively used and there was no carte blanche bombing of targets. IPKF operations were guided by use of minimum force and minimum collateral damage. The IPKF was extremely conscious of civilian casualties especially in the Tamil areas because of the fact that there were several Tamil speaking infantry units. IPKF also had to be mindful of the reaction in Tamil Nadu. Overall, great care and extreme sensitivity about civilian casualties prefaced military operations.

Q. What are your observations on Tamil Youth Militarism in Sri Lanka?

A: I think militancy is a hallmark of the young. I just feel it wasn't handled right – not in the case of the LTTE, not in the case of the JVP.

Q: Why did India support Tamil military movements in Sri Lanka in the past?

A: there was a specific geopolitical situation that warranted this. India did not want a problem on its shores and some Sri Lankan regimes tried to bring external powers into the Indian Ocean region that made India angry, alarmed and determined to retain some leverage in influencing politics in the region. There was a certain context.

Q: India is strongly opposed to terrorism but India strongly supports Sri Lanka Tamils and, it is no longer disputed, has even trained and armed Tamil militants. Why is this?

A: India strongly opposes terrorism, state sponsored or otherwise. If the Sri Lankan Government's minorities feel oppressed and find echoes in India, it could become an even greater problem for both our countries. It is better to engage and address issues instead of using coercion.

Q: If the LTTE didn't kill former Prime Minister Rajiv Gandhi could you please speculate on whether India would have backed the LTTE goal of Eelam?

A: Hard to say.

Q: How did Indian support, if any, help in recent defeats of the LTTE such as the loss of LTTE cargo vessels? In 2002 when the Sri Lankan army was trapped in Jaffna with some 30-40,000 troops close to being massacred, it is said that India stopped the advance of the LTTE. Is this true? What did India do?

A: India has provided usable intelligence and training to Sri Lankan Navy. The second part of your question is fiction

Q: A top level intelligence officer in Sri Lanka told me at a personal interview that India never supported the Sri Lankan military. Also he claimed that the joint patrol by both countries of the Indian Ocean is a joke. Is his comment true? Is this all an Indian drama with Sri Lanka?

A: I think you should ask the gentleman who told you, whether is he seems to enjoy a lively sense of humour! By the way India is the biggest trainer of Sri Lanka's military – Army, Navy and Air Force. No other country gets as many vacancies as Sri Lanka on training course in Indian military training institutions.

Q: Hilary Clinton, wife of former US President Bill Clinton has said during an interview with the London-based Guardian newspaper that the Tamil Tigers are a liberation movement, not terrorists. What is your opinion on her comment?

A: I am not sure how familiar she is with the realities of this region.

Q: Please comment on the international implications of the LTTE and its threats to peace and stability regionally and more widely.

A: The LTTE is militarily at its weakest today. Gone are the days when liberation movements and human rights violations could move nations to act. The LTTE may believe that support of the people of the north and east is with it, but the patience of international opinion is wearing thin with them. The overall international threshold of patience with 'liberation movements' is at an all-time low. So it should not expect any backing from any established regime. Yes, if they are content to call themselves liberation guerillas on the basis of equipment and money they extort, steal and smuggle, I have nothing today about them.

Q: What do you feel about the liberation of the East by Government of Sri Lanka? Does it advance the cause of peace by humbling the LTTE or retard the cause by making the GoSL feel it does not have to meet Tamil aspirations?

A: This is certainly a victory of sorts. One must remember that a guerilla force cannot be permanently defeated. The LTTE has been cleared from the East but retains a residual presence and over time can always recoup. The victory celebrations have a political connotation. They may be premature.

Q: After the arrest of the top arms procurer and smuggler of the LTTE, Kumaran Pathmanathan, better known as KP, you have said that this is the time to tame the Tiger. First, was KP really arrested? And second, could you give us your observations on LTTE's military capabilities?

A: I think Thai authorities have said clearly –and so have the Indians – that the arrested man wasn't KP. I don't believe in conspiracy theories, only facts. The LTTE has acquired military capabilities against heavy odds. But they must realize that a military victory against the Sri Lankan state is impossible to achieve.

Q: LTTE has just attacked the Sri Lankan Air Force base in Anuradhapura a few days ago. This is the first time Prabhakaran has used a suicide team and Air Wing on a single joint mission.

What do you think about the LTTE's latest attack?

A: Of the four air attacks carried out by the Tiger Air Force, this one is the most audacious and brilliant. The psychological payoff is much greater than the 21 out of the 24 Aircraft which have been disabled and resulting in the loss of $ 40 m The fact that the Black Tigers were able to damage or destroy almost every piece of equipment in sight barring the three helicopters which were parked away shows the skillful planning and execution of the operation. That 17 of the 20 Tigers blew themselves up shows nothing will stop them from carrying out even more daring attacks.

The combined ground and air attack also revealed big holes in Sri Lankan Air Forces' low level air defence and quick reaction capability. They have not been able to bring down a single Tiger aircraft. That says something for both sides.

Q: Please comment on the death of S.P. Tamilchelavan who was the political wing head of the LTTE?

A: It seems they got the wrong chap. The targeted killing by the SLAF of Mr SP Tamilchelvan, the head of the political wing of the LTTE and the international face of the botched peace process signals the virtual end of any prospect of a negotiated solution. While the Sri Lankan Air Force may have demonstrated its talent in acquiring actionable intelligence and precision bombing, Tamilchelvan's assassination is bound to lead to an eye for an eye and escalate the conflict still further.

The elimination of Tamilchelvan confirms the widely held belief that the Sri Lankan government is simply not interested in a political solution and is hell-bent on liberating the North as it has the East. The government is barking up the wrong tree.

Q: What are the responsibilities of Government of Sri Lanka?

A: To expeditiously evolve a devolution package which enjoys a southern consensus and offer it to the Tamils including the LTTE?

Q. Please comment on the ongoing operations against the LTTE by GoSL.

A: This question has been answered. The Northern offensive appears to be in two parts. The first is along the A 32 coastal road from Mannar to Pooneryn. This operation will ensure that LTTE guns will not be able to target Palaly airfield. The second front is in the Wanni area and it is believed that the Sri Lankan Army has made at least three incursions of battalion size in this area. But this is a long haul, fraught with risk and danger.

Q: What are the responsibilities of anti-LTTE Tamil political parties in this situation?

A: I think they must do everything possible to ensure devolution of power and a polytechnic polity. This is the fundamental issue and there is no point being in denial about it.

Q. What are the weak points in the Sri Lanka government and military for counter terrorism operations?

A: There is excessive use of force and military operations are not compatible with human rights and humanitarian law of conflict

Q: Can the LTTE win Eelam?

A: No.

Q. Please comment on what you expect to be the forthcoming military strategies of the LTTE, and how government forces can counter them?

A: LTTE will continue to wage its war by employing a mix of conventional and guerilla tactics and terrorism. Government forces have to fight on all three fronts.

Q: Can Government of Sri Lanka ever annihilate the LTTE? If so how long would it take?

A: Never.

Q. How can Sri Lanka find a sustainable solution for the ethnic crisis? Also what are the responsibilities of the other political parties?

A: The Southern parties must work together on power sharing and evolve a dignified devolution package that will satisfy the Tamils and the Muslims and which is acceptable to all the people in Sri Lanka.

November 3, 2007

6
INDO-LANKA: WE HAVE HISTORICAL BONDS GOING OVER MILLENNIA

"What applies to India , Pakistan , Afghanistan , Bangladesh similarly applies to Srilanka –the source of LTTE's funding was from Europe and UK based expatriates as well as other organizations . A policy to keep the pot boiling by extremist, fundamentalist groups and continue tensions and violence through fostering so called ethnic differences keeps us from a peaceful, harmonious society. "

- Vishnu Bhagwat

THERE is no need to tell much about who Admiral (Rtd) Vishnu Bhagwat is: a former chief of Naval staff (India) and remarkable person who is well known on military, political and strategic relations commentary. Admiral Vishnu Bagawat is the person who hunted down the first ship which belonged to the Liberation Tigers of Tamil Eelam. According to the press statement released by the former Chief Minister J. Jayalalitha in 1999 when Admiral Bagawat was sacked by the Government of India, "Admiral. Bhagwat had in 1994 done a "national service" by tracking down the vessel Ahat which was clandestinely bringing Krishnaswamy alias Kittu, the second most important LTTE leader, along with arms and narcotics, to India. So, he said, it needs to be probed if there was LTTE pressure on the minister to remove Bhagwat."

68

When I asked the reason behind this claim, the Admiral replied: "The short answer to your question is that one of the Ministers was closely associated with the LTTE, Narcotics and arms smuggling for them as well as into our North East."

Admiral Vishnu Bhagwat has openly shared his thoughts on the present political and military developments in Sri Lanka, India as well as Asia in general, with the writer.

Q: What are the current maritime security challenges in South Asia today? Is there any progress on training, join patrols, and join exercises?

A: Just as in 1991 when the political capitulation of the Soviet Union became an 'inflexion point' in the contemporary period of the historical process, and US Finance Capital and allied interests proclaimed the "Project for the New American Century" and the 'New World Order' (following such discourses as the 'End of History' and 'The Clash of Civilisations') dominated by 'unilateralist' interventions , invasions , threats of war, including attack, occupation to capture / control the oil and strategic mineral resources for monopolistic exploitation by their MNCs under a predominant culture of global militarisation underpinned by more than 700 military bases , plans to completely take over the oceans and the seabed as well as Space-----2007-08 mark the beginning of the terminal decline of the Western Alliance system –and all trends indicate a rapid descent and the end of the Asian Security Architecture they had planned and dreamt of for integrating the periphery with the Center, also widely refered to as 'Globalisation', another code-word for neo- colonialism and neo-imperialism or accumulation of the surpluses and savings on a world scale . Today we are witnessing the resurgence of Asia- West , South , South-East and East economically , politically and, therefore, in this context its security perspectives . South Asia is no longer a region to be viewed in isolation and 'disconnected', in geo-political terms from West Asia or East-South East- Asia .

Freed from its imperialist or globalist lenses , South Asia, enjoying as it does a geographical location right at the center of the east-west oil arteries and trade routes , can and must play a vital role in ensuring the security of these sea lanes for the benefit of all ,posing a threat to none . The same applies to the choke points in the Gulf of Hormuz , Aden , Cape of Good Hope and the Malacca Straits (including the narrows of the Lakshdweep/Maldives and South Sri Lanka) . This calls for mutual goodwill and reciprocity of economic relations between West Asia , South Asia , South East Asia and East Asia which would strengthen all and add to every one's security, rather than foster mutual suspicions which is currently the order of the day as far as the Western media and other speculative reports are concerned .

Incidents of piracy whether in the Malacca Straits or off the Gulf of Aden / Somalian coast, much hyped in the media can be easily managed by low –profile measures (remembering that the history of piracy is sourced to England) . Sri Lanka , India and the Indian Ocean littoral nations look forward to operationalistion of such a co-operative arrangement the dialogue for which was initiated in the New Delhi meeting of Heads of Navies of the littoral in recent months . I do not believe that extra –regional navies with their constant proposals for joint exercises and inter-operability banners help in peace and security in our region and neighborhood , when nations who are our immediate neighbors are under US- NATO occupation, daily bombings and threats of nuclear attack and war, all in gross violation of the UN Charter . India , despite the inclinations of its current dispensation in power has no ambition or basic national interest in working with any foreign power to formulate any joint plans for joint operations as has been demonstrated by a firm NO by the people to two Governments in Delhi, with respect to Iraq and Afghanistan and to the lobbies in support of US-Israeli planning for military action on Iran against a non-existent 'nuclear' Iran , proved to be a lie both by the IAEA and the NIEs of US Intelligence Agencies themselves in their October 1998 findings .

Q: How would you identify the concept of terrorism? What role has the West played in developing terrorism, especially in the light of their role in Afghanistan during the Soviet Occupation?

A: The New world order and the PNAC , such neo-con projects as 'Pre-emptive' unilateral Wars/ invasions and occupations need the camouflage or smoke-screen of Islamists terrorist creations like Osama bin Laden , Al Qaeda, all mythical para /pseudo agent-provocateurs in the service of US designed invasions/occupations . Brzezinski's " The Grand Chessboard" and Robert Gates' (former Director CIA) and currently US Defense Secretary's book, 'From the Shadows', substantiate the setting up of the insurgent Mujahideen groups with the Pakistan ISI's cooperation , at least six months ahead of the invitation to the Soviet Union for military assistance by the democratically elected Govt of Afghanistan , the MEK in Iran .Almost all the terrorist groups in India, past and present, in the North –East , LTTE, Khalistan (Sikh) insurgent groups in Punjab, various fundamentalist groups from amongst the majority and minority affiliations –all have been trained and funded(directly or covertly), in Europe , UK ,US , Canada and advised by their agencies from time to time. Lately the Mossad has been playing a deep, covert game.

Q: Please comment on the ethnic crisis in Sri Lanka. Who in your opinion is behind it? Why have we been unable to find out a sustainable solution during the last three decades?

A: What applies to India , Pakistan , Afghanistan , Bangladesh similarly applies to Sri Lanka –the source of LTTE's funding was from Europe and UK based expatriates as well as other organizations . A policy to keep the pot boiling by extremist , fundamentalist groups and continue tensions and violence through fostering so called ethnic differences keeps us from a peaceful , harmonious society . Susan George in her remarkable book '*The Lugano Report*' (1996-Pluto Press) describes the project for nurturing "Identity and Hate politics" as central to the furtherance of neo-liberal corporate globalisation in the 'countries of the 'Periphery', for control and dominance by the Imperial Center. When governments work for the benefit only of the oligarchy and big –business ,abandoning the slow but steady welfare state concept and the social contract implicit in electoral democracies they must find diversions , and therefore discriminate against national minorities to start with, hence the opportunities and solutions for reconciliation and harmony recede replaced by a chauvinism which feeds on itself.

Q: In the past, the Research and Analysis Wing (R&AW) provided training and arms to the Bangladeshi separatists known as Mukti Bahini. The R&AW's aid was instrumental in Bangladesh gaining her independence from Pakistan in 1971. India has been also giving arms to opponents in Pakistan. Does it mean that India is playing a double game in the region of South Asia?

A: It would be recalled that Sheikh Mujibur Rehman's Party, the Awami League, won the majority in the elections in Pakistan ,but he was not allowed to form a government and become the Prime Minister of Pakistan . Thereafter Pakistan unleashed a reign of terror and genocide in East Pakistan (East Bengal) which gave rise to the formation of the Mukti Bahini . India was also overwhelmed with 4 million refugees fleeing from East Pakistan into India . The Mukti Bahini's was a People's Army and the Indian armed forces went into Bangladesh after an unprovoked attack by the Pakistan Airforce on the evening of 3rd December 1971 . It is the Mukti Bahini that defeated the Pak forces in Bangladesh as documented by Lawrence Lifshultz in his brilliant history of events "The Unfinished Revolution". The Indian Armed Forces accepted the surrender of 90,000 Pakistani Army officers and soldiers , brought them to POW camps ,saved them from massacre by the Mukti Bahini and fed them ,till they were generously repatriated after the Shimla Agreement march 1972. The rest is history . The role of R&AW, if any, was only marginal. As far as Pakistan is concerned India's agencies have not been responsible for any arms supplies to any groups inside Pakistan .Other foreign agencies are playing dubious games.

Q: India gave arms and training to Sri Lankan Tamil military groups in the early 80s, but never supported separation in Sri Lanka. Why?

A: That was integral to India's policy which fortunately still continues intact.

Q: There is no doubt the Government of India has given their full strength to eliminate the Tamil Tigers in the final battle which ended last May. Meanwhile some security analysts claim that the present Government has failed over the Sri Lankan Tamil issue.

Others say India is more concerned about economic benefits than humanitarian issues in the Island nation. What do you think about the present political and security developments in both countries?

A: I have tried to summarise the political and security developments in Sri Lanka and India in response to your first two questions , they have also been analysed in the article," The Storm Sweeping South Asia " , by Niloufer Bhagwat published recently in your esteemed daily, *Sri Lanka Guardian.*

Q: I would like to know your experiences on counter-terrorism in India and more generally South Asia in your military career as a security officer.

A: This would require an expansive response . Very briefly 'counter intelligence' is the sanctum sanctorum of Intelligence agencies in pursuing counter terrorism and they must never allow entry of foreign intelligence personnel into CI, no matter how much their influence over the political apparatus of the State . If this happens the State and the government are subverted and suborned, leading to loss of sovereignty and even civil war. Our experience with terrorist outfits overall in the North –East , the South (DMK initially was separatist) , in Punjab and Jammu & Kashmir is that political dialogue /negotiations ,democratic elections , delegating administrative powers and a certain level of autonomy , development , dignity and respect as equal citizens of the country , removal of genuine grievances, respecting local customs , traditions and cultures is absolutely vital to enhance unity and integration of erstwhile separatist and terrorist groups . Trying a military solution is no solution at all in the long run for achieving stability and progress as a united people . Religion or ethnic origins do not form the basis of a modern nation state. Common interests ,a just and fair society woven by historical bonds is the basis for harmonious , happy peoples .

Q. Could you please explain to us the importance of espionage networks for counter terrorism within South Asia and the governments and military?

A. Espionage networks or the intelligence apparatus of the State is

73

an essential element of a sovereign state because the security of the country is underpinned by its information on the moves and plans of its adversaries , both state and non-state actors . Hence, the most important and vital need is to protect the integrity of the personnel staffing these agencies , because if they get subverted and the agencies themselves get infiltrated, the State's vital and key institutions get hollowed out , slowly but surely.

Q: Chief Minister M Karunanidhi announced that the government of Tamil Nadu wants to offer citizenship to about 100,000 Tamil refugees from Sri Lanka who have been living in the State for years. He said he had already submitted a request to that effect to the central government in New Delhi. Even Union Home Minister P Chidambaram said that the Centre would consider a proposal by the TN Government to grant Indian citizenship to all Sri Lankan Tamil refugees living in the state. Meanwhile some state politicians have been against the proposal. What comments do you have on this issue?

A: I have no comments about your information regarding Chief Minister of Tamil Nadu's proposals to the Home Minister as I do not know of this.

Q: What advice do you have for our military, Tamil politicians, and the people of Sri Lanka?

A: I am not competent to advise the Sri Lankan military , Tamil politicians or the people of Sri Lanka. We have historical bonds going over millennia. India's security and well-being are bound with Sri Lanka and if I may say so , so is Sri Lanka's, as it is always so with neighbours . In fact one famous strategic thinker some centuries ago described Sri Lanka as the 'Center' of the Indian sub-continent in the maritime context.

October 12, 2009

7

INDIA HAS A STAKE IN THE UNITY AND TERRITORIAL INTEGRITY OF SRI LANKA

"India should not and I think will not get involved in micro-managing matters internal to Sri Lanka. India can, however, help to create an atmosphere to promote a national consensus, without intrusively interfering in Sri Lanka's internal affairs."

- Gopalaswami Parthasarathy

"INDIAN Foreign Policy is not decided by any one individual. It is based largely on a national consensus. I do not see any great difference between the approach to relations with Sri Lanka of Prime Minister Atal Bihari Vajpayee on the one hand and Prime Minister Manmohan Sigh on the other," said Professor Gopalaswami Parthasarathy in an interview with the writer.

In New Delhi, Mr. Parthasarathy was Deputy Secretary in the Foreign Secretary's Office (1976-1978). He has served as Spokesman, Ministry of External Affairs and Information Adviser and Spokesman in the Prime Minister's Office with Prime Minister Rajiv Gandhi (1985-90). He has been a member of Indian Delegations in several international conferences including summits at United Nations, Non-Aligned Movement and SAARC.

Mr. Parthasarathy is presently Visiting Professor in the Centre for Policy Research in New Delhi. He is also a Senior Fellow and the Centre for Strategic and International Studies and a member of the Executive Committee of the Centre for Air Power Studies in New Delhi.

Excerpts of the interview;

Q: Your career as a diplomat, foreign ministerial positions and spokesperson of the late Prime Minister Rajiv Gandhi gives you in-depth knowledge of workings of the government and put you in a unique position to assess the mindset of the Indian government towards Sri Lanka and the other intricate regional issues. Amongst the several current positions, you are the visiting Professor for the Centre for Policy Research and a Senior Fellow of the Centre for Strategic and International Studies. My primary questing is why India is not taking a proactive engagement in Sri Lanka and giving room for other regional nauseates like Pakistan, China and Iran to fiddle in the affairs of that country?

A: I am not sure whether your assessment that India is not proactive in Sri Lanka is entirely correct. I think one has to understand that there has been a qualitative change in the global environment after the end of the Cold War. In today's world order, countries that may otherwise even be rivals in many areas cooperate in many areas. The Indo-Sri Lanka Agreement of 1987, therefore, reflected the rivalries of the Cold War which had a bearing on India's security concerns at that time.

Since 1987, there has been a qualitative improvement in the climate of India-Sri Lanka relations, which are now characterized by mutual trust and confidence. While there are no longer doubts in Sri Lanka about India's commitment to the unity and territorial integrity of the Island, there is also a measure of confidence in India that Sri Lanka will not allow any foreign presence detrimental to India's security on its soil. In these circumstances, while we in India are fully mindful of other countries fishing in our backyard, our two countries are rapidly expanding trade and economic cooperation and cooperating in regional and global forums. I was delighted to see and work together with representatives from Sri

Lanka, while participating recently in a Track II Meeting of the ASEAN Regional Forum, in Beijing. As democracies, we share common values and should cooperate for promoting peace, stability and cooperation in the Indian Ocean Region.

Q: Many opinions and thoughts are being reflected about India's non-interference policy in Sri Lanka. Poignant of all is that 'Once bitten always shy' position. India, understanding the complex situation in Sri Lanka, does not want to get involved to get hurt like its 1987 intervention when the President Ranasinghe Premadasa and LTTE leader Pirabaharan jointly booted the Indian intervention. Now that LTTE factor is not there, isn't it right to take an assertive stand to resolve the ever declining state of affairs in Sri Lanka.

A. As I said earlier India has a stake in the unity and territorial integrity of Sri Lanka. We are no longer confronted with a situation like in the 1980s when thousands of Sri Lankan Tamil refugees were compelled to flee to India. We believe that the 13th Amendment to the Sri Lanka Constitution, if implemented in letter and spirit, creates a basis for moving forward a process of reconciliation within Sri Lanka.

Let me clarify one point on the events leading to the induction of the IPKF in 1987. The IPKF was sent to Sri Lanka because of a request from President Jayawardene, who told Prime Minister Rajiv Gandhi that he feared that the insurrection in the South of the Island was getting out of hand and could lead to a situation, in which the entire island could be engulfed in chaos. Since he could not pull out Sri Lankan forces from the Northeast because this would result in a takeover of the Northeast by the LTTE, President Jayawardene asked for the deployment of an Indian Peace Keeping Force to enable him to move the Sri Lankan forces deployed there to the South. Prime Minister Rajiv Gandhi agreed to this request.

India had decided even in 1988 to reduce and thereafter withdraw its forces once elections were held and an elected Government took charge in the Northeastern Province under the 1987 Agreement. Rather than supporting the elected Provincial Government, President Premadasa chose to strike a deal with the

LTTE, in the belief that the LTTE would dance to his tune. We also know that President Premadasa's Government even provided arms to the LTTE. This decision was taken at a time when Sri Lanka's armed forces lacked the material and manpower resources to take on the LTTE. This naturally led to the IPKF being withdrawn somewhat sooner than earlier planned. It is for the people of Sri Lanka to judge whether the price they paid by way of two more decades of LTTE terrorism that followed President Premadasa's decision to "befriend" the LTTE, served their interests and welfare.

Q: Some say 'Sonia factor' is the determinant element in the remote dealing. What are your views on this?

A: Indian Foreign Policy is not decided by any one individual. It is based largely on a national consensus. I do not see any great difference between the approach to relations with Sri Lanka of Prime Minister Atal Bihari Vajpayee on the one hand and Prime Minister Manmohan Sigh on the other.

Q: With the Indian help, 13th Amendment was incorporated into the Sri Lanka constitution and powers were devolved to the provinces. 13th amendment is proving to be a nightmare as Colombo is not prepared to allow independent functioning of the provinces. Eastern Province is the good example as to how the government wants to control the provinces. The concurrent list that is part of the provision is being abused by the government. Instead of using them as a last resort, the government is using the provision as its primary powers and is undermining the provincial administrations. The Eastern Province experience is that the Chief Minister is even unable to appoint a toilet cleaner to his office without the approval of the centre. Is 13th amendment adequate to deal with the crisis facing Sri Lanka?

A: As I said earlier, it is my hope that President Rajapakse who now enjoys overwhelming public support in Sri Lanka will implement the 13th Amendment to the Sri Lanka Constitution, both in letter and in spirit. That would in itself be an important step forward. I also understand there are moves to transfer all subjects from the Concurrent list to the State list as a part of an overall package. Moreover, between 1995 and 2000 President Chandrika Kumaratunga and her constitutional advisers, Professor G.L. Peiris and Dr. Neelan Tiruchelvam put together a devolution package with provisions beyond what was envisaged in the 13th Amendment. Consequently, there are several ideas on the table and I think that given the mood of national confidence now prevailing in Sri Lanka, formulation and implementation of an effective devolution package would go a long way in addressing the deep scars of the prolonged ethnic conflict in the Island.

Q: Sources close to the President privately state there is a plan to have the Provincial Council as a facade and devolve real power to the smallest units, like village level and district level as a Machiavellian strategy to disrupt any move towards a Tamil homeland. The present All Party Representative Committee recommendations will be diluted to achieve this objective. Will India oppose such move?

A: Let me not offer comments on speculation. As I said, a credible devolution of powers going beyond the 13th Amendment would be welcome. In our own case, the Indian Constitution has been amended in 1993 to empower grass roots village level institutions, without in any was eroding the power of the States. I am sure similarly innovative solutions can be found in Sri Lanka.

Q: Sri Lankan constitutional and electoral provisions are so rigid that it is very difficult to get 2/3rd majority by a single party in the legislature to address the real needs of the nation. Only way this could be handled is by government entering into a bipartisan agreement with the opposition. All previous efforts to bring a bipartisan agreement have failed due to traditional mistrust between the parties. Don't you think India can play an important role to bring in the culture of accommodative politics by a bipartisan path? Has or will India move in this direction?

A: I have always believed that the people and Parliamentarians of Sri Lanka know best what is good for their country. India should not and I think will not get involved in micro-managing matters internal to Sri Lanka. India can, however, help to create an atmosphere to promote a national consensus, without intrusively interfering in Sri Lanka's internal affairs.

Q: It appears Tamil Nadu factor is not influencing the Centre unlike in the 1980's. Does the Centre understand that Tamil Nadu uproars are just bubbles that burst and they do not have long term influence on the Centre?

A: The Government of India represents the interests and respects the sentiments of all Indians. It is not a question of what is good for just Tamil Nadu, but for India as a whole. I think the Tamil Nadu Government and people in Tamil Nadu understand this very well. It is particularly important for India's friends to understand that in an era of coalition politics in India, no Government in New Delhi can be insensitive to sentiments and legitimate aspirations of people in Tamil Nadu, or in any other State in the country..

October 27, 2009

"I think the Governments of India and Sri Lanka have cooperated extensively on investigations into the tragic assassination of Prime Minister Rajiv Gandhi," said Professor G. Parthasarathy in an another interview with the writer. This interview was conducted two days before the passing of the 18th Amendment to constitution in Sri Lanka. The Amendment was passed by the parliament with two third majority.

Excerpts of the interview;

Q: What is your opinion of the forthcoming 18th Amendment to the Constitution introduced by the President that is going to be approved in the Parliament with a two thirds majority?

A: I think it is really for the Parliament and the elected Government in Sri Lanka to determine issues of governance in the country. The Constitution in India has been amended on over 90 occasions, with successor Parliaments sometimes rescinding earlier amendments, considered to be unwarranted or undesirable. The Supreme Court in India has, however, ruled that Parliament cannot alter the 'basic structure' of the Constitution.

It is perhaps for the Judiciary in Sri Lanka to determine the Constitutional propriety of any amendment to the Sri Lankan Constitution.

Q: Do you think that President Rajapaksa will solve the problems of the minorities in Sri Lanka?

A: I think President Rajapaksa is better placed than any of his predecessors to end the sense of alienation of the Tamils of Sri Lanka. He has shown grit and determination in wiping out LTTE terrorism. It would be a great pity if he does not use the huge mandate he currently enjoys to see the emergence of a pluralistic, prosperous Sri Lanka, developing with peace within the country. There can ultimately be no military solution to political problems.

Q: The UN Secretary General Moon has appointed a panel to investigate alleged War Crimes by the Sri Lankan forces as well as the LTTE during the final phase of the war. Do you think the panel will make crucial decisions over Sri Lanka? Do you think these decisions will have any effect on the governance of Sri Lanka?

A: It is really for the Government of Sri Lanka to persuade the international community that it acted with due restraint during the final stages of the war against the LTTE. But as I said earlier, there can be no military solution to political issues. To my mind, what is of crucial importance today is to heal the wounds of the war with compassion and foresight.

Q: In southern Sri Lanka a new harbour project, constructed with Chinese help was opened. On the same day the EU has decided to conclude the GSP plus offer to the Sri Lankan apparel sector. So, what is your assessment of the economic management of the government of Sri Lanka?

A: It is only natural for Sri Lanka to seek good relations with all major centres of power in the world. I am sure Sri Lanka's leaders will act with wisdom to see that the Island is not drawn into the vortex of great power rivalries. But the major lesson of the Cold War was that every country has to show due regard for the core security interests of others in its neighbourhood.

Q: Why do you think the government of India did not ask the Government of Sri Lanka to investigate the role of Kumaran Padmanadhan, a.k.a. KP, in the assassination of former Indian Premier Rajiv Gandhi?

A: I think the Governments of India and Sri Lanka have cooperated extensively on investigations into the tragic assassination of Prime Minister Rajiv Gandhi. No one needs to have any misgivings on this score, or on the commitment of the two Governments to bring those who were involved to justice.

September 9, 2010

8
INDO-LANKA RELATIONS PRESENTLY
SEEM TO BE MOVING ON AN EVEN KEEL

India's consistent opposition to the carving out of a separate sovereign state of Tamil Eelam is based both on the international requirement normally to preserve the integrity of existing states and her national interests. She has herself often had to struggle to preserve her national integrity against efforts by occasional local movements to secede from the Indian Union.

- R. Swaminathan
(1932-2010)

"I do not agree with the LTTE's claim to be the sole champion of Tamil interests in Sri Lanka," R. Swaminathan , President & DG of the International Institute of Security and Safety Management (New Delhi); and a Trustee of the Catalyst Trust (Chennai), said in an interview with the writer.

Mr. R. Swaminathan spoke his mind clearly on Sri Lanka's crisis and India's option. He also spoke about the current nightmarish political and military developments in South Asia in an interview with the writer. R. Swaminathan joined Indian Police Service in 1954 and also served for nearly 33 years in central intelligence and security organizations. He was retired in 1990 as Special Secretary, DG (Security), Cabinet Secretariat, Gov't of India. He has been actively associated with a few think-tanks since his retirement from service and has published papers on national security and international relations.

"LTTE may now seem to be facing a critical situation towards the end of 2007, but it has shown in the past great resilience and capacity to rebound,' he said.

Whatever, "India may then be able to deal with an LTTE without Pirabhaharan and others involved in the assassination of Rajiv Gandhi," he observed.

According to him, "Sea Tigers, a third navy in Indo-Sri Lankan waters is not in the interest of India's national security"

Even, "the Tamil Eelam is in a different category and a Unilateral Declaration of Independence by Pirabhaharan is very unlikely to find any supporters in the international community," he said.

He must state at the outset that he have been retired from government service for more than seventeen years and presently have no role in the government. Whatever he state in this interview, therefore, represents only my personal views and assessments.

Excerpts of the Interview,

Q: Could you please let us know your assessment of the Indian foreign policy within the context of its regional interests and influence?

A: It is my view that India is already a significant power - economically as a matter of fact, militarily as a matter of relative strengths, and politically if these can be leveraged to her national advantage. Many analysts have for long been used to India being strong on rhetoric but an under-achiever, and it may not be easy for them to see that the ugly duckling is growing into a beautiful swan (like in Hans Christian Anderson's fairy tale). India is trying to achieve and is achieving in a few years what many other significant powers could comfortably achieve in many decades or centuries - as the world gradually evolved from the Middle Ages to the modern era. In the process, many intermediate steps are being skipped (as has happened in many areas of India's technological development) and this accelerated growth is not easy to cope with. Though India may seemingly have allowed foreign invasions and colonial rule to make her forget her glory days (except perhaps in speeches and school text books), it has to be recognized that India has in reality grown out of her exploited under-dog status of nearly two centuries and is speeding on her way to becoming a big power. India's changed (and changing) status has also caused significant changes in the expectations of other countries about India's involvement in world affairs.

India should be expected increasingly to make overall national interest the primary and supreme consideration in formulating her foreign and security policies. Domestic politics and partisan interests should and would always provide major inputs during the stage of consultations, but are unlikely to become reasons for casting doubts on the credibility of the national foreign policy as it emerges out of those consultations.

India's "Look East" policy, the recent interactions with ASEAN and initiatives in SAARC are part of her efforts to further her regional interests and influence. The difficulties in maintaining friendly and cordial relations with her smaller neighbors may be due to her earlier inability to deal with them as total equals. The smaller neighbors may be justifiably worried by the asymmetry in size, human and material resources and economic and military strengths. India's readiness to assert her national interests (e.g. India's role in the creation of Bangladesh, Indian support to the Tamil movements in Sri Lanka; Indian encouragement and support to its political favorites in different countries of the region) and continuing differences relating to the utilization of water resources may also be matters of concern to the neighbors. The affected countries tend to guard themselves by avoiding the development of very close (and possibly dependent) economic and other linkages with India, by developing (balancing) economic and military linkages with other countries. This often results in positions of near hostility, suspicion and distrust. The Indian Prime Minister's statement that India is willing to consider asymmetric concessions to her less developed neighbors (as distinguished from the customary rule of reciprocity in matters of trade and commerce), as and when translated into practical policy, should help in removing or lessening the perception of India as the ubiquitous "Big Brother" in the neighborhood.

There is a lot of talk about India and China being rivals for influence in the region. The reality, as I see it, is that both countries are actively pursuing their own national interests. In the process, there will be areas of cooperation, as there will be areas of competition. This should not pose any major problem as long as both countries are also aware of and are sensitized to the interests of the other country.

Q: What do you think about the Indo–Lanka relations based on its historical experience and its current and future interest?

A: Though India and Sri Lanka are physically separated by a narrow strip of sea, the peoples of the two countries are bound together by bonds of geographic proximity, historical ties, religious and cultural affinities and similarities etc. State level relations tend to fluctuate from time to time, influenced by domestic political compulsions, international situation, economic needs etc. Stable state level relations are possible only when they closely reflect the reality of people-to-people ties.

Indo-Sri Lanka relations presently seem to be moving on an even keel. The political relations between the UPA government in India and the Rajapakse government in Sri Lanka are "correct", though not yet very close. Economic relations are improving gradually, but the dialogue on defense and security matters is progressing very slowly (mainly due to differing perceptions and lack of full trust).

There are two major irritants in Indo-Sri Lanka relations. The first is the "ethnic issue", which we will discuss later, and the other relates to Kachchativu. The latter issue is really less about ownership and sovereignty over the small island than about fishing rights around it. However, the issue of sovereignty over the island has been emotionalized to an unduly large extent, both in Tamil Nadu and Sri Lanka. The regional parties in Tamil Nadu have never been happy with the 1974 and 1976 Maritime Boundary Agreements between India and Sri Lanka. The issue has become an irritant also in the relations between the Central Government and the Government of Tamil Nadu; and has the potential of radicalizing Tamil nationalism.

Despite the Maritime Boundary Agreements, Indian fishermen have continued to fish in areas (including those in Sri Lankan territorial waters) where they have traditionally been carrying on their vocation. The Palk Strait has also become the conduit through which the Tamil militants move their men and materials. Though all the concerned entities seem to be happy to let the situation simmer and be available (whenever required) as a stick to beat the other entities with, it needs to be defused with a sense of urgency.

The fishing communities on both sides of Palk Strait had jointly exploited (with hardly any outside intervention) the marine resources for centuries. If the two governments could restore to those communities the right and responsibility to work out friendly, cooperative and sustainable fishing in these waters, the problem could probably be solved amicably. The two governments could encourage and facilitate whatever the fishermen are able to agree upon and reserve the waters of the Palk Strait for joint and co-operative fishing, exclusively by artisanal fishermen of the littoral fishing communities.

Apart from the fishing issue, it is possible that people to people relations and the media can act as pressure groups to evolve some kind of synthesis between differing security and political interests and priorities of India and Sri Lanka. Intellectuals, human rights advocates, lawyers, press corps, artistes and film stars could easily set in motion a closer understanding between the two countries and eventually compel their governments to agree that cooperation on ecology and efforts to eradicate poverty and deprivation should receive higher priorities than narrow political considerations. When the peoples of two countries develop a vested interest in peace and good relations between their countries, the governments would have to follow suit.

The repeated movement of Tamil refugees from Sri Lanka to India includes the possibility of LTTE cadres sneaking in with them. This could lead to instability and spillover of the culture of violence in Tamil Nadu, as experienced some years ago.

India may give the impression of being a helpless spectator of the developments in Sri Lanka, but it has to be appreciated that presently she has very little influence on either the Rajapaksa Government or the Tamil militants. However, India has to be concerned about the growing presence and influence of non-regional Powers in Sri Lanka. If this trend continues, India may have to consider taking a more active role in Sri Lanka, much against her natural inclination.

Q: What do you have to say about Indian assistance to curtail the Tamil terrorism in Sri Lanka?

A: India is basically opposed to terrorism of any form anywhere. She has been suffering from terrorist activities for some decades, and still continues to be a victim of terrorism, some indigenous and some foreign-inspired and supported. In my assessment, India is and would be prepared to share her experience and expertise in handling terrorism and in defusing issues that give raise to terrorism. However, memories of the manner in which IPKF suffered in Sri Lanka are unlikely to permit India to provide any material assistance to the Sri Lankan Government (SLG) in tackling what you describe as "Tamil terrorism".

Q: India has been always stated that it will never support carving out a separate state of Tamil Eelam for the Tamils in Sri Lanka. Will India support any Tamil movements to campaign against the Sri Lankan government as it did in the past by giving military training and practical support?

A: This question is in two parts and I will try to answer both, one after another.

India's consistent opposition to the carving out of a separate sovereign state of Tamil Eelam is based both on the international requirement normally to preserve the integrity of existing states and her national interests. She has herself often had to struggle to preserve her national integrity against efforts by occasional local movements to secede from the Indian Union. [India's support to the inevitable separation of Bangladesh from Pakistan should be seen in the different context of an intolerable situation of "genocide" and large scale refugee movement.] A separate sovereign state of Tamil Eelam is unlikely to function of a classical "buffer state", but is more likely to have the potential to become a focus for pan-Tamil parochialism and nationalism.

On the issue of Indian support to Tamil movements campaigning against GOSL, I would like to draw attention to India's normal policy of "non-involvement" in differences between sovereign states and their populations of Indian origin. But non-involvement should not be interpreted as lack of concern. In Sri Lanka, Indian involvement was essentially triggered by GOSL's attempt to deny citizenship to a large number of Tamils who had been staying and working in Sri Lanka for generations. Subsequent efforts at discrimination and marginalization of the Tamil population, coupled with the non-addressing of legitimate grievances, led to a deepening crisis in the ethnic issue. The radicalization and polarization on this issue could probably have been avoided by tolerance of diversity and sympathetic understanding of grievances and aspirations. India has to discharge her moral responsibility to support the aspiration of the Tamils to be "equal" citizens of Sri Lanka.

It is unfair to second guess, with the benefit of hindsight, the Indian decision (more than twenty years ago) to provide military training and practical support to Tamil movements in Sri Lanka. It was obviously based on an objective analysis of the available facts and the prevailing ground realities. I am extremely doubtful if, in the current circumstances, India would repeat those actions.

Q: What is your assessment about the Liberation Tigers of Tamil Eelam (LTTE). Can you tell your views on their past, present and the anticipated future?

A: The LTTE was one of the many parallel Tamil movements that came up in protest against GOSL's decisions that were seen as discriminatory against the Tamils. It was, however, one of the most radical of those organizations and believed from the beginning that an independent sovereign state of Tamil Eelam was the real solution to the problem. LTTE was initially very reluctant to join the other Tamil movements in the 1985 talks at Thimpu, aimed at finding a solution through the devolution of powers to the Tamils, within an integrated state of Sri Lanka. Over a period of time, mainly through the free use of the weapons of violence and assassination, LTTE eliminated or marginalized most other Tamil movements. In the areas controlled by it, the LTTE has been able to establish a rudimentary state structure, without letting those areas become ungoverned and chaotic. Despite all this, I do not agree with LTTE's claim to be the sole champion of Tamil interests in Sri Lanka.

LTTE has had two faces - one as arguably the most effective champion of the Tamil cause and another as a dreaded terrorist organization. While there would be wide-spread support for LTTE's basic objective of getting justice for the Tamils, its use of terrorist methods and insistence on having a separate state perhaps do not elicit the same extent of support from the Tamils. There would, of course, be considerable reluctance to express any different point of view, as Prabhakaran and LTTE have shown total intolerance of any dissent or even any difference of opinion – with "elimination" being the favorite solution. Over the years, LTTE has shown itself to be one of the most ruthless, determined and murderous terrorist organizations.

LTTE may now seem to be facing a critical situation towards the end of 2007, but it has shown in the past great resilience and capacity to rebound. However, it would appear that the best days of LTTE are behind it. The differences between the eastern and northern cadres of LTTE may or may not lead to a change in leadership, but there may still be scope for that. India may then be able to deal with an LTTE without Pirabhaharan and others involved in the assassination of Rajiv Gandhi. It would anyway be unwise for India or any other concerned party to ignore the reality of LTTE.

The development and activities of the Sea Tigers and the fledgling air capability are major matters of concern, even after the damages claimed to have been inflicted by GOSL. A third navy in Indo-Sri Lankan waters is not in the interest of India's national security. The Bengal Bay is very sensitive from India's security point of view, not necessarily in the military sense only. India has to ensure the integrity of the Gulf of Mannar and Palk Strait, lest LTTE misuses them to smuggle material useful for waging war. The capability and potential of Sea Tigers to disrupt fishing in the Bengal Bay and for maritime terrorist acts cannot be under-estimated. The Government of India has made precautionary deployment of Coast Guard and Naval vessels in the area, but has been surprisingly quiet about the threat posed by Sea Tigers. This may be due to the peculiar compulsion of coalition politics, but the stage may soon come when India may have to take some hard decisions about the Sea Tigers. India may have to work towards the constitution of an international coalition against maritime terrorism, which could force LTTE (through diplomatic pressure if possible and through naval action, if necessary) to dismantle its maritime capability. The last unenviable option, if Indian security gets seriously threatened, may be for India unilaterally (or in collaboration with Sri Lanka) to take the necessary naval actions.

Q: In his recent Hero's day speech V. Prabhakaran, the leader of the LTTE demanded the international community to rethink their approach to support the Sri Lanka government on the conflict and also asked the Tamil Diaspora community to support the LTTE struggle. Will his appeal have sympathetic hearing?

A: It is my assessment that Prabhakaran's appeal displays elements of frustration and desperation at the present situation. I personally doubt if the appeal would have any effect, unless accompanied by changes in the behavior of the LTTE.

Q: If V. Prahakaran declares Unilateral Declaration of Independence will the international community support his effort like they did to recognize the independence of Kosovo, Montenegro and East Timor? What do you think about his present predicament and Prabakaran's war tactics?

A: I hope that Prabhakaran would not feel compelled to take such an ill-advised step. Kosovo and Montenegro had "voluntarily" joined the Socialist Federal Republic of Jugoslavia at the end of World War II. They were, in effect, retracting their earlier merger. Tamil Eelam is in a different category and a Unilateral Declaration of Independence by Prabhakaran is very unlikely to find any supporters in the international community. I doubt if the step (and the possibility of consequent isolation and sanctions) would even get the support of all the Tamils in Sri Lanka.

I feel that Prabhakaran and the LTTE would have to undertake a serious exercise of introspection, take into account all the realities and decide whether or not to pursue the goal of an independent state.

Q: How will the present politics in Tamil Nadu influence the Central government to intervene in the crisis in Sri Lanka?

A: The coalition regime in Indian politics produces some strange situations. Regional and ideological positions, which would normally be considered to be of marginal consequence, tend to acquire greater importance. In the case of Tamil Nadu, the regional political parties find it difficult to adopt moderate positions on many issues, lest they surrender ground to the more radical political parties like the Pattali Makkal Katchi. Even considering their present disproportionate influence in decision-making by the Central Government, I do not think that the mainstream politicians in Tamil Nadu would attempt to make the Central Government agree to intervene physically in the crisis in Sri Lanka; or that they would succeed if they made the attempt.

Q: How could the Government of Sri Lanka deal with the crisis it is facing for many decades now?

A: It was a complex situation to start with and successive governments, as well as many Sinhala politicians, helped to increase its complexity over many decades. It is therefore unrealistic to expect that there could be a miracle cure for this problem. The existing crisis of confidence needs to be overcome first. The first essential step would seem to be take measures to convince the majority of the Tamils that their legitimate grievances and aspirations would be attended to without their having to resort to coercive actions merely to be heard. The Tamils require to be convinced that Sinhala political parties do not consider them to be enemies or second-class citizens. If a comprehensive agreement cannot be reached with the Tamils, GOSL should be prepared to consider taking the initial steps unilaterally and hope that the Tamils would respond favorably to those gestures of reconciliation. Such an action would take the wind out of the sails of radical Tamil elements and strengthen the presently-silent moderates amongst them. This, however, calls for a major shift in the thinking of the Sinhala majority and its leadership. It is as yet a matter of doubt if they can summon up the necessary moral strength, maturity and pragmatism to take the step.

When Mahinda Rajapaksa won the Presidential election in November 2005, with the support of Janatha Vimukthi Peramuna (JVP) and Jathika Hela Urumaya (JHU), it was expected that the government would move away from Chandrika's federal formula for handling the Tamil insurgency.

Q: What is your observation (negative and positives) about the present Rajapaksa government in Sri Lanka?

A: I will answer this question only in the limited and narrow context of the ethnic problem. I am afraid that I cannot say anything positive about the present GOSL in that context. When Mahinda Rajapaksa won the Presidential election in November 2005, with the support of Janatha Vimukthi Peramuna (JVP) and Jathika Hela Urumaya (JHU), it was expected that the government would move away from Chandrika's federal formula for handling the Tamil insurgency. The President's approach to the ethnic problem appears to carry sufficient credibility to attract at least the guarded support not only of his electoral allies of JVP and JHU, but also of the erstwhile electoral opponents of Sri Lanka Muslim Congress (SLMC) and the Ceylon Workers' Congress (CWC). Though the LTTE was initially nudged back to the negotiating table at Geneva, the repeated provocative attacks by the Tigers on the security forces and the retaliatory attacks by GOSL on Tamil areas led to a situation where the Cease-Fire Agreement (CFA) has died, though short of a formal revocation by the signatories. On its part, the LTTE has clearly demonstrated that it is not prepared to work within the existing (or a slightly modified) system. After each hopeful pause, it resumes its violent methods. Along with the proclaimed terrorist outfit, the legitimate and democratically elected GOSL has done little to help in resolving the "Tamil problem". If anything, the Mahinda government has been equally responsible for escalating an intractable problem into one that is becoming near-impossible to solve.

Q: What do you think about present Military offensives against the LTTE by the state forces?

A: There have been many claimed successes. It would appear that the capabilities of the Sea Tigers have been severely crippled, at least for the present. Limited advances on the ground have also been reported. However, aerial bombardment of one's own territory (not under foreign occupation), with resultant casualties amongst innocent civilians, does not show GOSL as being in control of the situation. Some of the counter-attacks by LTTE have highlighted the weaknesses of the government. The military offensives cannot obviously be carried to their logical conclusion. I doubt the ability of the Sri Lankan Security Forces totally to eradicate the presence or influence of militant LTTE cadres from the areas presently controlled by them, much less from all of Sri Lanka.

Armies that have fought long wars are aware of the phenomenon of battle fatigue, resulting in lack of motivation and vigor. Similarly, historical evidence is that ethnic or ideological insurrections or revolutionary movements lead to their own versions of revolutionary fatigue. Sometime after the CFA stabilized to a certain extent, LTTE showed signs of having reached that critical stage. The intensified military offensives by GOSL has probably done more to remotivate and reinvigorate the fighting cadres of LTTE than any exhortation by Prabhakaran could have achieved.

Further, the continued offensives ignore the lessons of history. Any movement by an ethnic minority, based essentially on legitimate grievances of discrimination and perceived suppression, cannot be eradicated totally by military means alone. Military measures should be accompanied by sincere and sympathetic efforts to address the legitimate grievances and to minimize any discrimination by the state.

Q: Can Sri Lanka find an effective and a durable solution for the problem on its own?

A: The question should not be whether Sri Lanka can find an effective and durable solution, but whether Sri Lanka can afford not to find such a solution. Ideally, the solution should be totally indigenous and arrived at by consensus. Less ideally, it can be achieved with the help of mediators or intermediaries from outside. It is very clear to me that any solution imposed only by military force or majoritarian fiat would neither be effective nor durable.

December 8, 2007

9

HUMAN RIGHTS ARE BASIC TO
GOOD GOVERNANCE

*But I am not so sure even now I was wrong. The LTTE has an
elephantine memory. Is Karuna sure that a man with a loaded gun is not
roaming around even now to wreak vengeance on him for his sins of
parting with Prabhakaran? I am sure he is not; you can ask him. He
will agree with me.*

-R. Hariharan

I don't think even the TNA takes their own rhetoric seriously. My
suggestion to them is to cut off their umbilical chord with LTTE
quickly and work out a political package that is realistic in the
present context and sell it to the APRC, President Rajapaksa and, if
need be, India. (I don't know whether India would bet on them;
they did that in 1987 and got burnt.) Otherwise they will be
sidelined by Tamil people, said Col. R. Hariharan, retired Military
Intelligence specialist on South Asia, served as the head of
intelligence of the Indian Peace Keeping Force in Sri Lanka 1987-
90.He is associated with the South Asia Analysis Group and the
Chennai Centre for China Studies.

Here is the full text of Col. R. Hariharan's (retd) interview with the
writer.

Q: Are you optimistic about progress of the Sri Lankan Security Forces approach to wiping out the Tamil Tigers?

A: Yes; as of now the Sri Lanka security forces are poised to finish off the military capability of the LTTE. They will do it in the coming days it seems. When we are dealing with non-state actors - insurgents and terrorists - the terms "wiping out" has little meaning because a single suicide bomber in the wrong place at the right time can wipe out a leader as happened to President Premadasa or Rajiv Gandhi and that can cause immense changes. So I would not call LTTE's defeat as "wiping out" but military defeat.

There are many reasons for the present success against the LTTE but President Rajapaksa's single minded pursuit of the goal of "finishing off" the LTTE (regardless of the cost, national and international contrarian views, and other negative aspects of war) is the most important one.

The other important factor is Prabhakaran losing touch with the changed world attitude towards terrorist bodies. Now, after 8 years of 9/11, the world is making it more and more difficult for terrorist bodies to operate globally freely as they used to. Look at Pakistan and see the high price it is paying now for nurturing the Taliban. Prabhakaran did not factor this though Anton Balasingham probably understood this when he sold the idea of joining the Oslo peace process to the LTTE. After his death Prabhakaran probably lost even the little touch he had with the world as understood everywhere else.

The 3rd factor was Prabhakaran's fall out with Karuna. Karuna's exit from the LTTE and its important contribution to Sri Lanka's success is not given the credit it deserves. Strategically it freed the army from the burden of the east after the LTTE was swept out, while closing the recruiting base of the LTTE. It also split the Tamil ranks.

Lastly, the armed forces deserve full credit for fighting a well planned operation with effective military leadership and the coordination of the navy and air force which also rose to the occasion. It was a professional job. However, as we have limited information at this stage I don't know how much the victory cost the armed forces and the nation. But that does not diminish their successes.

Q: What in your opinion are the root causes of this very complicated and chronic war? The conflict in Sri Lanka is now internationalised. What is your assessment on this horrible problem and its root causes and its future?

A: In all wars root causes are of non-military in origin. Sri Lanka is no exception. In Sri Lanka you are not fighting with an external enemy but a segment of your own population. It became internationalised because the national polity could not cope with it politically when the opportunity was there. And it got out of hand.

In the closely, globally networked environment of the present days, no conflict - whether local or international - is going to go unreported. So in a way there are going to be no more national wars anymore because there is a huge international lobby for preserving the basic rights of every man - even if he is a murderer or a terrorist. Nations have to be prepared for this changing dynamics of war. On the plus side it has the advantage of drawing international support for a national war effort as President Rajapaksa has done.

But the turning point was the disenchantment of the Tamil population with Sri Lanka's leadership after the Black July riots. That ended their feeling of security and trust in the Sri Lankan state. Even now I wonder whether it is fully restored because too much blood has been shed on both sides.

The LTTE emerged as a powerful force because it cashed in on the failure of the TULF and the Sri Lankan State to resolve Tamil grievances politically. It provided use of force as the only alternative answer to achieve results. And for the next 30 years internal political differences in Sri Lanka hobbled the State from taking decisive political action to remove Tamil grievances. Similarly military action against the LTTE was in fits and starts. That was at the root of survival of LTTE.

Even now I am not too sure how speedily the Sri Lankan State is going to address the Tamil issue. Like most Sri Lankan Tamils (though I am not one) my level of optimism on this count is around 40 per cent only. I know this will offend many of your readers. But it can be turned to 60 per cent if the 13th Amendment is implemented in letter and spirit. It will go further to 75 percent if the APRC is allowed to present its unbiased recommendations and if they are implemented. Sounds unreasonable? No; that is because political solutions are not as neat as military ones. There are a lot of grey areas that cloud them. And both sides have to make sacrifices as much in a political solution as in a military solution. But politicians are generally reluctant to make sacrifices. But I live on hope.

Q: You were the head of intelligence on Sri Lanka, when the Indian Peace Keep Force was active in the Island nation, cracking down on the Tamil Tigers. The IPKF suffered around 1,255 killed in action and several thousand wounded; LTTE casualties are not known reliably. I know you have spoken and written so many times about that era and its strategies, and on countering, losing and winning against the Tigers. I would be happy if you can compare the past situation under the IPKF with the present situation under the Sri Lankan Forces.

A: I think the two situations should not be compared. Both are unique in their own way.

1. The IPKF was fighting with a half-baked mandate in a foreign nation - I am still not clear what its mandate was. So ours was not a national commitment but a political one reduced to a military responsibility; after all the country was not ours. We were operating in a Sri Lanka where both Sinhalese and Tamils were suspicious of us because their dreams and our reality were different. The change in national leadership in both countries created problems for the army both at home and abroad. We could not fulfil even our half-understood mandate because politicians in both countries did not want us to do it. All these things do not happen within your own country though politicians will always have their

own agenda but we are accustomed to dealing with them.

2. The LTTE then was learning conventional operations then but probably it is so fit now that it can teach others. It now has had both air and naval wings though the air wing was rudimentary. This showed the way it was thinking ahead of waging war always. Its international supply and support structure was now fully in place, as it could not depend upon India even for reliable covert supplies after it murdered Rajiv Gandhi. It was the unfinished job of the IPKF that opened up the world for LTTE's dream of building a conventional army. It was indirectly underwritten because the Tamil diaspora was terribly disappointed with India. (Even now they send me more hate mails than Sri Lankans from Sri Lanka!)

3. Our warfare was more restrictive. We did not use artillery and airpower (except gunships which were mostly used in Vanni; we had very few of them). We did not get any support from Tamil Nadu where the ruling party ensured that the pro-LTTE elements got the maximum leeway from our action. This was bad for the morale of troops.

I can keep on adding. But in the 20 years since we went there, warfare has become more deadly on both sides. That is the bottom line. I am glad I retired. Otherwise I might not have been here.

Q: If the LTTE hadn't assassinated your friendly and young Leader on your own soil, do you think India would never have turned against the Tamil Tigers?

A: In Tamil there is a proverb; *"Aththaikku meesai mulaithaal sithappa"*. In English it would be "If the aunt grows a moustache she would be uncle." Your question is like that. In India and Sri Lanka so many things have changed in the last 20 years. Tami Nadu is more global than local after the IT revolution. India has no more a soft spot for Moscow as in the Cold War period. The US is its strategic ally now. Both India and Sri Lanka are closer in relations than ever before. So we should not attach too much importance to Rajiv's death in India's deciding its Sri Lanka policy. But it did affect India's perceptions of the LTTE that had gone sour after the 1987 war. It closed the official door for it. If it had not happened perhaps India would have joined the co-chairs when the Oslo peace process 2002 came into being. That's what I feel.

You have given six points in 2004 of Karuna Amman and his newly built movement against the Tamil Tigers. According to your assessment in 2004, "Politically Karuna appears to be in a no-win situation. With so many issues loaded against him, can Karuna emerge victorious? Politics is the art of the possible; so the story may not end here. In Karuna's case he has started with the end move; he has to leave the gun to take to the political rostrum. But he cannot do that as long as the LTTE's threat to his person exists." But today Karuna has become a Member of Parliament through the Government. Actually I think he has won. But what do you think of his political career and his future?

But I am not so sure even now that I was wrong. The LTTE has an elephantine memory. Is Karuna sure that a man with a loaded gun is not roaming around even now to wreak vengeance on him for his sin of parting with Prabhakaran? I am sure he is not; you can ask him. He will agree with me. After all for lesser sins people like Amirthalingam and Neelan were done to death by the LTTE. Probably that is why Karuna hopes to join the SLFP; that would at least minimise the risk of meeting an infiltrator from the LTTE among the TMVP cadres.

About his politics, my answer is simple. I don't know. But as I said then, politics is the art of the possible. If he can do good as an MP I am sure he can establish himself politically. Let us give him some peaceful time before he does that. He is making the difficult journey into the political field which is no less dangerous than a military mine field. And in Sri Lanka in both fields people die.

Norway, Japan, USA and EU have asked the Tigers and the government of Sri Lanka to negotiate terms for the LTTE's capitulation. At the same time, the four countries are determined that the government in Colombo must demonstrate that it can respect its international human rights obligations and give international representatives unimpeded access to inspect camps where Tamils are held in custody or under supervision. But the

GoSL rejected the truce with the Tigers and also at the same time the Tigers didn't give any comment on their laying down arms. In this context what is the responsibility of the International Community on the Lankan issue?

Human rights are basic to good governance. It is essential for the State to demonstrate to its citizens that it gives them these rights that are denied by totalitarian organisations like the LTTE. Each state has to make its decision on this, not because others have a better or worse record, but because it has to make a difference to win the war against insurgents. And so Sri Lanka has no choice on this if it truly wants to win the war. It does not matter that the US has Guantanamo Bay, and Israel uses cluster bombs on Palestine refugees. Sri Lanka is not their country; Sri Lanka is yours.

International responsibility is a nebulous thing. It is elusive. Look at the Palestine problem. The least they can do is to ensure that the LTTE does not flourish on their soil while helping Sri Lanka's polity to ensure that the Tamil issue is resolved amicably and quickly. They should use non-military leverage that nations use in such situations. Otherwise again there will be the growth of a second generation insurgency that nobody including the international community wants.

In the meantime the Tamil National alliance has said to the Tokyo Co-chairs who called on the Tamil Tigers to lay down their arms and surrender to the Sri Lankan government, that it has been the firm and consistent position of the Tamil people that the island of Sri Lanka is inhabited by the Tamil nation and the Sinhala nation. What do you think of the TNA's concept of two nations within one country? Do not forget that the TNA MPs are paid and maintained by the Sri Lankan Government, and when they take oath they promise to protect and uphold the constitution of the Sri Lanka.

I don't think even the TNA takes all this rhetoric seriously. My suggestion to them is to cut off their umbilical cord to the LTTE quickly and work out a political package that is realistic in the present context and sell it to the APRC, President Rajapaksa and if need be India (I don't know whether India would bet on them; they did that in 1987 and got burnt). Otherwise they will be sidelined by the Tamil people. I am not too sure that it has not happened already. Except for a few of them most TNA leaders are not to be seen in parliament so what is all this talk about the oath and so on.

At the end of the War, the post War situation in Sri Lanka will be as important a period as the present situation in the country. Nowhere in the World can we see an easy "mission totally accomplished" end in guerrilla warfare. A good example is eastern Sri Lanka which the Government declared liberated many months ago, but there are still some serious military incidents happening there. According to your reading, how does Sri Lanka totally accomplish mission over the civil war?

First don't promise too much to the public. I think patience is a Buddhist virtue. But that does not mean the government should take its own time. I think the most important thing is for Tamil people everywhere to feel secure. So if you have an army garrisons in every town in the North and the East for the next 5 years, your mission is going to be dismantled invisibly in the minds of people. People must be involved in development plans and restoration of normal life. That means local governments must become operational. Accessibility to government benefits must be without discrimination. Government should learn to talk Tamil. There is a Tamil description for Lord Murugan: "Thamizhil waidharyum Vazhthuvan," meaning the God is supposed to bless even those who abuse him in Tamil. That is the power of this language over its people. (Probably it is the same for the Sinhalese people; but I don't know Sinhalese; but I can imagine.)

If you carry out military operations while the visible results of peace gradually come up, people will help you to win the war against the insurgency. This is what we have seen in the Punjab and Mizoram. And this is what we have to do in Kashmir I have no doubt. So that is what Sri Lanka should do if it wants to prevent a resurgence of the LTTE; not by occupying HSZ forever (we are vacating our own version of HSZ in Kashmir now).

People should feel they are better off after the war than before. It is as simple and as complex as that depending upon how you want to go about it. In the East the more difficult option is being adopted. I hope they change it.

February 7, 2009

10
INDIA IS CLEAR IN ITS SUPPORT TO THE SRI LANKAN GOVERNMENT

Acquiring basic flying skills to fly the type of aircraft acquired by the LTTE is relatively an easy task. Any of the flying schools today could train an aspirant to fly an aircraft in a matter of months if not weeks. However, the consolidation of flying skills and particularly night flying skills would require little more application and training. The ingenuity of the LTTE in modifying a simple aircraft for use against well-defended targets needs to be appreciated.

- RS Vasan

COMMODORE RS Vasan IN Retd has rendered distinguished military service of over 34 years. His shore assignments include command of two naval air stations, Maritime Air Squadron, Air Crew Examiner, member of the faculty at the College of Naval Warfare and Chief Staff Officer of the Southern Naval Command at Kochin.

He commanded a patrol vessel for the IPKF. Prior to his retirement, he was the Regional Commander of the Eastern Region of the Indian Coast Guard. Presently, he is steering the Maritime Security Programme at the Observer Research Foundation a major

Indian think-tank.

Question (Q) : Could you please explain to us the current political and military developments in Sri Lanka and their implications?

Answer (A): For any observer and analyst it would be quite clear that the SL military has an upper hand now despite some daring attacks of the Anuradhapura kind by the LTTE. The LTTE undoubtedly is militarily weak. However, any additional pressure applied by the Sri Lankan Military would invite more such suicidal attacks by the black tigers. It is perhaps the ripe time to ensure that there is some kind of concrete acceptable proposal that is both face saving for the LTTE and is practical enough to be considered and speedily implemented. If this time were missed out, the agony of this struggle would be prolonged. Both Sri Lanka and the LTTE would then be responsible for not utilizing the opportunity to break the ice.

Q. Who in your opinion are the persons with responsibility for the growth of military capabilities within the Liberation Tigers of Tamil Eelam?

A. This question has answers in the historical aspects of whatever has happened since the struggle for Eelam began. The impressive growth in the initial stages is obviously due to the massive support received from expatriate Tamils in Western countries. The LTTE leadership was well aware of the need to strengthen its capability primarily at sea, then land and of course in the air dimension. If it was the late Mr. Balasingham who orchestrated the cause and found support in the UK and the EU, closer home, it was the team of KP, late Kittu, Soosai, Colonel Shankar ably guided by Mr Prabhakaran himself.

Activities of KP in procuring high-end technology weapons and sensors are too well known to bear repetition. If he succeeded it was also largely due to both the easy availability of military hardware from diverse sources across the globe at that time. It was also possible to procure second hand ships to be registered as Flags of Convenience (FOC) to promote both legal and illegal sea trade. The primary market apparently remained in the Southeastern countries.

As per reports, money came from donations, taxes, extortion and even drug trafficking. It must be acknowledged that the LTTE has outsmarted its adversary in the past by thinking out of the box and coming out with innovative ways to deal with the SL Military and the Government. The LTTE by and large scouted for highly sophisticated equipment to outwit the security forces. The break-up of the Soviet Union and the Afghan war also threw up many sources for illegal arms procurement.

The only reason why it is becoming increasingly difficult for the LTTE to procure freely and transport essentially required military hardware is the scenario post- 9/11. This has brought in so many restrictive regimes across the globe that it has become difficult if not impossible to continue in the same manner for procurement of essential and critical military hardware. The implementation of security regimes such as the International Ship and Port Security code (ISPS) in July 2004, Maritime Security Operations (MSO), Regional Maritime Security Initiatives (RMSI), Proliferation Security Initiative (PSI), and Container Security Initiative has succeeded in plugging loopholes in the entire maritime domain where mischiefs are better detected and handled. In addition the strict surveillance control on financial transactions of large-scale has rendered it difficult for such transactions to go unnoticed.

Q: What exactly is the air threat that seems to have sent a shiver down the spines of the countries of South Asia?

A: First of all it must be understood that the air assets that the LTTE has acquired are not of the highly sophisticated variety nor do they have high payload carrying capacity to make a difference. The aircraft as now established are the Czeck built Zlin 142, which has been modified to undertake both night missions and attack missions. The dropping of a few hundred pound bombs on three occasions has unnerved the observers. Acquisition of air capability does add a new dimension to the ongoing warfare. However, the limited numbers and the type of aircraft do not pose such grave danger. The aircraft procured are no match for the SLAF. The only reason for the success is some excellent planning based on sound intelligence and well-coordinated simultaneous /advance ground commando operations as in the case of the recent attack on Anuradhapura.

Q: What are the weaknesses of Government of Sri Lanka from the perspective of their own security?

A: From the military point of view, in fact the Sri Lankan military is in a much better position today due to the sustained operations against the LTTE, which have nullified the claim of invincibility of the LTTE. However, any conventional military would suffer losses due to the guerilla operations once in a while. The aspect of suicide attacks has the most damaging effect on the military as such attacks are dramatic and cause extensive damage to life and property.

The suicide squads as in Iraq are already ready to die so they are not inhibited by the nature of the target or terrain or other obstacles. On the part of the LTTE this would continue to bring down the number of able-bodied youth who can sustain the guerilla operations or suicide missions.

Q: One day you mentioned that the aircrews of the LTTE would have been trained abroad in one of the flying schools. Can you tell us more about the skills of the LTTE aircrews and when and where they might have finished their training?

A: Acquiring basic flying skills to fly the type of aircraft acquired by the LTTE is relatively an easy task. Any of the flying schools today could train an aspirant to fly an aircraft in a matter of months if not weeks. However, the consolidation of flying skills and particularly night flying skills would require little more application and training. The ingenuity of the LTTE in modifying a simple aircraft for use against well-defended targets needs to be appreciated.

As I have brought out elsewhere, it is clear that the foundations laid for the growth of the air tigers by late Col Shankar are really strong. Due to the spurt in aviation growth worldwide, there has been a proliferation of aviation training schools in the US, Canada, South Africa, Australia, Singapore, Southeastern countries and many more corners of the world. After acquiring the basic skills some advanced training to meet the standards set by air tigers could be undertaken in any of the flying schools on payment.

Q: So many times the Sri Lanka Air Force has been found to use Israel made K-Fir in bombing LTTE areas. Also they have claimed to destroy LTTE military targets. What do you think of their Air Strikes against the LTTE? Are they effective?

A: The success of any air attack is dependent on the precise knowledge of the targets and enemy movement at the time of such attacks. In addition the training level of the air crew, the capability of the aircraft and the enemy's air defence would decide, indeed largely dictate the success or otherwise of an air mission. The SLAF has been successful on many of the missions undertaken. Both the Kfirs and the Migs are good aircraft and have the potential to take on identified targets. There would be always claims and counterclaims about the efficacy and effectiveness of the attacks. It is clear that the SLAF has made a great difference to the course of the war against LTTE which has not been able to shore up its anti-aircraft capability. The skies are virtually ruled by the SLAF.

Q: What are the differences between LTTE Air Wing attacks and Sri Lanka Air Force Attacks?

A: The difference essentially in the nature of attacks. The attacks by the SLAF are largely conventional against targets identified for attack. Such identification could be based on intelligence, surveillance and or on request of the ground forces that are advancing. The Air tigers have been innovative, motivated, daring in their exploits and yet extremely careful thus far in preventing neutralization of their assets both in the air and on the ground.

Q: LTTE have for the first time used Black Tigers and their light aircraft together in their latest attack on the Air Force base in Anuradhapura. Is there any significance to this?

A: This is what led to the success of the LTTE. The rest of the world was led to believe in the initial stages that it was the air attack of the LTTE that destroyed the aircraft and helicopters on the ground. It is only some hours later that the actual picture emerged.

It just brought out the excellent way in which this attack was planned. The destruction of the aircraft was on the ground by the commandos of LTTE and not by the air attacks. The aircraft arrived on the scene only after the commandos were in control and had given a green signal for the aircraft to attack. In fact, after the success of the black tigers, which caused such extensive damage, the air attack would be viewed by the LTTE itself as only an icing on the cake in an operation that was executed to perfection.

Q: Please comment on the government of Sri Lanka's implementing strategy behind the war against the LTTE .

A: As I have indicated earlier in an answer to another question, at this time, militarily the Sri Lanka Military has an upper hand. From that point of view, the Government has succeeded in weakening the LTTE. The strategy was essential if the Government had to negotiate from a position of strengthen. In the past it has been observed that the LTTE normally comes to the negotiating table only if it is perceived to be in a powerful position. It is necessary therefore to avoid a stalemate situation. However, the present spate of successes should only pave way for a dialogue that would enable some devolution of power and cessation of hostilities so that Sri Lanka can concentrate on its welfare, social and economic progress of all its integrated citizens.

Q: Can Government of Sri Lanka ever annihilate the LTTE?

A: Theoretically yes. However, this is something that is not dependent on the Sri Lankan Government alone. As long as there is support for the Tamil cause, however weak, it would be difficult. There is perhaps a need to allow the LTTE to change its face and give it an opportunity to participate in the political process. There is a misconception that the LTTE alone represents the viewpoint of all the Tamils. This is hardly the position. Other moderates who are willing to bring about peace by other alternative methods need to be encouraged.

Q: Please comment on India's role in Sri Lanka under the present situation? Is India playing any role at all? How should India's position change?

A: India has looked at this as an internal problem to be sorted out by the Sri Lankans themselves. Despite some voices of support from some political parties in Tami Nadu, the ruling party is not interested in supporting the LTTE which itself stands banned in India. There is definitely lot of behind the scene activity to facilitate the process of normalization. As long as the LTTE is at the head of the political process, India would not be in a position to accept a mediatory role even if invited. It would choose to support the actions of the Sri Lankan Government to come out with a package that would protect the interests of the Tamils in a united unified Sri Lanka without any division.

India is clear in its support to the Sri Lankan Government on the need to find a solution soon. India can only wait and watch while the elected Government in Sri Lanka headed by the President is indirectly helped to expedite the peace process.

October 29, 2007

11

LTTE SHOULD HAVE SENT OUT 'POSITIVE SIGNAL' TO 48-HOUR CEASEFIRE

There is overall agreement among all major political parties at the national-level that there can be no military solution to the Sri Lankan issue and that a permanent political solution should address the legitimate concerns of all communities within a united Sri Lanka. This has also been the position of the Indian Central Government all along, and whichever party is in power, there is no reason to believe that this position would undergo any drastic change.

- N. Sathiya Moorthy

DESPITE various speculation to the contrary, I presume that President Rajapaksa is as keen as anyone else to usher in peace and prosperity, based on power-devolution that derives from a political solution. I guess he is alive to the political possibilities and even electoral necessities deriving from the Tamil constituency, said N. Sathiya Moorthy, Director, Chennai Chapter of the Observer research Foundation, a well-known Think Tank in India in an interview with the writer.

Question (Q): The Co-Chairs and many other nations have called upon the LTTE to lay down arms, and the Sri Lankan Government to end hostilities. Neither has obliged. What is your comment?

Answer (A) : Disappointing as it maybe, the reaction of the two sides was not wholly unexpected. Clearly, the LTTE's ranks are dwindling. Minus the civilian population, which they seem to use as 'human shields' in whatever form, they may have to give in to the superior force of the Sri Lankan armed forces, both in terms of men and material. The Government, at the instance of the Indian neighbour, announced a 48-hour informal ceasefire, couching the announcement more as a warning to satisfy the local constituency. The LTTE did not respond favourably. Obviously, the LTTE was concerned about the post-evacuation scenario, where it would have become indefensible. A 'positive signal' at that stage might have helped the international community to try and prevail upon the Sri Lankan Government to look beyond civilian evacuation. It is anybody's guess how the Government would have reacted under the circumstances. Yet, there was no harm in the LTTE sending out a positive signal that it was ready to consider a ceasefire of sorts, if modalities could be worked out through mutual exchanges, or through facilitators. It would not have changed the ground situation for either – whatever the final outcome of such a strategy. In the absence of any such an initiative on the part of the LTTE, the Government might have decided that enough was enough – and that the LTTE was using the civilians as a fodder in their defensive war on the battle-front and propaganda war, overseas.

Q: Do you think an end to the LTTE is the end to the ethnic problem in Sri Lanka?

A: No. Any end of the LTTE on the conventional battlefront could still leave behind remnants that could become a thorn in the flesh for the Sri Lankan State in the form of guerrilla warfare. I think the security forces would have thought about strategies to nullify such possibilities. However, we need to remember that all Tamil militant groups, starting with the LTTE, had started off only as guerrilla groups and had excelled in the art and craft of the same. The Government also needs to remember that apart from incidents like 'Pogorm-83', it was the search-and-destroy operations targeting the Tamil militants in the North and the East that ended up alienating the local population so very completely, through the late Seventies and the Eighties. Unlike in the conventional war, the security forces would be fighting ghosts at best and shadows otherwise, if and when the current phase of war reverts into a guerrilla affair.

We also need to remember that many of the LTTE cadres now would be in the 30-minus age-group. They would have been born after the early incidents of the Seventies and the Eighties. They are as much the victims of the hate-campaign that the LTTE would have indoctrinated them in *vis a vis* the Sri Lankan State apparatus as they are the progenies of the early victims of the ethnic issue. They need to be convinced that there is life beyond this hate-campaign, and the Sri Lankan State is not a single-agenda institution. They also need time to readjust themselves to the changing situation, which alone would teach them that all may not be as bad as has been told to them. Only a honest political process and sincere implementation would help extinguish Sri Lankan Tamil militancy from within. Military measures are but only the first step – to facilitate such a process, by ensuring that the LTTE does not continue to be a hurdle, with its monopolist views, enforced by a monolithic leadership.

Q: How early do you think is peace possible in Sri Lanka?

A: In physical terms, early signs to an early peace are already visible, but it all depends on what we see as peace. If one is talking only about a peace of the graveyard, enforced through a military victory, it might already be here. I hope, neither the Sri Lankan Government, nor the security forces are not looking at it that way – as some observers would like to believe. Real peace would have arrived only when the political processes are set in motion – and a permanent solution is found on the power devolution front, preferably through the inclusive process of negotiations.

Q: What do you think is President Mahinda Rajapaksa's doctrine as far as the future phase of the current situation is concerned?

A: Despite various speculation to the contrary, I presume that President Rajapaksa is as keen as anyone else to usher in peace and prosperity, based on power-devolution that derives from a political solution. I guess he is alive to the political possibilities and even electoral necessities deriving from the Tamil constituency. The Government seems to have concluded, and not without reason, that for a political process to be set in motion and a power-devolution plan to be implemented on the ground, the LTTE needed to be de-fanged. There are going to be hitches and hurdles, interpretations and imputations. I expect President Rajapaksa to raise above petty political considerations and appeal to the entire Sri Lankan nation, and not just a section thereof, as is being made out by some. After all, he had the strategy to win the war. I think he has a strategy to win peace, as well.

Q: What is your assessment of the post-war era of Sri Lanka and the Tamil political power in the island-nation?

A: Rather than assessment, I would outline my expectation. For anything to be achieved, the Tamil polity has to remain united. They cannot remain divided and keep complaining about the Sinhala polity or the Sri Lankan State alone – not that the divisions within them is a justification or excuse for the other two to run rough shod over their legitimate aspirations. Not many people would have noticed it, but there are over 45 Tamil-speaking members in the 225-seat Parliament. They are divided under three broad categories – of Sri Lankan Tamils, Muslims and the Indian Tamils, but the political divisions are countless. There are no great ideological divisions among any or all of them, unlike in the case of the majority Sinhala polity. If only they remain united and put their societal demands ahead of personal perceptions of the self and their own groupings, they could command the respect not only of the larger Tamil-speaking population but also of the Sri Lankan nation as a whole. I hope the post-war scenario provides the environment and creates the mood for such a turn.

Q: Former LTTE militant leader 'Col' Karuna has joined the ruling SLFP. How do you view this development?

A: Independent of the internal squabbles within the LTTE first, and the ruling Tamil Makkal Viduthalai Puligal (TMVP) in his native Eastern Province, the cross-over by 'Col' Karuna to the

SLFP should be a welcome sign of sorts. His reasons and explanations might not be acceptable to all Tamils – but then it has opened up the possibilities. After all, there were and are also other Tamil members of Parliament in the two Sinhala political majors, namely, the UNP and the SLFP. Until his assassination last year, you had Jeyaraj Fernadopulle, a Tamil who had been winning parliamentary elections from a traditional 'Sinhala majority' electorate. He was a Minister, Government Chief Whip in Parliament and also the treasurer of the ruling party. Even very few Sinhala leaders had reached that stage. It's easy to dismiss elevations like this, of Tamil-speaking leaders even in the Sinhala polity. Why, you even have Tamil-speaking members of Parliament in the JVP, which is dubbed the 'Sinhala nationalist' party from deep South.

Q: There is a lot of political action in Tamil Nadu over the ethnic issue. How do you think it will play out?

A: I think things are slowly evening out. DMK Chief Minister Karunanidhi has taken the initiative to put the position of larger Tamil Nadu in perspective. He has even publicly invited the Opposition AIADMK to join hands with the DMK parent and the State Government to move forward together on the 'Sri Lankan Tamil issue'. More than ever he has since clarified that the LTTE issue and the larger Sri Lankan Tamil cause are distinctively different. This has been the position of the two Dravidian majors, namely, the DMK and the AIADMK, all along, but the clarification has helped. It also gels with the overall position of successive Indian Governments, particularly after the Indo-Sri Lanka Accord, and more so after the 'Rajiv Gandhi assassination'. As is known, the Congress, the BJP and the CPM, from among the national parties have always maintained such a stance. Minus the minor aberrations in the State CPI, overall, the party holds a near-similar line on the issue at the national-level.

Q: At the national-level in India, BJP Opposition Leader and former Deputy Prime Minister L K Advani has criticised the Congress-led UPA Government for its handling of the Sri Lankan situation? How do you view this?

A: The differences, if any, between the Congress-UPA and the BJP-NDA pertain only to details. They have all drawn the distinction between the LTTE's needs and demands on the one hand, and the larger Tamil concerns and cause, on the other. There is overall agreement among all major political parties at the national-level that there can be no military solution to the Sri Lankan issue and that a permanent political solution should address the legitimate concerns of all communities within a united Sri Lanka. This has also been the position of the Indian Central Government all along, and whichever party is in power, there is no reason to believe that this position would undergo any drastic change. Whichever party or alliance comes to power after the upcoming parliamentary polls, they would pursue a political course to find a permanent solution to the ethnic process, without interfering with the schemes and systems of a sovereign nation that Sri Lanka is. To them all, a permanent solution does not flow either from the barrel of the gun or the military neutralisation of the LTTE.

12

SITUATION IN SRI LANKA
ABSOLUTELY GRIM

That the Indian government armed and trained the LTTE is well known. But then it switched sides. India has done everything it can, including blocking the demand for an investigation into the possibility that the Sri Lankan government might be guilty of having committed war crimes in this war against the Tamil people of Sri Lanka.

- Arundhati Roy

"THAT the Indian government armed and trained the LTTE is well known. But then it switched sides. India has done everything it can, including blocking the demand for an investigation into the possibility that the Sri Lankan government might be guilty of having committed war crimes in this war against the Tamil people of Sri Lanka."

"Her voice is calm but the words in her vocabulary are the strongest in the world." This is my assessment on Arundhati Roy, a well-known author and social activist in India whom I met recently. In an exclusive interview with the writer, Ms. Roy has shared her views on the present situation in Sri Lanka. "The situation sounds in Sri Lanka absolutely grim, she exclaimed. There are no need write about Arundhati Roy, although, her name rings across the world. Her books and her essays; even her other social activities are very controversial. "Indian civil society is a vast and varied creature. Most people in India have absolutely no idea what happened in Sri Lanka, because the Indian media was careful not to report it," she said when I asked about present gloomy interests of an Indian civil society towards situation in Sri Lanka.

Speaking about war in Sri Lanka which has ended last May, Ms. Roy suggested, "I believe that the Government of Sri Lanka should be investigated for committing war crimes." "I am in no way pro LTTE nor have I ever been. I cannot admire those whose vision can only accommodate justice for their own and not for everybody," she has pointed out on her view regarding the Tamil Tiger rebels a.k.a Liberation Tigers of Tamil Eelam.

Even talking about the policy of the Government of Sri Lanka, Ms. Roy asserted, "I do believe that the LTTE and its fetish for violence was cultured in the crucible of monstrous, racist, and injustice acts that the Sri Lankan government and to a great extent Sinhalese society visited on the Tamil people for decades." Has the Rajapaksa Government's openly nationalized almost fascist rhetoric? What has Arundhati Roy said? Read full text of the interview is below;

I would like you to share your thoughts with our readers on the present political and military climate in Sri Lanka as well as your thoughts on the ongoing war against Naxalite in India, that is considered as deadly threat to the internal security of India, according to the Leaders of the Government of India.

Q: So how do you summarize the present political developments in Sri Lanka six months after the elimination of the Tamil Tiger rebels?

A: The situation sounds absolutely grim. I have not visited the camps myself, but from the reports that are emerging it is obvious that there is an unconscionable humanitarian crisis unfolding which the world seems to be turning it's eyes away from. For hundreds of thousands of people to be herded into camps and held there by a government that is so blatantly gloating over its military victory over them is a terrifying situation. Mind-numbing. The use of the term 'concentration camp' does seem appropriate given the few testimonies that have made their way out of the steel wall of silence the government has erected around them. If these testimonies are untrue, and if the Government of Sri Lanka has nothing to hide it should allow the media free access to the camps so they can see what is going on.

Q: How is the Naxalite terror impacting on India?

A: Many of us here feel that the Indian Government has paid close attention to the Sri Lankan government's methods and will try to reproduce them to some extent in the region where the Maoist (Also called Naxalite) guerillas are, which also happen to be the mineral rich forest regions which the government wishes to clear for mining. I have just written a very long piece about it that you may like to read it's too a complex situation to discuss in a couple of sentences. However, unlike the Rajapaksa Government's openly Nationalist almost fascist rhetoric, which is even more extreme than the rhetoric of the Hindu nationalists—the BJP and its goon squads (the VHP and the Bajrang Dal)— the current Indian government has a different rhetoric, a different self-image. ..it is in a way, far more sophisticated and would not penly use such language. People in India are very disturbed by what is happening, and we hope our protests will be heard. But there are huge corporate interests at stake, running into trillions of dollars. So they won't back off all that easily. In this part of the world, so many countries are falling into civil war...Iraq, Afghanistan, Pakistan, Sri Lanka and now India. It is very worrying.

Q: The Government of Sri Lanka is saying it will resettle all Internally Displaced People (IDPs) before end of January 2010. It is interesting to read that the Government is ready to offer Colombo schools to ex-Child Soldiers of Tamil Tigers. Always we can hear victory euphoria from the Government side and its tune all the time is very optimal. Meanwhile, many Rights groups and some countries like the United States criticized the action of the Government of Sri Lanka, and are saying the Government is violating basic human rights, as well as there are some critical issues over war crimes by the Government in the final battle against the Tamil Tigers. But it seems the Indian civil society is having very little sympathy to the suffering of Sri Lankan Tamils. Let me know your views on War on Terror in Sri Lanka and the minority's future in the Island Nation?

A: Indian civil society is a vast and varied creature. Most people in India have absolutely no idea what happened in Sri Lanka, because the Indian media was careful not to report it. The section of the Indian establishment - those with a 'voice' are increasingly developing a ghoulish fascination for State power and its ability to crush people. There is a great admiration for Israel and its methods among this crowd. It is shameful. So this section has no problem with what has been done to an ethic minority. They have tolerated a huge amount of state brutality in their own country, in Kashmir, in Nagaland, in Manipur for years. My views on the Sri Lankan War? I believe that the Government of Sri Lanka should be investigated for committing war crimes.

Q: It is claimed by some quarters that India was behind the conflict from the beginning and gave weapons and other logistical support and also training facilities in her soil for the Tamil militancy few decades ago. But later India went against the Tamil militancy and went close to the Government of the Island nation. Let me know your views on the India's approach towards its southern neighbour in the future?

A: That the Indian government armed and trained the LTTE is well known. But then it switched sides. India has done everything it can, including blocking the demand for an investigation into the possibility that the Sri Lankan government might be guilty of having committed war crimes in this war against the Tamil people of Sri Lanka. India, China and Pakistan came together to block it. International politics is a cold, unforgiving game.

Q: The Prevention of Terrorism Act–or as you have called it, the 'Production of Terrorism Act'–is still in force in Sri Lanka, whilst hundreds of youth, most of them ethnic Tamils are being arrested under the PTA and held prisons or in undisclosed clandestine camps. It seems Patriotism, National Security, Humanitarian

Mission etc. of the government are overshadowing the Law and Order in the country. It is easy for people to be branded as patriots or traitors by under these missions thus undermining the law and order needed at this difficult juncture. If this continued what will be the long term consequences for Sri Lanka?

A: That is exactly what anti-terror laws are meant for. They are never meant for real terrorists. They are meant to terrorize ordinary people, to criminalize democratic space. In Gujarat in 2002 after Hindu mobs massacred Muslims on the streets, only Muslims were booked as 'terrorists'. Today India is passing laws that allows the government to call anyone it wants to a Maoist, a Naxalite. In India the bogey of 'Islamist terrorism' had an inherent flaw - the minimum qualification for a person to be booked was that he or she had to be Muslim. Now with the 'Maoist Terror' bogey that flaw has been rectified. The media's wild stories about Maoist terror has allowed the Indian Government to vastly expanded the catchment area of suspects. It can apply to any one of us. In Sri Lanka the long term consequences cannot be good. I don't believe that people who have been brutalized and robbed of their dignity will just keep taking it. The Tamils will rise again, not now, but some years from now.

Q: Whenever you came out with your views on the ground realities, you came under severe criticism of the Sri Lanka government as a supporter of the LTTE. Is this because your comments are considered pro-LTTE sentiments?

A: That is a pretty standard, self-serving way that most right wing governments have of dealing with criticism. It's the old Bush doctrine 'If you are not with us you are with the terrorists." I refuse to submit to it. I am in no way pro LTTE nor have I ever been. I cannot admire those whose vision can only accommodate justice for their own and not for everybody. However I do believe that the LTTE and its fetish for violence was cultured in the crucible of monstrous, racist, injustice that the Sri Lankan government and to a great extent Sinhala society visited on the Tamil people for decades. I also believe that the LTTE must take at least some responsibility for the cataclysm that has befallen the people it claimed it spoke for, and fought for. The tragedy of Sri Lanka's

Tamil people is one that all armed struggles, including the Maoists of India ought to learn from.

Q: My last question in this worthy meeting is about former US President George W. Bush's comment in the Hindustan Leadership summit that "the US recognised India's nuclear weapons programme and it is considered India's passport to the world,". While in her resent visit in Pakistan, US state Secretary Hillary Rodham Clinton said, Pakistan has failed in its mission against Islamic militancy while the Pentagon is giving millions of dollars to Islamabad. However, Pakistan has blamed India for fueling the war in Pakistan. What are your views on the cold war between Delhi and Islamabad, and the current US's Foreign policy towards South Asia.

A: My views on this are well known. What I fear, just from reading some stray signs, is that given the worsening of the situation in Pakistan, the Indian Government may be being 'persuaded' to send Indian troops to help the US out in Afghanistan. I really hope I am wrong. I also fear that the ratcheting up of the rhetoric between India and China may result in the US offering India 'protection' (which actually means India offering the US use of its airbases on the border…) And that like other countries that have been thus 'protected' by the US in the past- Iraq, Afghanistan, Pakistan - India too will devolve into chaos. I fear that greatly. We have enough trouble brewing internally without this added catalyst. I hope this Indian government can reign in its almost child-like desire to please the US. India's nuclear weapons did not make India a superpower. They made India buy into a game that it cannot hope to win. Once it was a proudly Non-aligned country. Now it is completely aligned, and feels no embarrassment in calling itself the 'natural ally' of countries like the US and Israel. Sad.

Nov 3, 2009

13
PRESENTING A THEME TO PERFECTION IS CREATIVE ART

"Art can be a tool for social change of political awareness. While art doesn't create revolutions, it impacts thought processes, responses and attitudes in a sub-conscious way. And often this has a lasting impacting in making us who we are."

- Nandita Das

"DURING my visits to Sri Lanka, which have always been memorable, I have always felt deeply saddened by the situation," said Nandita Das, an award-winning Indian independent film actress and filmmaker in an exclusive interview with the writer.

Nandita Das was born in New Delhi. Her father was the celebrated Indian painter, Jatin Das, originally from Orissa. And her mother was a writer, Varsha Das.

As an actress, Nandita is known for her critically acclaimed performances in Fire (1996), Earth (1998), Bawandar (2000) and Aamaar Bhuvan (2002). As a director, she is known for her directorial debut Firaaq (2008), which has won a number of national and international awards.

According to Nandita, "I think no violence can be justified and I hope the sane voices there are heard and the innocents don't continue to suffer."

We discussed several issues on her life as artists who are involved with social issues. "Art can be a tool for social change of political awareness," she has pointed out when I asked is art a tool of politics?

Question (Q): As a director, Nandita Das is known for her directorial debut Firaaq (2008), which has won a number of national and international awards. Why do you think Firaaq has been gathering so much adulation?

Answer (A) : During my many travels and interactions around the world, I have sensed a collective desire to understand the complex and violent world we inhabit and a palpable need for peace. I think Firaaq reflects that spirit and therefore touches the hearts and minds of those who have watched it.

Human emotions are universal and I see that with the kind of feedback I have got in different parts of the world. Across the board people have been able to empathize with the journeys of the characters. While the film has made the audiences aware of the context of the film they are also able to relate it to their own experiences. After every screening I had people wanting to engage, share their stories and ask a hundred questions.

People of all race, community, age and nationality have had similar responses, and so I feel it resonates at a very basic human level. At the end of the day, Firaaq is a human interest film, about the impact of violence on our lives and relationships. But there is hardly any violence in the film and yet you feel fear, tension, prejudice…the lingering effects of violence. It explores the fierce and delicate emotions of fear, anxiety, prejudice and ambivalence in human relationships during such times. And this reflects the situation around the world.

Q: What is it that inspired Nandita to move beyond the space in front of the camera to the one behind it?

A: As an actor, it was always exciting to watch the rest of crew work towards shaping up a scene. Often I would get involved with suggestions or just observe the whole process. Slowly the desire to tell stories, the way I wanted to, started growing stronger. So I thought maybe making a film and going through all its phases and having the space and freedom to tell one's own story would be more satisfying.

But I didn't think Firaaq would be my first film. Firaaq was born differently. It had to do with waking up to newspapers with stories full of violence; having conversations about religion and identity and soon finding oneself in a polarized 'them and us' debate; meeting many who were victims, and many more who remained silent .Firaaq is a reaction to all that and more.. It is an expression of all the helplessness, anguish, anger, frustration, and the fluctuating optimism I have felt over the years. I think what happened in Gujarat was deeply disturbing and I started engaging with the issue of communalism in a much deeper way. For me, making the film has been a cathartic experience.

I didn't think Firaaq would be my first film. Firaaq was born differently. It had to do with waking up to newspapers with stories full of violence; having conversations about religion and identity and soon finding oneself in a polarized 'them and us' debate; meeting many who were victims, and many more who remained silent ...Firaaq is a reaction to all that and more.

Q: How did Nandita go about casting her film?

A: While writing the script, I had mentally started casting. Although I was not lucky enough to get all of them, the four I did were precious- Naseeruddin Shah, Paresh Rawal, Raghubir Yadav and Deepti Naval. I got to experience a diverse range of talent as I searched for my characters; and finally an incredible cast came together. In addition to the four gems we have Sanjay Suri, Tisca Chopra, Shahana Goswami and Nowaz, and each one of them is no less. But the most challenging casting was for Mohsin, a six-year-old child in the film. I looked at many children in about ten schools and finally found Mohamed Samad. His eyes are full of wonderment, innocence, intelligence and resilience and that makes him a perfect Mohsin.

Q: How exciting was the transition from an actor to a director?

A: For me, in many ways acting to directing was a natural progression. But directing is far more consuming and obviously very different from acting, as it challenges every aspect of one's personality. The journey of making Firaaq has pushed my boundaries and by this I don't mean only creatively.

As an actor one doesn't realize how much more goes into a film than just the shoot. Also having gone through this experience I feel, a film is not the sum total of its parts. Directing entails making choices and decisions at every step and taking responsibility for all its aspects. There are 100 odd people who work on the shoot and as a director, you become like a parent! Also the post production has many technicalities and learning all of that on the job, was both challenging and exciting. However being an actor myself definitely helped my interactions with the actors in the way one could communicate to them.

Q: Have you followed the conflict in Sri Lanka?

A: It is very sad indeed that a country with such gentle people, those who respect nature, have had so much conflict and violence for so many years. During my visits to Sri Lanka, which have always been memorable, I have always felt deeply saddened by the situation. It is a global phenomenon that we are seeing where violence and identity politics are taking such dangerous roots. I think no violence can be justified and I hope the sane voices there are heard and the innocents don't continue to suffer.

Q: Is art a tool of politics?

A: Art can be a tool for social change of political awareness. While art doesn't create revolutions, it impacts thought processes, responses and attitudes in a sub-conscious way. And often this has a lasting impacting in making us who we are. In fact that is the reason art often threatens fundamentalists and that is why they choose to attack it or indulge in cultural policing. Art can trigger a dialogue that can make an individual or a society grow. It raises questions that stirs the stagnancy and helps to move towards finding solutions.

Q: Peace is a challenge in the region as well for the whole world. As a director, how do you read the present situation?

A: Yes, the whole world is in the siege of violence in the name of race, religion, language, caste or region. Till we don't take the responsibility of engaging with what is happening and speak out for those who are suffering, things won't change. Irrespective of our professions and other identities, we can't think that it is happening far away and will not touch our lives. It will, and it has. So the way to peace is by questioning one's own prejudices, reducing one's own anger and being the change we want to see in the world, as Mahatma Gandhi said, ' *violence can only be countered with empathy, compassion and love.* '

Mar 30, 2009

14
PAKISTAN HELPED THE SRI LANKAN
STATE FOR THREE REASONS

Winning the conflict primarily means winning hearts and minds in Tamil dominated areas and giving the ethnic minority and other political groups a sense of ownership. I don't think that the present leadership has the capacity to bridge the divide within the society.

- Ayesha Siddaqa

"THIS is a place where freaks get together to say and discuss anything under the sun, the moon and the stars. The faint-hearted or who suffer from high temper and anxiety may not join. Other categories not encouraged are those whose sense of political correctness doesn't usually allow them to be at peace with themselves. At a time when authoritarian regimes have found national and international partners and have learnt to control the mind, let's use this technology to stay connected and alive," Dr. Ayesha Siddaqa pointed this out a few months ago.

Ayesha is one of best military analysts in Pakistan who have diversified into other areas as well such as sociology of power politics, Islam and society and civil-military relations in South Asia.

"I am a gypsy writer and a social scientist," she said. She did her Ph.D. in War Studies from king's College, University of London. She also author of few books including (a) Pakistan's Arms

Procurement and Military Build-up, 1979-99 In Search of a Policy, and (b) Military Inc: Inside Pakistan's Military Economy.

In an exclusive interview with the writer, Dr. Siddaqa talks on current political and military trends in Pakistan as well as in Sri Lanka.

Question (Q): Please let us know your observation on present situation in Pakistan?

Answer (A): Like other states, especially in South Asia, Pakistan's present and future is defined by its past. The character of powerful stakeholders, their competing interests and relationship with each other have an impact on the state of the state. The country is a post-colonial state ruled by a predatory elite and constantly struggling to find a stable political path. This means that Pakistan at present is and will remain a weak democracy. The military no longer directly controls the state but that does not mean that it is powerless. The army decides all strategic matters pertaining to defense, national security, foreign policy, etc. The military just sits at the backseat, controlling the affairs of the state. Given the incompetence of the politicians and lack of vision, this situation is not likely to change. Another issue where we will not see a change either is Pakistan's relations with India which will remain hostile for the foreseeable future. The nature of the civil-military conflict and myopia of the ruling elite is creating continued instability in the country. We are in a whirlpool from where we seem unable to emerge.

Pakistan has a lot of potential. It has a trained bureaucracy, it has natural resources, and it has a fairly 'OK' infrastructure. However, what we lack is a vision -- the ability of the leadership to give a sense of ownership to its citizens and motivate them to operate jointly as a team. In many ways, Pakistan and Sri Lanka are similar. We have a similar kind of leadership which is unable to transcend their personal biases, personal greed and ethnic prejudices. We lack truly national leaders.

Q: Now that the LTTE has been defeated militarily, the Tigers no longer exist according to the Sri Lankan Government, and the general who led the country to its historic victory has now been arrested by the very government he used to work for after he ran as an opposition candidate in recent presidential election, what do you think of the post-War situation in Sri Lanka?

A: On the surface, not allowing General Fonseka to contest elections looks like a good idea. But the decision is more about the political and personal greed of the political masters and the present regime. It was equally responsible for the human rights atrocities. Is the current leadership able to bring peace and reconciliation between the different communities? I don't think so. Pakistan and Sri Lanka are similar. Both have a predatory ruling elite. This means a leadership which thinks mainly in terms of short term goals rather than long term objectives. Winning a military conflict is a short term goal but integrating a community to make a wholesome well-connected society is a long term goal that the Sri Lankan leadership is unable to achieve.

Personally, I have seen Sri Lanka change. The first time I visited Sri Lanka was in the summer of 1977, the year ethnic trouble started. But it was still relatively peaceful. Beaches were pristine and the level of education and communication of ordinary people was impressive. Even the beggars used to read English newspapers. Later, I re-visited Sri Lanka in 1996 and have been going there every year until my last visit, which was a longer stay, in 2006. The difference between the Sri Lanka of 1977 and 2006 is phenomenal. People find it harder to communicate in English and are becoming increasingly parochial. Changing the language from English to Sinhalese was a myopic decision and represents the predatory mindset of the ruling elite. This basically means that the leadership has limited capacity to repair the wounds which they have struck themselves.

Winning the conflict primarily means winning hearts and minds in Tamil dominated areas and giving the ethnic minority and other political groups a sense of ownership. I don't think that the present leadership has the capacity to bridge the divide within the society.

Q: When the military is used to circumvent the rule of law in a nation, how, from a practical perspective does this affect the basic freedoms of the citizens?

A: Of course, using the military internally is harmful from a human rights perspective. However, there are times when a state has to use oppression. We have to be carefully in understanding and analyzing the impact of the use of military by the state. A military, anywhere in the world, is the highest form of oppression that must be avoided. In South Asia there is a tendency to use military as a policy tool to solve internal conflicts. But this always exacerbates conflicts. Sri Lanka's problem is complex because here the politicians have opted to use the military as a tool of violence to solve political issues. Politicians often forget that allowing the military to use violence will eventually empower it and will be detrimental to the state and its political system.

Q: Do you think the current political situation in Sri Lanka is a sustainable one?

A: I haven't visited Sri Lanka after 2006 but what one sees through the media, winning the battle is less than half a victory. There must be a plan for socio-political appeasement. The Sinhala majority should show patience and tolerance in offering the Tamil minority greater political space. Without such voluntary concessions and effort at truth and reconciliation, things will not takeoff.

Q: It's obvious that the Government of Pakistan provided a great deal of help to Sri Lanka during the War and some reports go so far as to claim that a small number of Pakistani Air Force pilots participated in air raids against the Tamil Tigers. How do you see Sri Lanka/Pakistan military relations, and do these claims of Pakistani and Sri Lankan military personnel fighting alongside each other have merit?

A: Pakistan helped the Sri Lankan state for three reasons. First, increasing Pakistan's ability to participate in South Asian politics and posing itself as a counter-balance to India. Second: increasing its nuisance value in the region. Third: fighting Tamil militant forces which are considered a product of Indian intelligence agencies. A very minor objective may also be marketing and selling its locally produced weapons. I would say a better role would have been to put diplomatic pressure on the Tamils as well as the Sinhalese state in Colombo to negotiate peace. Sadly, while the Sri Lankan government has good ties with Islamabad, the same cannot be said about the majority of Tamil people who will always consider Pakistan as the culprit.

Q: Let us talk about Pakistan, specifically. How you see the developments after the passage of the Kerry Logger Bill passed by the US congress?

A: The Kerry-Lugar bill resulted in enhanced tension between the civilian government and the military. The later would never allow a civilian government to strengthen itself. Since the introduction of the said bill, the military is trying its best to weaken and destabilize the government. The rumor mill is constantly active churning out stories that undermine the government. This is not to suggest that the government is not incompetent. It becomes hugely problematic when the government is incompetent and inefficient. However, none of the stories against the government have an ending. Today, the popular opinion seems to be that remove President Asif Zardari and Pakistan will be saved. His departure through extra-political means will not solve the corruption or the political instability problem. The military is corrupt itself. It is punishing the political government for trying to counterpoise itself as an alternative to the army in front of the US.

Q: How do you view the role of the Army in Pakistani politics after the 18th amendment in the constitution?

A: I don't see things change in Pakistan, at least, in the foreseeable future. The NRO issue is still alive. This pertains to the National Reconciliation Ordinance signed between the (late) Benazir Bhutto and former President and army chief Pervez Musharraf according to which all cases of corruption and other charges will be withdrawn against her and she will be allowed to return to Pakistan in return for providing support to the dictator. Later, they parted ways and we witnessed her assassination. Bhutto's husband Asif Ali Zardari, who became the President of Pakistan, tried to weaken the military through the 18th amendment which basically introduces provincial autonomy in the country. It is not just political autonomy but financial autonomy as well which will eventually weaken the state bureaucracy. However, this also means that the military and its intelligence agencies will continue to weaken the political leadership in the provinces to ensure that provincial autonomy doesn't become effective. In any case, the provincial political leadership and bureaucracy is too fragile and major issues still unresolved regarding the command and control of bureaucracy for provincial autonomy to become effective.

Q: Many people claim that the Armed Forces, particularly the Pakistani Army, are behind the Islamic militancy in the country as well as in Afghanistan and India. There seems to be a double standard in the Pakistani military of going to great lengths to fight Islamic militants, yet politically actually sympathizing with them in many regards. What is your assessment on both the loyalty of the military to the cause of defeating militancy and protecting the stability of the state and the effectiveness of the military's efforts over the last few years?

A: The different form of militants is the creation of Pakistan army. Proxy war is a fairly popular policy tool in South Asia which got perfected starting from the early 1980s. This is when Pakistan military volunteered to raise an army of mujahideen jointly with the US to fight the Soviet military in Afghanistan. Later, the militant forces were used at other fronts particularly Kashmir. The Rawalpindi GHQ uses militants to fight India in Kashmir and Afghanistan.

Qs: There are reports that during the army action against the Taliban in North West Frontier Province there were killings of many civilians which were not revealed because the army has control of the media. What is your understanding of the fact or fiction behind these "mass grave" reports?

Did the military strike a significant blow to the militants in the North West Frontier Province? What do you know about claims the Taliban knew before hand when attacks were coming?

A: I would not want to address such specific issues but the fact of the matter is that there is the strategic linkage between the military and the militants. Such a policy means that information may reach the militants which may be passed on to them institutionally or individually. It is important for Pakistan to change this policy.

Q: What is your opinion about the restoration of the Judiciary and chief justice of Pakistan, do you think that the Judiciary is still independent? Or will it be able to enforce the rule of law?

A: Judiciary seems to have a mind of its own. It appears to be taking decisions without listening to dictates from the civilian government. But this does not make the judiciary less of a stakeholder in the country's power politics. Perhaps, more information and details about the moral health of judiciary might come out only if people did not have fear of being tried under treason. The state should have the capacity to judge people according to the same criterion. It was only a couple of days ago that a press report appeared in one of the newspapers claiming that the chief justice of the supreme court was also a beneficiary of free land distribution by the previous military government. I believe the political and legal system would be able to look at this case with the same lens as it uses in other cases.

Q: There are reports of more than 5000 people are missing in Pakistan after 9/11. Most of them are from Balochistan. How do you see the issue of disappearances being resolved?

A: There is no single institution of the state which has a concrete policy to address the issue. The military and its intelligence agencies, since they are involved in the cases of disappearance of the Baluchis, are not willing to talk about it. Similarly, the military, the political government is not ready to talk about the disappearance of people who were picked up at the behest of Islamabad's western allies. I don't see the issue seeing a logical end.

Q: Torture in custody is very common in Pakistan. Even the military is running torture cells in different containment areas. The ISI is also thought to have "safe houses" where torture is used to obtain confessional statements. There is no law in the Pakistan Penal Code which mentions torture as a crime. Would you like to participate in the movement against torture, through research, your analytical reports, or through your columns?

A: Of course, I would like to be part of such a movement. By the way, I have also written about this issue along with other columnists.

Q: In a recent interview former President Musharraf says that Kashmir is out of control, and he vowed to started politics again. So do you think that Musharraf will successful in Pakistan ?

A: Musharraf has no real future in Pakistan. There are many a people who will be after his life if he dares return. The army and the present service chief are not happy with Musharraf either. I don't see him returning to the country in the foreseeable future.

Q: Finally, do you feel that long-term peace is an achievable goal in the region? How can this be achieved, if it is possible at all?

A: Peace is achievable as long as the leadership in the region can have a vision about South Asia. Be it leaders in Pakistan, India, Bangladesh, Nepal or Sri Lanka, most are driven by their real political short-term objectives. Peace requires that we see each other as relevant. This means greater trade and all those opportunities that make people appreciate the worth of the 'other.' This is the only way that things will improve. Greater interaction is the key.

November 29, 2010

15
OLD GHOSTS WILL RISE AGAIN IF THE GOSL CANNOT ADDRESS CORE ISSUES OF THE ETHNIC PROBLEMS

If the concerns of the Tamils are not satisfied by mutual dialogue, even if militarily defeated, the old ghosts will rise again to torment later

I do not think India would ever plan to involve itself in Sri Lanka as it did in 1987.

- A. K. Verma

FORMER head of the Research and Analysis Wing (R&AW), an Indian External Intelligence agency, Mr. Anand Kumar Verma has given an interview to the writer, in which he shared his thoughts on the present situation in Sri Lanka and India.

Mr. A. K. Verma served as the head of the R&AW from 1987 to 1990, during which period he led mainly two external operations were known worldwide. One was "Operation Cactus" in November 1988, when the People's Liberation Front of Tamil Eelam (PLOTE) comprising about 200 Tamil secessionists' invaded Maldives. At the request of the President of Maldives, Maumoon Abdul Gayoom, Indian Armed Forces with the active assistance of the Research and Analysis Wing launched a military campaign to fight the mercenaries out of Maldives. The second operation was the Indian Peace Keeping Force offensive on Liberation Tigers of Tamil Eelam (LTTE) from 1987 to 1990.

He has explained why an Indian was involved with case the in Sri Lanka during 87-89, ignoring even the Tamil Nadu factor and Tamil nationalism, the ongoing military operations against the Liberation Tigers of Tamil Eelam (LTTE) and other complicated issues.

According to Mr. V. K. Verma, "training of Sri Lankan Tamils in India was, therefore, not a good idea. The situation in Sri Lanka was not comparable to East Pakistan in 1971, which became Bangladesh towards the end of that year. As later events were to prove Sri Lankan Tamils did not hold themselves beholden to India for all the assistance they received."

He doesn't believe military solution is the right one to the problems in Sri Lanka. He urged to find a sustainable political solution politically. "If the concerns of the Tamils are not satisfied by mutual dialogue, even if militarily defeated, the old ghosts will rise again to torment later," he pointed out.

Question (Q): How would you identify the concept of terrorism in South Asia?

Answer (A): Modern terrorism is linked to one's perception of violation of one's identity. It could be religious, ethnic or linguistic. This places terrorism on both sides of morality. A terrorist could be a freedom fighter in which case he does not see himself as a terrorist while the state against which he has taken arms would not think so. This conundrum has so far prevented the evolution of a universal definition of terrorism and the UN has been unable to get a resolution on the subject.

Q: Please comment on the state's rights to kill terrorists? Since the US uses water-boarding, why can't Sri Lanka use similar techniques in interrogation? Does India use anything like water-boarding?

A: In a modern state governed by principles of human rights no state can claim an executive right to kill anybody. Laws have to be followed always which can award a death sentence only after a due process. However certain states like the US do reserve such a right but here also there is a legal cover available by special laws of the state. Public opinion in such a state generally does not approve such special provisions. India has no laws of this kind nor do I think Sri Lanka.

Terrorists are like ordinary criminals who must face all legal consequences for their actions. From the point of view of a state their defining themselves as freedom fighters gives them no immunity.

The state has many options to guard its national interests some of which may lie in the covert field and can therefore be denied publicly.

Q: Please comment on the crisis in Sri Lanka. Who in your opinion is principally behind it? Why have we been unable to find out a sustainable solution during the last three decades?

A: India displayed no interest in the Sri Lankan Tamil ethnic questions till early 1980s. Prior to that the Indian interest had gravitated around the plantation Tamil immigrants from South India, who for more than 150 years had become the backbone of the plantation economy of Sri Lanka. After Sri Lanka's independence, the Sinhala authorities wanted them, now numbering a million with several of them with residence in Sri Lanka for more than one generation, to be treated as Indian citizens. The Sri Lankan Tamils looked upon the plantation Tamil as a distinct group, separate from them. Consequently, the former did not enter India's focus at that time.

But the rumblings of what was to follow had already started. The Sinhala leadership had displayed consistent insensitivity to implementation of their agreements with Tamil leadership over questions of regional autonomy and other rights of equal citizenship. The communal tempers were constantly rising and erupting in clashes. In July 1983, riots broke out which eventually catapulted ethnicity to the top of the agenda and marked that a point of no return had been reached for the Tamils of North East. The riots had erupted in Colombo and elsewhere after LTTE killed 13 Sri Lankan soldiers in the North on July 13 after an ambush. In these riots several Tamils were killed, including those locked up in prisons. There was credible suspicion of involvement of Sri Lankan Govt.

Q. Meanwhile in Tamil Nadu politicians also have interests in a Dream State; they have given energy to Sri Lankan Tamil youth for thru uprising. Can you explain the Tamil Nadu factor and case for Eelam?

A: The communal riots led to an exodus of Tamils from Sri Lanka into Tamil Nadu, bringing into focus for the first time the Government of India and people of Tamil Nadu the intensity of the ethnic question. The Indian reactions were guided by its political and strategic interests which required that while Sri Lanka must remain a united country, it should be advised against seeking a military solution to the ethnic problem through internal and external resources. Fearing that the influx might arouse fires of Tamil or Dravidian nationalism in Tamil Nadu also, it was felt, an option should be kept in hand to neutralize any effort by Sri Lankan Government to enforce a military solution in the North and East. A decision was therefore taken to keep pressure on Sri Lanka by giving military training to Sri Lanka Tamil groups in India.

Actually there was no danger of igniting Tamil or Dravidian nationalism in Tamil Nadu. Dravidian nationalism had been just an intellectual concept of its progenitor Periyar EV Ramaswami Naicker, not based on ground reality. This theoretical formulation had also not even included Sri Lankan Tamils in its sweep. Besides in 1962, the idea of even Tamil separatist nationalism had been buried for good by CN Annadurai, founder of DMK.

Q: According to history, R&AW provided training and arms to the Bangladeshi freedom fighters known as Mukti Bahini. RAW's aid was instrumental in Bangladesh's gaining independence from Pakistan in 1971. India has been also giving arms to opponents in Pakistan. Also India has been giving arms and arms training for Sri

Lankan Tamil military groups in the early 80s.But India never supported separation in Sri Lanka. Why? Does it mean that India is playing a double game in the region of South Asia?

A: Training of Sri Lankan Tamils in India was, therefore, not a good idea. The situation in Sri Lanka was not comparable to East Pakistan in 1971, which became Bangladesh towards the end of that year. As later events were to prove Sri Lankan Tamils did not hold themselves beholden to India for all the assistance they received.

As Sri Lanka, in panic, looked for assistance from outside powers like US, UK, even China and Pakistan, Indian diplomacy tried to checkmate such efforts and to persuade the Sri Lankan Government to devolve substantially central powers to North and East by creating regional councils. Indian efforts came to naught as Sri Lanka feared such devolution would lead to secession, with Trincomalee becoming the natural capital of Eelam Tamil region. How deep such fears ran was illustrated later by how quickly the demerger of North and East was brought about by the Sri Lankan Government after the IPKF left Sri Lanka.

India did not give up and hosted meetings in Thimpu in July and August 1985 between Sri Lankan Government and Tamil militants. It was the first time that all the Tamil militant groups came together to make a united set of proposals to the Sri Lankan Government, seeking recognition of identity, self-determination and dignity. Unfortunately, the Sri Lankan Government failed to appreciate that this was an occasion to explore various options with the young leadership of the Tamil movement. The talks failed as the Sri Lankan Government could not offer anything to meet the Tamil aspirations. It also became evident that Indian influence did not count for much either with the Sri Lankan Government or the Tamil militant groups.

Failure at Thimpu also indicated that the negotiating process had reached a dead end. Sri Lankan Government felt that it must get back to a military campaign to vanquish the Tamils. The siege of Jaffna followed with bombing raids and starving of Tamils in the Jaffna Peninsula. This caused a tremendous sense of outrage in

Tamil Nadu. India was left with no option except to send IAF relief flights over Jaffna to air drop supplies.

Q: Please comment on India's intervention in the internal problems in Sri Lanka.

A: The July 29, 1987 Indo-Sri Lankan agreement inevitably followed as yet another manifestation of Indian concerns for arresting the drift towards a long civil war. However, the agreement was another example of a flawed exercise. President Jayewardene of Sri Lanka might have sued for peace with the Tamils through the pact but obviously enough notice had not been taken of the seeds of insurrection which were sprouting in the south among militant Buddhist Sri Lankans who were dead set against any compromise towards Tamil aspirations. Their party JVP was an off shoot of the rural youth movement of the sixties. By 1980s it had acquired formidable strength in urban and quasi-urban regions also.

The agreement incorporated two major concessions to the Tamils, a single administrative unit with devolved powers in North and East with a single provincial council and elections to this council before December 1987. Prabhakaran's heart was not in it as by that time he had already decided that Tamils deserved nothing short of Eelam. Indian assumptions that he would accept less were illusory. Similarly the dream expectation that a merger of North and East would be genuinely acceptable to the Sri Lankan Government was unreal. The agreement was doomed from the beginning. Indian Intelligence had misgivings about this agreement and had advised against the induction of Indian Military into Sri Lanka which followed the signing of the agreement.

The intransigent attitude of Prabhakaran's LTTE came to surface soon enough. It refused to surrender all the arms which the agreement required. It refused to take part in the elections to the provincial council of the merged North-East. The IPKF had in the meanwhile been inducted in Sri Lanka to organize de-militarization of the Tamil areas. In the absence of LTTE co-operation, the Indian authorities allowed IPKF to become coercive.

The Indian decision to opt for military operations against LTTE was based on the army assessment that IPKF would take no more than a week to drive LTTE to its knees. Indian Intelligence was not aware how this assessment had been arrived at. Unfortunately, this assessment was not subjected to any deeper scrutiny and became the basis for Indian army operations against the LLTE. Subsequent events proved that the so called assessment was just wishful thinking.

Q: Why did the IPKF fail in its war with the LTTE?

A: The failure of the Government of India was largely systemic because policy decisions in the past were often made without the benefit of well conducted policy research and analysis. Structures did not exist which could carry out an objective study of a situation, examining its short term and long term dynamics and throwing up a set of options with likely scenarios, for the policy maker to make his choice.

It is evident that a study of this nature would try to reconcile various contradictions and their implications before recommending policy steps. In point of fact, policies those days were made through discussions in a core group, with rarely a position paper being ever presented to the discussants by anyone. No minutes were ever recorded and circulated after discussions which were often attended by bureaucratic overlords whose sole qualification for inclusion in the core group was their over lordship, not expertise, knowledge or understanding of the issues at stake.

Q: What do you think of the current military operations against the LTTE by the security forces in Sri Lanka?

A: I am not sure that only military measures can solve the problems between the Sri Lankans and the Tamils of the North and East. If the concerns of the Tamils are not satisfied by mutual dialogue, even if militarily defeated, the old ghosts will rise again to torment later.

Q: Please comment on the future of the LTTE and the fate of Prabhakaran. Where will this all end? Can he ever hold office even if it is through a negotiated settlement given that he is wanted in

India?

A: The LTTE should be seen as the embodiment of Tamil aspirations. Whether or not the LTTE is vanquished, these aspirations have a life of their own and will keep looking for fulfillment.

Prabhakaran is a wanted criminal in India and will remain so as long as his wanted status is not altered legally. But I do not think India would ever plan to involve itself in Sri Lanka as it did in 1987.

Q: I would like to know your experiences on action against terrorism in India and more generally South Asia in your career as a security officer

A: If the terrorists are not aided from outside they can be neutralized fairly easily. Many terrorist groups in India have been persuaded to join the mainstream through dialogue and offer of participation in governance. Most difficulties arise where a state is a nonactor supporter of terrorism. It is common knowledge that such states exist in South Asia.

Q: More than 20 terrorist organisations have been activating in South Asia. Thousands of people are victims in this conflict every year. Please explain what should be done by the governments of South Asia to wipe out terrorism?

A: States should not offer mere lip sympathy and instead be ready to alter their creed and philosophy to fight terrorism. Unfortunately such an approach is not visible.

Q: All our terrorist organizations have been building up networks. But we can't see any strong tendency for political cohabitations within a country or between states within the Region of South Asia. How does it influence the stability of the region?

It is true that without peace and harmony stability will remain a distant dream.

Q: Could you please explain to us the importance of espionage networks for counter terrorism within South Asia and the governments and military?

A: It is very difficult to deal with terrorism by military means alone. A considered counterstrategy is necessary. In this espionage plays an important role. Good human agents inside a terrorist network are worth their weight in gold but recruitment of such agents is almost next to impossible.

Q: Finally, do you think the present regime under President Mahinda Rajapaksa can find a sustainable solution to the ethnic crisis in Sri Lanka?

A: The Indo-Sri Lankan Agreement served some useful purposes in that Sri Lanka agreed not to allow hostile use of Trincomalee port or VOA facilities in Sri Lanka for prejudiced propaganda. But IPKF had ultimately to withdraw, leaving over 1200 dead and with over 3000 injured. The strange spectacle was also witnessed of LTTE and the Sri Lankan Government, under the successor President Premadasa, cooperating against IPKF. The merger of North and East has now been undone. The current President Rajapaksa is offering no more than district development councils to the Tamils in a unitary set up which had been rejected way back in 1985 at Thimpu by the Tamils. The Sinhala leadership has come full circle in its attitude towards the Tamils.

In my view, based on the wisdom that hind sight generates, the induction of IPKF into Sri Lanka, cannot but be considered flawed. The real cause was the consistent non realization by the Government of India that the issue at stake, of conflicting identities, was held non-negotiable by both the Tamils as well as Sri Lankans. The enigma of Prabhakaran could never be comprehended.

His experience with the Sinhalese has taught him that the Sinhala leadership of whatever hue cannot be trusted. He had implicit faith that Eelam is an achievable objective and he will be the one who will lead his people to this destination. His confidence in himself and his mission makes him in his own eyes the sole arbitrator of what can or cannot be accepted on behalf of the Sri Lankan Tamils from the Sri Lankan Government.

- October 4, 2008

16
'YOGIC FLYERS' CAN
KEEP LANKA UNITED

Sri Lanka is a progressive and modern industrial country with a multi-religious and multi-ethnic society. It is so easy for the armed forces of Sri Lanka to implement the Invincible Defence Technology.

- Gunter Chassé

"SRI LANKA is a progressive and modern industrial country with a multi-religious and multi-ethnic society. It is so easy for the armed forces of Sri Lanka to implement the Invincible Defence Technology," Lt. Col Gunter Chassé, Rtd Air Force Officer in German Air Force , said on present situation in Sri Lanka in an exclusive interview with the writer.

Lieutenant Colonel Gunter Chassé (Retired)—decorated with the Honourary Cross of the Bundeswehr in Gold—began his military career in 1969 by completing officer training at the German Air Force Officers' School in Munich. Chassé's specialized military training includes courses on Air Defence Weapon Systems at the German Air Force Air Defence School and the US Army Air Defence School, both in Fort Bliss, Texas, USA. He served in the

German Air Force mainly in the Integrated NATO-Air Defence, alternately in commanding and staff positions. From 1992 to his retirement in 1997, he was employed in Home Defence with territorial tasks.

We discussed several issues on him life as senior security officer who are involved with defence issues. "Largely shaped by Germany's role as a trade partner, political relations between the two countries are good and straightforward.," he has pointed out when I asked about German-Sri Lanka relations.

Question (Q): To introduce you, if anyone asks you, who is Gunter Chasse, from which country is he, and what is his role and status, what would you say?

Answer (A): I am a retired Lieutenant Colonel with nearly 40 years of military service, mainly employed in NATO Integrated Air Defence. With this background I founded the Institute of Invincible Defence, Germany, whose director I am. I am also a member of the International Advisory Board of the Center for Advanced Military Science of the Institute of Science, Technology and Public Policy, USA.

With more than 30 years' experience with Invincible Defence Technology (IDT) in theory and practice I can state that IDT provides the opportunity to make the nation invincible. IDT prevents the birth of an enemy so that fighting is not necessary anymore. This makes the nation invincible

I am a teacher of Transcendental Meditation, which is the key technology of the Invincible Defence Technology. I travelled in Europe, Africa, the Middle East, India, Sri Lanka, South East Asia, Australia and New Zealand lecturing about Maharishi's Vedic System of Defence.

Q: Can you describe the main challenges and difficulties you faced as a military officer in the battlefields?

A: I served in NATO Integrated Air Defence during the Cold War with its dangerous East-West confrontation. At this time of high political and military tension in Europe and in the divided Germany, it was a great challenge for me to know that even with the successful engagement of the first enemy air crafts the war could not have been avoided. It was obvious that defence had to begin much earlier. It was necessary to change the enemy's hostile intention into friendly behavior so that the danger is averted before it arises.

I was looking into alternative defence programs and found out that through the Invincible Defence Technology it is possible to prevent the outbreak of hostilities and war. IDT is rooted in the ancient Vedic Technology of Defence, the group practice of Transcendental Meditation and Yogic Flying. Scientists see its basis in the latest discovery of quantum physics – the Unified Field of all the Laws of Nature. We can call the IDT an ancient and yet an ultra-modern Technology of Defence whose effect lies in the field of consciousness.

Q: Did you use special tactics to defeat enemies?

A: NATO's special strategy and tactics to defeat enemies were deterrence by means of highly sophisticated destructive military power and the readiness to use it when necessary. This created threat, fear and even more enmity and was actually counterproductive to peace and defence. The great military potential was in reality a sign of weakness and a lack of power.

It is not the weapons that save the country but the strength and coherence of an integrated national consciousness. Such a strong and indomitable national consciousness can be achieved by a group of soldiers – the square root of one percent of the population is enough – which are trained in the Invincible Defence Technology and practice it together as a new kind of exercise. This is the superior tactics to prevent the war from the level of silence. Real power lies in the ability to prevent the birth of an enemy.

Q: Air strikes on enemy territories cause more casualties. There are some allegations against the Sri Lankan Air Force that they hurt civilians trapped in enemy-held areas. Same things happen in Iraq. How do you protect civilians, while targeting enemies?

A: To protect the civilians it is necessary to target the enmity instead of the enemy and to change the enemy into a friend. When a group of Yogic Flyers practices the Invincible Defence Technology the terrorists are bathed in the harmony of the Unified Field and are just coming back to friendly and life supporting behavior. The Yogic Flyers enliven peace from the level of silence which is a field of transcendental consciousness. They neutralize any oncoming danger with the mighty power of the Unified Field. They purify the collective consciousness so that no violence, terrorism and war will be possible. They use the mechanics of transformation to change negative trends into positive tendencies.

As a result the need for air strikes will never arise and casualties among the civilians will not occur anymore.

Q: You have been to Sri Lanka many years ago. What do you think people in Sri Lanka and their customs etc.

A: I was overwhelmed by the natural beauty of Sri Lanka, the Pearl of the Indian Ocean. I have met wonderful people of different ethnic backgrounds and religions, among them Buddhist monks, Christians and Muslims who practiced Transcendental Meditation. I could witness their sorrows about the ethnic conflicts and violence in Sri Lanka. All people I met had a deep understanding for Transcendental Meditation. I have learned that Sri Lanka has also some roots in the Vedic tradition.

Q: What is your reading on terrorism?

A: The charter of UNESCO states in its preamble that wars begin in the mind of men and that therefore peace must be defended also in the mind of men. Why do violence, terrorism and wars break out? They break out due to the accumulation of stress and tension in consciousness and the nervous system of the people. If stress exceeds a certain level it must erupt. The result will be aggression, violence and terrorism and eventually war. It is not because of ethnic, religious or social differences that groups or nations fight each other. Rather it is stress fighting stress.

Group practice of Transcendental Meditation and Yogic Flying effectively removes collective stress – the breeding ground for terrorism - and develops friendliness, cordiality, and love. IDT purifies the human consciousness and nervous system and enables the individual and the nation as a whole to spontaneously think and act in a cordial and peaceful way. The causes of violence, crime, terrorism, and war are eliminated at their roots. Every nation should have a permanent group of Yogic Flyers to bring lasting peace to the family of nations.

Q: As a senior German military officer, what do you think of the current political and military developments in Sri Lanka?

A: Sri Lanka is a progressive and modern industrial country with a multi-religious and multi-ethnic society. It is so easy for the armed forces of Sri Lanka to implement the Invincible Defence Technology. Sri Lanka with its population of little over 20 million people needs only about 500 Yogic Flyers which practice daily Yogic Flying together in a group. The rest of the armed forces can continue with its normal duty. The group of Yogic Flyers will ensure that unity is growing in the awareness of the nation and differences in religion, culture, language and political opinions will no longer dominate.

The unique effectiveness of the Invincible Defense Technology in preventing social violence, terrorism, and war has been confirmed by more than 50 demonstrations and 23 scientific studies. They showed that war deaths dropped by 76% (Lebanon 1983), that crime, traffic accidents, fires, and other indicators of social stress decreased significantly. Other studies showed a decrease of war-related fatalities by 71%, war-related injuries fell by 68%, the level of conflict dropped by 48% and cooperation among antagonists increased by 66%. During a National Demonstration Project conducted in Washington, D.C., in 1993, violent crime dropped by 23%.

So with IDT Sri Lanka will become a light house of peace and enjoy unity in diversity and diversity in unity.

Q: In an interview you say 'no armed force today is able to protect the nation if the enemy really wants to strike.... In the last 3,000 years, [there have been] over 9,000 peace treaties, and each one lasted on average no longer than 8 years.... Therefore military means and diplomacy [are] not a means to ensure protection of a nation and lasting peace...' But there is a different perspective view of the Sri Lankan conflict. Now the Tamil Tiger rebels are being finished off. They are reportedly losing on all fronts. Do you think your previous comment is applicable to the conflict in Sri Lanka?

A: Today, every nation is vulnerable. Not even the strongest military power in the world, the USA, could prevent this terrorist attack on the World Trade Center. Conventional military approaches are increasingly powerless to protect a nation against terrorist attack, against new destructive technologies, or against missiles with pinpoint accuracy.

According to recent research, traditional approaches to defence fail because they do not address the underlying cause of violence and conflict: they do not relieve the acute political, ethnic, and religious tensions that fuel terrorism and conflict. IDT offers an effective means to eliminate these deep-seated tensions—a proven approach that can safeguard a nation against violence and promote peace and prosperity in the world.

I am not so much familiar with the situation in Sri Lanka. With military force, diplomacy and treaties you may calm down the situation on the surface and bring a temporary relief. But it is just a matter of time until collective stress increases and terrorism starts again. As long as the root cause is not dissolved, as long invincibility is not gained there will be no lasting peace.

Q: What is your assessment on the "war on terror" as a senior military official and later a teacher of the Transcendental Meditation programme?

A: The "war on terror" has been a failure. What is necessary is the immediate establishment of large national groups of peace-creating experts in every country practicing IDT which has given scientific evidence to neutralize acute ethnic, political, and religious tensions that fuel violence, terrorism, and social conflict. By defusing tensions and neutralizing animosity, this field-tested approach will immediately defuse enmity in a potential adversary. It will create coherent and harmonious national consciousness and a peaceful and cooperative global environment and will ensure lasting peace, security, and economic stability at home and in the family of nations.

The extensive body of scientific research makes the IDT the most thoroughly tested and rigorously established technology for a successful "war on terror".

Q: I know we face many difficulties when we think about this subject (Transcendental Meditation programme). I would be happy if you can explain the programme briefly?

A: The Transcendental Meditation Technique is a simple, natural, effortless procedure practiced 20 minutes twice each day while sitting comfortably with the eyes closed. It's not a religion or philosophy, and involves no change in lifestyle. It's the most widely practiced, most researched, and most effective method of self-development. The technique is distinguished by its naturalness, effortlessness and profound effectiveness.

The Transcendental Meditation technique is based on the ancient Vedic tradition of enlightenment in India. This knowledge has been handed down by Vedic masters from generation to generation for thousands of years. About 50 years ago, Maharishi — the representative in our age of the Vedic tradition — introduced Transcendental Meditation to the world, restoring the knowledge and experience of higher states of consciousness at this critical time for humanity.

Q: What is your view about German-Sri Lanka relations?

A: Largely shaped by Germany's role as a trade partner, political relations between the two countries are good and straightforward. Germany is engaged in a variety of ways in Sri Lanka (cultural institute, political foundations, German Archaeological Institute, German Academic Exchange Service, the South Asia Institute, friendship societies) and is respected and valued as a reliable partner. Germany is traditionally one of Sri Lanka's most important partners in the tourist industry. Alongside language courses, a Goethe Institute in Colombo runs a multifaceted cultural programme and provides a mediatheque with a good assortment of German books, CDs and feature films.

April 1, 2009

17
END OF LTTE HAS NOT FINISHED
THE PROBLEMS OF THE
MINORITY TAMILS

I live in India, a constitutional democracy governed by the legislature, judiciary and the Parliament. I do not feel comfortable with the 18th amendment that has given unbridled power to the President and mutilated the systemic machineries. I feel the people of Sri Lanka should protest and opt for open and systemic democracy standing on the tripod of Parliament, Executive and the Judiciary. That is the universal symbol of democracy.

- Maloy Krishna Dhar

"END of LTTE has not finished the problems of the minority Tamils. As I said they require full rehabilitation with equal rights," said Mr. Maloy Krishna Dhar (1937- 2012) , the former joint director, Intelligence Bureau of India, in an interview with the writer at his residence in New Delhi.

M K Dhar's career with the Intelligence Bureau spanned for nearly three decades, during which he witnessed innumerable counter-terrorism, counter- espionage and political operations. He specialized in counterintelligence measures against Pakistan's covert and overt aggressions and the proxy war Pakistan had unleashed in the past few decades against India. Mr. Dhar is also the author of several books including Open Secret: India's Intelligence Unveiled,

Mission to Pakistan- An Intelligence Agent in Pakistan, Train to India: Memories of Another Bengal and Fulcrum of Evil - ISI, CIA, Al Qaeda Nexus.

About Maloy Krishna Dhar: He was born in Kamalpur, Bhairab-Mymensingh in East Bengal. As a youngster, he and his family migrated to India walking through a bloodbath. He taught in a college and worked as a junior staff reporter before joining the Indian Police Service in 1964. He was drafted to the Central Intelligence Bureau in 1968.

When we first met a few months ago in New Delhi we talked about the political situation in Sri Lanka. I recall that you told me there was little possibility of General Sarath Fonseka, the common opposition candidate of winning the presidential election which was held last January. It has now happened that Fonseka, the man who led the Army in the war against the LTTE which ended in May 2009, is now a prisoner. Let us start our discussion with this development.

Question (Q): How do you feel about the present situation in Sri Lanka one and a half years after the historic victory against what is considered to be the world's most ruthless terrorist organisation?

Answer (A): I feel happy that terrorism has been vanquished and peace has been restored. I look forward to see complete rehabilitation of the Tamil people and their integration with the country with equal opportunities.

Q: Recently Sri Lanka passed the 18th Amendment to the Constitution which ended the limit of the terms of the President and dissolved the independent commissions against corruption, free and fair elections, the police service and promotions of servicemen. A well-known newspaper in India pointed this out as a serious threat to democracy. What do you think about that?

A: I live in India, a constitutional democracy governed by the legislature, judiciary and the Parliament. I do not feel comfortable with the 18th amendment that has given unbridled power to the President and mutilated the systemic machineries. I feel the people of Sri Lanka should protest and opt for open and systemic democracy standing on the tripod of Parliament, Executive and the Judiciary. That is the universal symbol of democracy. With LTTE gone there is no need for special power of the President. I am afraid it is another form of dictatorship.

Q: What is your assessment of Indo-Lanka relations, in the past, the present and the possibilities for the future?

A: Indo-Lanka relationship has undergone some rough periods. But the present situation is happy and it is hoped that as our closest neighbor Lanka will develop healthier ties with India for mutual benefits.

Q: You were director of the IB (Indian Intelligence Bureau). Do you think there is common understanding between the intelligence organisations in the region with regard to terrorism?

A: There exists lack of cooperation. Indian and Sri Lankan intelligence may like to establish institutional arrangements for exchange of information on terrorism as terrorists have emerged as a global theat.

Q: Do you think the end of the war against the LTTE was the solution for minority people in Sri Lanka? If not please tell us your opinions of the armed conflicts and ethnic problems in South Asian in the context of your experience?

A: End of LTTE has not finished the problems of the minority Tamils. As I said they require full rehabilitation with equal rights. It is the duty of the majority community to help them to gain self-respect and self-reliance.

October 24, 2010

18
THE SRI LANKAN GOVERNMENT HAS TARNISHED ITS OWN IMAGE

Sri Lankan diplomatic missions have been a partisan disgrace.
                                            - Bruce Douglas Haig

THE Sri Lankan Government has tarnished its own image, without help from anyone else, Bruce Douglas Haig, former Deputy High Commissioner of Australia to Sri Lanka in 1994, said in an interview with the writer.

Bruce Haigh joined the Department of Foreign Affairs and Trade in 1972. He served in South Africa from 1976/79 with the Australian Embassy.

He worked in the Australian Embassy in Saudi Arabia from 1982/84. From 1984/86 he was Director of the Indonesia Section. During that time he travelled within the Indonesian archipelago. From 1986/88, he was at the Australian Embassy, Islamabad. He travelled to Afghanistan where he reported on the war and other aspects of the Soviet occupation. He also undertook the photographic recording of Soviet activities and installations.

Bruce has visited or worked in Zimbabwe, Tanzania, Kenya, Israel, Egypt, Iran, Saudi Arabia, Kuwait, Bahrain, the Yemen, Pakistan, India, Afghanistan, Sri Lanka, Thailand, Malaysia, Singapore, Indonesia, Papua New Guinea, Canada, the United States and Europe. He was involved in high level trade and foreign policy negotiations.

Question (Q): I would like to start by inviting you to give us an introduction about your present role as a retired diplomat. You have worked as Deputy High Commissioner of Australia in Colombo. Later you wrote many articles and made a number of speeches on Sri Lanka's ethnic issues as well as the situation involving the Sri Lankan Diaspora. Could you also please give us an introduction of your role prior to retiring as a diplomat and how you have helped to build Australian-Lankan relations?

Answer (A): I don't have a role as a retired diplomat. That profession plus my earlier studies equipped me to analyse people, policies and politics and that is what I do. Australian/Sri Lankan relations have yet to be built on a proper and sound basis. Australian security agencies have driven the relationship in the wake of 9/11, when the Sri Lankan Government convinced some Western governments that it was waging a war against terror. That veil has been lifted and it is plain for all to see and now widely accepted that it was a civil war.

Q: Sri Lanka's diplomatic missions have gone through rapid changes over the past decade. It is also the case with the Sri Lanka's foreign policy. Unfortunately, Sri Lanka lacks a strong establishment and its foreign missions have become heavily politicized fronts with the political appointees. Are these politicized missions healthy for Sri Lanka?

A: Sri Lankan diplomatic missions have been a partisan disgrace. Thoroughly politicised; they have been vehicles of propaganda and harassment of expatriate Tamils, often with the compliance of host governments. That is now changing, as host governments question their role.

Q: Going further, it is general knowledge that political appointments have weakened Sri Lanka in many fronts? This includes inexperienced political diplomats unable to do their jobs properly. Further, these missions are unable to bring fusion between the Diaspora communities and tend to work with heavily politicized extreme Sinhala nationalist groups. This is not helping Sri Lanka to reach to the minority Sri Lankan communities to build bridges. What is your advice to Sri Lanka on this?

A: Enter the real world, embrace the new realities.

Q: The Government of Sri Lanka celebrated its first anniversary of crushing the Tamil Tigers, which is banned and listed as a terrorist organization in many countries including Australia. So what is your assessment of the post military victory against the so-called terrorist organization?

A: The LTTE is not listed as a terror organisation in Australia. There is no victory in the humiliation of the vanquished. The root cause of the civil war has not been addressed. Look at Palestine.

Q: Sri Lanka has crushed the LTTE militarily? The LTTE outfit is the product of the political failures of Sri Lanka for over six decades in not positively addressing the legitimate political demands of the Tamils. This underling political issue is haunting Sri Lanka in spite of defeating the LTTE. Can Sri Lanka continue to prolong the agony by engaging in heavy handedness towards its minorities?

A: No, but you have answered your own question.

Q: The Sri Lankan President Mahinda Rajapaksa is undertaking an important visit to India. What is your assessment of the Indo-Lanka relationship in the post –War Sri Lanka? Meanwhile Chinese vice premier is scheduled to visit Sri Lanka with a huge loan that is expected to help galvanize the semi-dead economy of Sri Lanka. Do you think President Rajapaksa's anti-west foreign policy will archive its goal?

A: Sri Lanka wrongly believes that it can be very clever and play China and India off against one another for advantage to the GOSL. It will end in tears with Sri Lanka losing autonomy. It was a big mistake to get into bed with China, particularly under the nose of India. The Sri Lanka Government has stupidly, in my opinion, stupidly transgressed Indian notions of its sphere of influence. My own government has behaved just as stupidly and clumsily toward India.

Q: There are so many allegations against the government over corruption, war crimes, human rights violence, nepotism, manipulations, sexual abuses etc. Despite these, in the last few elections the majority of the people are with the President Rajapaksa. Why there is wide gap on the opinion of the President within and outside Sri Lanka. Is the West's attitude towards Sri Lanka justified?

A: The Sri Lanka Government killed press freedom. Debate is at best stifled and at worst crushed. Ordinary people look for financial security, a level playing field, they are desperate for jobs, prosperity, predictability, voting for Rajapaksa, partly represents that and also represents the lack of choice. Expectations relating to politics and politicians are low. How could they be otherwise in a corrupt, quasi police state?

Q: The section of the pro-LTTE Diaspora has formulated a Transnational Government which the government of Sri Lanka is vehemently opposing. Do you think a Transnational Government will be an impediment rather than a constructive effort to build bridges between communities in Sri Lanka?

A: No. It was done to influence the thinking and perceptions of Western governments and peoples.

Q: Once again the UN Special Rapporteur urged the Government of Sri Lanka to allow international access to investigate War Crimes during the final battle between the government forces and the Tamil Tigers rebels. But in his reply to Prof. Philip Alston, the Attorney General of Sri Lanka says, the allegations are baseless and issues raised are strictly the internal matters of Sri Lanka. It is alleged that Prof. Alton is tarnishing the image of Sri Lanka internationally. What is your opinion on Sri Lanka opening its door for an international inquiry into war crimes? Do you think Sri Lanka can continue to halt the process to investigate war crimes?

A: The Sri Lankan Government has tarnished its own image, without help from anyone else. Not opening the door to an international UN backed investigation relating to war crimes is a significant statement in itself. Through the movement of segments of its population around the world the issues relating to the murder of prisoners of war, rape and killing of non-combatants have become issues of international concern. They are not internal matters, just as the issue of widespread corruption in government and other institutions impacts upon the ability to conduct international trade.

Q: What is your opinion of Tamil political parties and their role in the conflict? How can they involve themselves to achieve a sustainable solution?

A: Sincere and honest discussion, negotiation and other positive interactions, of which we have seen no sign of from the government.

June 10, 2010

19

I REMAIN A FRIEND OF THE
SINHALA PEOPLE AND OF BUDDHISM

The Tamil diaspora, in so far as they were forced to leave their homeland, go through much suffering in exile and wanting to return,, are also stakeholders in reaching a solution. Hence the diaspora are called to play a supportive-role in the struggle. This they do in the context of their present living.

- S. J. Emmanuel

REV Fr Dr S. J. Emmanuel is an eminent theologian and an academic who devoted much of his time for political upliftment of the Tamil people in Sri Lanka. The 78 pontiff is the President of the Global Tamil Forum (GTF) and even at his prime age is energetically campaigning for the just cause of the Tamil people.

Question (Q): Even at your prime age, you are boldly campaigning for justice. It is because of your passion for Tamil people or your Christian mission?

163

Answer (A) : I was born a Tamil and baptized as a Christian (1934). Birth as a Tamil and call to be a Christian are both God's gifts and call to me.

My life is to live faithfully to my vocation, vision and mission – all from God. In the changing contexts and challenges of my life, I act according to existential identities derived from birth, faith and profession. Hence my campaigning for justice springs, not from a mere superficial passion for Tamil people, but from my existential identities and mission to fight injustices anywhere and for all peoples.

If I may be allowed to narrate from my own life, it is a conviction and sensibility, from my young age against all forms of injustice, that keeps me struggling for justice.

Already as a young man in my own family, I fought against my own father discriminating others on the basis of caste, as an undergraduate at the University of Colombo (1954-8), I lobbied people on the streets of Pettah against the Paddy Lands Bill of Philip Gunawardene, as a Mannar correspondent for Lake House, Colombo (1959-61), inviting Sinhala politicians from the South, I fought against the Take-over of catholic schools.

After I resigned from my teaching(1962)studied philosophy and theology and ordained in Rome(1962-67),I returned to Sri Lanka where I was Parish Priest, Professor of theology (Kandy,1976-86) Rector of St. Francis Xavier's Seminary, Jaffna and Vicar General of the Jaffna Diocese till 1997.

As a young priest, I stood against a crowd of over 1000 people in Sillalai giving equal status to a so called "low caste" couple at their wedding in the church, as theologian I fought for the rights of lay people in the church and helped the Asian Bishops at the Roman Synod in 1987, stood in defense of the once excommunicated Father Tissa Balasuriya OMI, both inside and outside Sri Lanka.

I have always encouraged my colleagues and students- priests and bishops – to follow Jesus Christ, the true Liberator of the whole man.

Hence my speaking up for the victimized Tamils is only a part of my mission based on my Christian convictions. That is why I spoke out as Vicar General against the bombing of churches and schools and killing of innocent children.

People accused me as being political and supportive of the LTTE. But that does not stop me from condemning anyone who behaves unjustly against fellow human beings. Silence in the midst of such carnage is connivance and sinful.

I wish my sisters and brothers in Sri Lanka of all religions and races serve the island and its peoples by standing up for truth and justice.

In my view, *vis a vis* the long ethnic conflict and war, all the four religions have rendered mostly humanitarian services sure, but not done enough by way of courageous protest against evil, standing up for truth and justice to build up a peaceful island.

Religions have their share of blame in our country losing its moral values and standards. Sabbath is for man, not man for the Sabbath, said Jesus. Religions and governments are to serve man, not vice versa.

Q: The *status quo* has changed following defeat of the LTTE (Liberation Tigers of Tamil Eelam) . Do you still hold the objective of a separate state for Tamils to make life more difficult for them back home or is GTF you represent is willing to tone down the claim. The status quo has changed, sure, but what is it now?

A: It is true that LTTE has been militarily and as an organization defeated. But the political aspirations and ideologies live on among the people.

LTTE, born after 1976, was not merely a terrorist or military outfit as the majority Sinhalese and their governments still make out to be. They fought for political aspirations and goals which were there before them. Hence those aspirations and goals do not die or get defeated, they still have much support among the people. And the new status quo as at present is strengthening them.

After May 2009, we see a victorious sand arrogant Government drunk with power, headed by a dictatorial family, executing its Mahinda Chinthanaya mainly against the Tamil people inside and outside the country.

Bulldozing cemeteries and memorials built by the LTTE, but were sacred places also for Tamil parents and people to venerate their sons and daughters are barbaric acts against a people.

Building new military bases on those places is an uncivilized way of showing anger against an enemy!

Are these forces truly descendants of a magnanimous Sinhalese Dutugemunu who built a memorial for a defeated Tamil Elara ?!

Now the Government and its military are eradicating the roots of Tamil claims for nationhood and homeland by militarization, Sinhalisation and Buddhistisation.

And this new status quo, with all these acts of hatred and anger,

  a) further illustrates the hegemonic intentions of the government and of the majority supporting them,
  b) further justify and strengthen the calls for separation which was never an arrogant claim of the Tamils but a helpless cry "leave us alone" for a survival free of oppression
  and
  c) shows how the majority have misunderstood the LTTE as mere separatists and terrorists and nothing beyond.

The majority Sinhalese and their governments seem to forget that LTTE was born 3 decades after the conflict started and was born as anti-state-terror outfit.

The birth of the LTTE is a military response of Tamil youth pushed to the wall, both by discriminatory laws passed by a Sinhala majoritarian democracy and executed with the help of a terrorizing military stationed in the Tamil provinces.

Hence "the objective of a separate state for Tamils" is not dead with the defeat of the LTTE. It will remain among the Tamils as a last resort for survival. This objective is not our seeking, but thrust upon us and will remain with us all Tamils inside and outside Sri Lanka, till a just and peaceful solution is found.

There is no question of the diaspora "toning it down for something lower to make life comfortable back at home". It is up to the Governments of the majority to offer a political solution respecting the fundamental rights of the Tamils and make the objective of a separate state meaningless.

Let us not forget that a people fighting for their basic and fundamental rights and having suffered and sacrificed enormously during the last six decades will now give up their noble aspirations of freedom and human dignity just for a better looking or comfortable life.

The Colombo government has succeeded, even now succeeds, in buying over some Tamils by offering petty gifts. But that will not truly win over the hearts and minds of the Tamils towards genuine reconciliation.

It is the Tamils in Sri Lanka along with their elected parliamentary representatives, who have the primary responsibility and right to decide and determine the final goal or solution of the struggle.

The Tamil diaspora, in so far as they were forced to leave their homeland, go through much suffering in exile and wanting to return,, are also stake-holders in reaching a solution. Hence the diaspora are called to play a supportive-role in the struggle. This they do in the context of their present living.

And GTF, being a network of diaspora Tamil organizations, is in contact with the Tamils and their representatives in Sri Lanka. In spite of the Sri Lankan Government's continued propaganda and activities against the diaspora Tamils as terrorists or potential terrorists, we are lobbying support from the international community for a just and peaceful solution.

Q: The GTF (Global Tamil Forum) issued statements to have dialogue with the GoSL. Did you have any response?

A: We never issued any statements to have dialogue with GoSL and we expect no response.

Q: A delegation of Tamils consisting of over 20 persons from all over the world are in Sri Lanka to discuss a resolution to the conflict. What is your views?

A: I came to know of it only from the SL government media. Why is the Government giving out such news items?

The SLG is obviously under pressure from within and without Sri Lanka with respect to its efforts towards finding a political solution. The international community cannot be deceived longer by development as a way to reconciliation. It expects the Government to seek a political solution through Talks.

If there is to be a genuine dialogue to discuss a resolution to the conflict, it should be foremost with the elected representatives of the Tamils in Sri Lanka.

The GoSL has failed miserably in such sincere dialogues. It wants to talk only to those who will listen and accept their own views. Unfortunately there are a few Tamils who are "coolies" or "loyal servants" of the Government.

With 18 rounds of Talks with the TNA coming to noght, the Government has introduced another delaying cum deceptive mechanism of a Parliamentary Commission but without success.

Hence another government delaying/ distracting effort is to show that they are talking with diaspora Tamils.

Unfortunately there are Tamils in the diaspora, who have their self-interests. They are friends of the already bought over Tamils like Douglas and KP, who will respond to the Government's call, and invest for their own profit in some development projects of the government. Their cooperation cannot benefit the Tamils living there nor can they help a political solution.

As it stands no self-respecting diaspora Tamils will go for Talks with the Government and betray the Tamils and their representatives within Sri Lanka.

Q:. This is a difficult question for you. But I must ask in the best interest. Is GTF a mouthpiece of the defeated LTTE or represent the wider global Tamils. When screams of the flag holding LTTE activists are strong, there is clearly no room for the wider Tamils and moderate Tamils. Isn't it not time for the GTF to declare its stand to represent cross section of the Tamils without being heavily influenced by the pro-LTTE activists.

A: GTF is a post-LTTE organization and definitely not a mouthpiece of the defeated LTTE nor of any other group.

It is a democratic transparent diaspora network-organization of many country-organisations of Tamils. Hence it is a global organization representing a majority of diaspora Tamils *vis a vis* the international community and engaged with governments and international NGOs related to Human Rights and Conflict resolution.

It is wrong to conclude that "when screams of the flag holding LTTE activists are strong, there is no room for the wider Tamils and moderate Tamils".

The Tamils as a whole have been victimized, but in expressing their reactions against oppression there have been varying degrees – some expressing it in the most violent, some by screaming in pain, and others through their writing and speaking a moderate language.

At the same time there were Tamils who were either anti-LTTE or distanced themselves from the LTTE for other reasons.
But after the defeat of the LTTE, angered by the arrogant attitudes and actions of the government, many of so called "wider Tamils and moderate Tamils" are joining the majority of diaspora Tamils.

For the majority Sinhalese and their government, LTTE was purely a terrorist organization, without any political ideology, but hell bent on terror, nothing more.

They do not ask how or why they came into existence.

They forget the two factors which gave birth to the LTTE, namely, the discriminatory laws of the government and the anti-Tamil terror of the State forces.

Hence the majority of Sinhalese and their governments were allergic to anything of the LTTE.

Even if a post LTTE organization puts demands for a political solution, the government labels it as an LTTE- demand and try to justify its denial.

The just demands of a people have to be met irrespective of those who shout for it or not.

It is time for the government to stop labeling people and aspirations as LTTE and deal with the demands in a civilized manner.

GTF represents country organizations of Tamils who agree to the vision and mission as articulated in our constitution and in the web page.

We do not cut off or distance ourselves from the screaming and the flag-waving. We understand their feelings. We are in touch with the ground-realities as well as representatives of people inside and outside the country.

What we seek as a solution is not any exclusive privilege for Tamils living on the island, nor robbing anyone else of their birthrights. It is a solution for the Tamils who have inhabited the island as a distinct nation, to live along with other nationalities, side by side, not one on top of another, but as friends and good neighbors.

Q: Thousands of Tamils including civilians and the LTTE cadres have died in the decades old war. But Tamils are limiting the remembrance to the LTTE warriors only. It is nothing wrong in LTTE celebrating the sacrifices of their cadres, but the groups like GTF subscribing to this is causing concerns. Will the GTF move away for a larger agenda.

A: The victims of this war has been from all communities and from various sections of these communities.

Tamils have special commemorations for the LTTE cadres who gave their lives voluntarily and consciously for the cause they espoused, namely the Tamils and their homeland.

Besides there are also political and religious leaders and media personnel who were targeted and killed in action.

Then, not the least, there were the innocent civilians killed by state terrorism as in the case of churches and schools bombed. All these are remembered and honored in different ways.

I am happy that you state "it is nothing wrong in LTTE celebrating the sacrifices of their cadres" – But the reality is the GOSL with the support of the majority have bulldozed all the cemeteries and war memorials and now eradicating even the roots of Tamil ethnic and religious identities under the military boots.

While the Sinhalese can erect huge war memorials and heroes and have victory celebrations, Tamil people who have lost their sons and daughters have no place, memorials or freedom to mourn!

GTF as an organization of Tamil people victimized and still groaning in pain for survival as a people.

It cannot distance itself from its wounded-identity. For the surviving Tamils, it is not exclusively remembering only those of the LTTE.

It is much more a national remembrance. It is a "remembrance of the past INTO the future". It is with this consciousness and reality of being a suffering people, the GTF engage with everyone who can help find an end to the suffering and a way to reconciliation and peace.GTF does not hide its identity, nor give up the true aspirations of the people to gain any advantage or acceptance.

Q: The BBC reporter Frances Harrison has said the Tamils are shying away from dealing with the war crimes committed by the LTTE and their campaigns are conditioned and as a result the issue of war crimes against Sri Lanka will wither away. What are your views on this.

A: The main intention of Francis Harrison in coming out with her story is to focus attention on the last stage of the war and its continuation in other forms. She has done well.

Her opinion that," the issue of war crimes against Sri Lanka will wither away" may be pleasing to the SLG.

But, we of the GTF and many others have been saying from the beginning, that both sides must be investigated and we hold on to it. Without justice there is no true reconciliation.

Q: Having raised some difficult questions, I must also say GTF is playing a much broader play of international politics. What do you wish say to the Tamils in the wider world to help build this process?

A: The role GTF has undertaken to play at the international level is by no means easy.

It has many challenges with regard to the nature of the new phase of the struggle, with regard to mobilizing people and talents and with regard to leadership.

Firstly, the SL propaganda through their embassies since the time of Lakshman Kadirgamar has been "that all diaspora organizations are front-organizations of the LTTE".

Rajapaksas have raised the embassies as military- watchdogs to organize anti Tamil infiltrators.

This has instilled a justified fear among the diaspora Tamils. And keep away even from any form of associations or lawful activities.

And after Mullivaikal, SLG has openly started a new war against the diaspora as announced by the Defence Ministry and its propaganda. It has also sent its trained/brainwashed agents to do some dirty work among the diaspora.

With the defense ministry's web page portraying me as a key-supporter of terrorism, I too have fears.

Hence, we Tamils in the diaspora, while living as law abiding citizens in democratic and transparent societies, should not allow ourselves to be victims of infiltrators or divisions caused by them.

Let us not dissipate our energies in in-fighting or in competitions but with unity of vision and mission struggle on behalf of our people.

I call upon the diaspora Tamils to play their supportive role for a noble cause of liberation in a responsible manner, not with anger and revenge against a people or religion, but as sincerely wishing a reconciliation and peace based on truth and justice.

We should not engage in any anti-Sinhala or anti-Buddhist activities.

What GTF is doing is to engage with the international community and its organizations within the democratic space available in favour of a just and peaceful solution in Sri Lanka.

But true reconciliation or peace is not possible without truth and justice. Demanding justice for crimes committed does not mean unwilling to forgive.

Forgiveness is due to those who acknowledge their crimes. That is why we demand an independent international inquiry which will establish the truth of what happened on that island and will identify the crimes and their perpetrators.

This is by no means a revengeful act.

Q: If you get an opportunity to meet President Mahinda Rajapaksa what will you say to him?

A: I have no thoughts about such a meeting or about what to say to him.

But on a lighter vein, I recall what I wrote to President Premadasa:- Sir, please turn the lion on the National flag the other way, so as not to threaten the two minorities with the sword!

To His Excellency President Rajapaksa, I may quote a Chinese proverb from Wang Suo of Hans dynasty: –Nothing brings greater misfortune than killing those who have already surrendered.

Q: What do you wish to say to the Tamil speaking people in Sri Lanka?

A: As a Tamil catholic priest, who has accompanied you for a long time, and suffered with you in Jaffna and in Wanni, I continue to hear your cries, agonies and aspirations.

I like to assure you all my continued solidarity and struggle at the international level for a better life for you all. I will not betray the trust you have placed on me.

Q:. Also, the Sinhala people?

A: I have spent happy days as an undergraduate in Colombo and later as a priest and professor at the National Seminary in Kandy.

A greater part of my 30 years of priestly life was spent in educating priests at the Kandy National Seminary and in Jaffna.

I have been to the Dalada Maligawa in Kandy to invite a Buddhist monk to teach Buddhism to our students, started getting teachers from outside the seminary to teach Sinhalese and Tamil for our students, drafted for the Provincial Synod of the Church in April 1995 a document titled – Church as Communication between North and South that was read out by the then Auxiliary Bishop Malcolm Ranjith and accepted with applause.

Sadly there was no follow up of actions.

I remain a friend of the Sinhala people and of Buddhism.

Sinhalese are a people only in Sri Lanka and your language and culture must be guarded and nurtured there on that island.

You have a right to bloom as a great nation and also be proud of Buddhism, but not at the expense of destroying or eradicating or oppressing another people, their nationhood and their human and religious rights.

Instead of using me as an instrument in the North-South dialogue, GOSL have falsely accused me as promoting terrorism and separatism.

Some irresponsible Sinhalese have spread wild and baseless rumors about me.

But my work in Sri Lanka till 1996 and afterwards in self-exile through speeches and writings will prove my innocence.

I love Sri Lanka and wish all the peoples peace and prosperity.

Sri Lanka has enough place and resources and ways of coexisting for its multiethnic, multi religious population.

Do not allow the politicians to use the Mahavamsa chronicles to politicize or overtake the noble teachings of Buddha.

There are many good courageous political and religious leaders as well as human rights activists and media people among you.

But they are threatened to become a fearful minority. Identify and support them before they are forced to leave the country for their survival.

If we have the courage and wisdom, to cling on only to Truth of history and Justice as due to all human beings irrespective of our ethnic and religious differences, then we can build a peaceful unity in diversity on that paradise isle.

Mr. D.S. Senanayake, the first Prime Minister, who knew the birth pangs and fears of the non-Sinhalese on the eve of Independence, loudly proclaimed to the world: United we stand, divided we fall!

20
MEDIA CAN NEVER GIVE
THE FULL TRUTH

I recommend objective activism. By that I mean present as many sides as possible. And let the readers decide. Media can never give the truth. It can only give some truths. Make sure you give every shade of opinion on a subject.

- P N Balji

"I empathize with the journalists in your country. It is a difficult terrain they have to walk. "If I have one recommendation to make, it will be this: Focus on the future by tackling the fundamental issues Sri Lanka are likely to face", Professor P N Balji of Asia Journalism Fellowship at Nanyang Technological University (NTU) in Singapore exclaimed in an interview with the writer.

After spending the last 20 years building two of Singapore's most successful newspaper start-ups, veteran editor P. N. Balji is turning his attention to professional development as the Director of the new Asia Journalism Fellowship at Nanyang Technological University (NTU) in Singapore.

Balji has been much sought after as a consultant, and as a speaker at press and media seminars overseas. His unique experience as editor of one of the most successful newspapers in the world is his calling card.

He has been a consultant to both *The Malay Mail* in Malaysia and also an Indian weekly magazine. He was also approached to kick start a new newspaper in India, and was also offered the post of editor-in-chief by a European publisher wanting a foothold in the region.

Prof. Balji has openly shared his thoughts on the present political developments, role of media, and responsibilities of journalists to make excellent media that can be focused on people that are, with the writer.

Q: In many countries some political groups are barred by the government from being able to express their views in newspapers and on the radio and television. In other places, governments impose on news companies to provide avenues for all political groups to express themselves, even fringe or radical groups. Many people, especially in the United States and in Western Europe, oppose both of these systems, feeling that, while any government clampdown on freedom of expression is an act of tyranny, the government would also be acting tyrannically if it dictates how much coverage each point of view is allowed to have by implementing a 'fairness doctrine,' as it is called in the United States. What are your views on the role of government in regulating the media?

A: The fundamental question here is whether media should be regulated. And if so, who should do be the regulator? Ideally, newspapers should have staff who see the profession as a calling, not just as another job. They should make sure that their publications stand to the objective scrutiny of newsmakers and readers.

Generally speaking, the media has fewer of such people around. The result is an erosion of standards, which then results in somebody else stepping into the vacuum to control the media,

As a guiding principle, I am against government control of media. But, we don't live in an ideal world.

Q: Throughout history, the media has often played a key role in the political side of military conflicts and as such, governments have often sought to control content during times of crisis. From the Alien and Sedition Acts in the United States at the end of the 18th Century to the media blackout in Sri Lanka precipitated by the final campaign of the civil war there, how do you feel emergency government censorship has helped or hurt the nations that employ this tactic over the years? Are there any examples where you feel government intervention in the press has been beneficial?

A: A lot depends on whether the Government does it for the good of the nation. The problem is that such intervention usually starts with altruistic intentions. But then the good intentions degenerate into something more sinister and an interventionist gov't continues to dominate the media as a way to rule for ever. The taste of such control can give them such a high that they don't want to let go after that.

Also, the world is so driven by monetary gains and power politics that inhumanities committed are ignored by foreign gov'ts in search of the gravy train. The Sri Lankan example is illuminating. Look at the foreign gov'ts trying to jump on to the train to cash in on business potentials being laid bare in the aftermath of the annihilation of the LTTE.

Q: Many of those who remain in Sri Lanka are harassed and threatened. What advice do you have for Sri Lankan journalists seeking to continue writing despite their hostile environment?

A: I empathise with the journalists in your country. It is a difficult terrain they have to walk. If I have one recommendation to make, it will be this: Focus on the future by tackling the fundamental issues Sri Lanka are likely to face. I suggest two paths: One, learn to live and let live. Nelson Mandela was a target of the repressive apartheid regime. Still, after he became the leader of South Africa he got the entire nation to focus on forgiveness. The winners in Sri Lanka should learn to be magnanimous in victory.

Second, the gov't must do some soul searching and realise that the continued marginalisation of the Tamil minority can only be the breeding ground for more bloodletting in future. Malaysia is realising the hopelessness of its policy of forcing the Malay language down the throats of the minority Chinese and Indian communities. That policy and the discrimination in favour of Malays is exposing that country's racial and religious fault lines only to be exploited by opportunists and trouble makers. Economic growth and peace are the victims.

Q: It has often been argued that biased media networks and sensationalist journalism can put a nation at risk in a wartime situation. Some even argue that there are groups of journalists who seek to aid and abet the opposing forces their country is fighting because they oppose their own country's government. In Sri Lanka, it seems that nearly every media company that doesn't simply accept government press releases at face value is accused of being a front for the defeated Tamil Tiger rebels. More famously, many Americans have blamed activist journalism for deceiving the American people during the *Tet* Offensive by cherry picking facts and stories to give the appearance that America and South Vietnam were facing a disaster, when in fact they were winning the most decisive military victories of the entire war. This resulting in the failed offensive becoming a political victory for the North Vietnamese and Viet Cong. Can you comment on how accurate you feel these views are and how great is the danger to a nation or government of being destabilized by activists in the media?

A: I recommend objective activism. By that I mean present as many sides as possible. And let the readers decide. Media can never give the truth. It can only give some truths. Make sure you give every shade of opinion on a subject. Don't rush into print with unconfirmed stories. Check and double check. Make corrections the next day if there are inaccuracies.

Q: Can you share with us your experiences as a journalist, what kind of challenges you faced how you work with deadlines. What is your advice for young journalists and students who want to be journalists?

A: If you don't have the passion for the profession, please don't get into it. With the world becoming more complex and major shifts taking place, we need journalists who can slice and dice the issues and say with confidence and some certainty what it all means to your reader.

Oct 30, 2009

21
INSIDE STORY OF "WAR ON TERROR"

It's not strictly true to say that the US created al-Qaeda, although they did pour billions of dollars into Afghanistan in the 1980s to fund the mujahideen resistance to the Soviet Union. As a member of the Arab mujahideen in Afghanistan at this time, Osama bin Laden, and others who went on to form al-Qaeda, were therefore at least indirectly funded by the US, but the most significant side-effect of the US funding for the anti-Soviet fighters was that they -- along with the Saudis, who matched US funding, or provided even more -- literally swamped this poor country with weapons, to lingering and brutal effect.

- Andy Worthington

"I visited Sri Lanka about ten years ago. The island is beautiful, and the people charming and welcoming, although I was, of course, saddened by the violence that has torn a hole in the country's heart," says Andy Worthington well-known historian and a journalist from the UK in an exclusive interview with the writer.

Question (Q): To introduce you, if anyone asks you, who is Andy Worthington, from which country is he, and what is his role and status, what would you say?

Answer (A): I'm a historian and journalist from the UK, living in London, and the author of three books. My latest, The Guantánamo Files: The Stories of the 774 Detainees in America's Illegal Prison, is the first book to look in detail at the stories of all the men held in Guantánamo. I've also just started work as the Communications Officer for Reprieve, the legal action charity founded by Clive Stafford Smith. Reprieve represents 31 Guantánamo prisoners, and also works on behalf of prisoners facing the death penalty.

Q: What do you think of the current political and military developments in Sri Lanka as a senior journalist who is dealing with the international media?

A: I'm not qualified to report on the current situation in Sri Lanka, although I sincerely hope that peace will prevail for all the Sri Lankan people.

Q: You have visited Sri Lanka a few years ago as a tourist. What do you think of the people in Sri Lanka and our customs, problems and the solutions we are pursuing?

A: Yes, I visited Sri Lanka about ten years ago. The island is beautiful, and the people charming and welcoming, although I was, of course, saddened by the violence that has torn a hole in the country's heart.

Q: Well, I would like to change our topic to discuss your current position. We know you are the best writer on some intelligence agencies including the Central Intelligence Agency (CIA) and their dirty tricks. How do you identify terrorism as a concept and the CIA's perceptions of terrorism and effectiveness in countering it?

A: I'm sure I don't deserve that first accolade, although I have certainly undertaken research into the workings of the US intelligence agencies. To keep my response succinct, I would say that terrorism -- as it relates to al-Qaeda and the 9/11 attacks -- is the work of criminals, that it should not be confused with the precepts of Islam and the beliefs and actions of the overwhelming majority of Muslims worldwide, and that combating al-Qaeda by declaring a "war" on terrorism has been profoundly misguided.

Q: How do you as a historian exhaustively trace terrorism and its historical development?

A: Essentially, with the help of some extraordinary researchers who have come before me. If we're talking about Islamist terrorism, it's important to understand its roots in terms of the radical ideologues who first promoted the idea of violent jihad -- and in the modern era that includes pivotal figures like the Egyptian Sayyid Qutb. Also of crucial importance is the trajectory from colonization to independence in the Muslim world, the struggle of political Islamists and the manner in which that struggle has largely been superseded by notions of violent jihad, and the role in this development of Egyptian militants and, in some cases, their bloodthirsty radicalization by the Egyptian state (as in the case of Ayman al-Zawahiri, usually described as "number two in al-Qaeda", but clearly an enormous influence on the radicalization of Osama bin Laden).

Another crucial trajectory concerns Afghanistan, from the Soviet invasion in 1979, through the funding of the mujahideen resistance by the United States (via Pakistan, an untrustworthy intermediary, to put it mildly) and Saudi Arabia, the ruinous civil war of the early 1990s and the rise of the Taliban. Two of many books that I would recommend, which have helped me along the way, are Ghost Wars by Steve Coll and Al-Qaeda by Jason Burke.

Q: Could you tell us about current developments in global terrorism since 9/11 in the US and 7/7 in the UK?

A: Again, to keep my response manageable, I'd say that the US response to 9/11 has been misguided and counter-productive in three particular ways: the invasion of Afghanistan seems to have served primarily to push al-Qaeda into the border areas of Pakistan, where they remain; the invasion of Iraq created a whole new country-wide battlefield for al-Qaeda, and could have been dictated from a script prepared by Osama bin Laden and Ayman al-Zawahiri, and the processes -- at Guantánamo and beyond -- of imprisonment without charge or trial, "extraordinary rendition", torture and secret prisons have been corrosively damaging for the moral standing of the United States.

In the UK, the government paranoia and tough posturing on terrorism has been equally misguided, in particular through the politicians' unwillingness to equate their involvement in the carnage of Iraq with discontent amongst parts of the Muslim community, and their insistence that they have the right to hold terror suspects either without charge or trial or -- when rebuffed by the courts -- under control orders that amount to virtual house arrest. Speaking as a British citizen, it's an absolute disgrace that these kinds of developments are taking place in the UK, and that they're allowed to proceed virtually unchallenged. Where is the public's outrage, and why are we almost solely dependent upon judges to combat an increasingly paranoid and authoritarian government?

Q: Please comment on counter terrorism activities by the United States and the United Kingdom and their effectiveness. Would you do things differently?

A: The huge issues that are being ducked by both the US and the UK are that we should be seeking to decrease, rather than increase our violent involvement in the affairs of the Middle East, and that we should not confuse the actions of a small number of criminals with a supposed "Clash of Civilizations."

Q: Osama bin Laden and his terror movement are said to have been created by the USA in the early 1980s. But now they are the enemies of the USA. First, is it true that the US created al-Qaeda? And can leaders in the United States and United Kingdom ever eliminate al-Qaeda?

A: It's not strictly true to say that the US created al-Qaeda, although they did pour billions of dollars into Afghanistan in the 1980s to fund the mujahideen resistance to the Soviet Union. As a member of the Arab mujahideen in Afghanistan at this time, Osama bin Laden, and others who went on to form al-Qaeda, were therefore at least indirectly funded by the US, but the most significant side-effect of the US funding for the anti-Soviet fighters was that they -- along with the Saudis, who matched US funding, or provided even more -- literally swamped this poor country with weapons, to lingering and brutal effect.

The US also stepped back from Afghanistan when the Soviet regime fell and the mujahideen embarked on a brutal civil war, and were also sidelined -- in particular by the Pakistanis -- when the Taliban, supported by Pakistan, either directly or covertly, rose up to restore order in the mid-1990s. This combination of neglect and of manipulation by Pakistan meant that the military training camp system in Afghanistan, which had initially arisen during the US-funded resistance to the Soviet Union, and of which al-Qaeda was but a small part (from 1996 onwards, after Osama bin Laden returned from a four-year hiatus in the Sudan), was allowed to expand in a largely unchecked manner.

As for whether al-Qaeda can ever be eliminated, I have to return to my observations above about Western foreign policy and the need to regain the moral high ground.

Q: What is the hidden agenda, if any, behind the US War on Terror?

A: Clearly, as Iraq demonstrates, the hidden agenda of the United States is geopolitical influence and the control of oil. Both factors also apply to Afghanistan, of course, but are somewhat muddied by the fact that the US was also involved in the pursuit of al-Qaeda. With Afghanistan in particular, it's not enough to say simply that the "War on Terror" is a smokescreen for installing a pro-American regime that will cooperate with the construction of a pipeline from the Caucasus to Pakistan. Guantánamo, Bagram and the secret prisons are not just a front; they are, sadly, the fruits of an administration mired in a mix of vengeance, blinkered self-righteousness and the misguided pursuit of "actionable intelligence" through the use of torture.

Q: You have launched an important book on Guantánamo Bay, The Guantánamo Files: The Stories of the 774 Detainees in America's Illegal Prison. The book reveals how American soldiers have held innocent people like slaves and how they are finishing them off. Please tell us why Americans are playing with human life like this.

A: Bluntly, because they believed their own hype that they were picking up "the worst of the worst" from the battlefield, even though at least 85% of those who ended up in US custody were handed over to US forces by their Afghan or Pakistani allies, at a time when substantial bounty payments for al-Qaeda or Taliban suspects were widespread.

Specifically, as well, the administration, at the highest levels (Bush, Cheney, Rumsfeld), authorized the use of torture on these poor men, when they failed to produce "actionable intelligence" (for the most part, because they were either innocent men or simple foot soldiers, and had no knowledge to impart), and were also directly responsible for all the other lawless innovations of the last six years: holding prisoners without charge or trial, authorizing the kidnap and "extraordinary rendition" of terror suspects anywhere in the world, and empowering the CIA to run secret prisons or to "render" those kidnapped to third countries, particularly in North Africa, where they could be interrogated by proxy torturers.

Q: Have you visited Guantánamo Bay camp or Abu Ghraib in Iraq? What are the conditions prevailing there?

A: I haven't. Abu Ghraib, like all the Iraqi prisons, is totally off-limits to all outsiders (except the Red Cross) and visitors to Guantánamo are only allowed to meet the prisoners if they are their legal representatives. For this, you need to be both a lawyer and an American, and I'm neither. As a journalist, I wouldn't want to be given the military's PR tour of the prison, although I admire journalists like Carol Rosenberg of the Miami Herald, who has been a persistent and critical visitor to the prison since it opened, and I also appreciate that, as a journalist, the trials at Guantánamo -- the Military Commissions, dreamt up in November 2001, and still struggling to establish their legitimacy -- are important events to cover.

Q: Pakistan, Afghanistan and some pro-USA countries have been giving their support to capturing al-Qaeda suspects. In Pakistan hundreds of youths have been disappeared. Some have been arrested and handed over to the CIA/FBI without proper investigations, according to some independent analysts. Could you let us know the contributory countries to the catastrophe in Guantánamo Bay? Asian countries?

A: As you correctly point out, both Pakistan and Afghanistan have been involved in these processes, although it should be noted that in Afghanistan this was down to the actions of individual warlords, whereas in Pakistan, as President Musharraf admitted in his autobiography in 2006, the government received millions of dollars for handing over hundreds of terror suspects.

What we also need to remember is that, after 9/11, the US administration put pressure on almost every country on earth to provide assistance in the pursuit of terrorists. European countries complied, if not by assisting in the direct apprehension of suspects (as was sometimes the case), then in facilitating -- or turning a blind eye -- to the passage of "extraordinary rendition" planes through their airspace. Other countries were leaned on -- or volunteered -- for deeper involvement. Thailand and Indonesia were involved in kidnapping and rendition, for example, and for a while the Thais also allowed -- or tolerated -- the existence of a secret CIA prison in their country, as the Poles and Romanians apparently did later.

This is too big a topic to cover here in any depth, but your readers will probably be interested to know that the prisoners in Guantánamo were captured in 17 different countries, and that some, like those captured in the Gambia and Zambia, were some considerable distance from the battlefields of Afghanistan.

Q: It seems to us that Americans truly believe that they are fighting for freedom and democracy and cannot see what they end up doing. What is the mechanism behind this? Surely they are not brainwashed with books like yours freely available to them?

A: Well, that's very kind of you to say so, but the simple truth is that millions of Americans believe what the President tells them, and that many of those involved in prosecuting the "War on Terror" -- in the government, and in the military -- also believe the hype that the illegal prisons are full of "the worst of the worst." It's still the after-effect of 9/11. The truth, which can only be perceived when you step back from these assertions, is that you can't legitimately describe people as dangerous terrorists when they haven't actually been through any valid screening process, and have been denied any legitimate manner in which they can question the basis of their detention. It's as simple as that. You have to follow internationally acceptable methods of establishing guilt; you can't just trust the President to say so, without having to provide any evidence, which is essentially the deplorable situation that still prevails.

Q: How is flawed American public opinion on matters like this different from public opinion in closed countries like, say, China or North Korea?

A: Oh, I'd have to say that it's very different. People complain that the right-wing controls too much of the media in the United States, and it's certainly true that some media proprietors have a shockingly wide and baleful influence. People also complain that there are few good newspapers in the US either, but the truth is that some extraordinarily important stories about the conduct of the "War on Terror" have been broken by journalists at newspapers including the Washington Post and the New York Times, and it's also apparent, of course, that there is a thriving alternative world of news that exists on the internet in the US, unlike, to use your example, China and North Korea.

Q: Regarding Iran, it is now conceded that the US deposed the elected leader Mohammed Mossadegh in 1952 and imposed the Shah. Many believe that it is this natural anger within Iran that led to the growth of extremism in Iran. It is also said that, however flawed, it is the most democratic of Islamic countries. And yet the US is allied with nearly all oppressive Islamic countries while always berating Iran. How does this happen with the American polity being democratic and the public having access to a wide variety of opinions?

A: Just because people have access, or potential access to information doesn't mean that they exercise that choice. You're right to point out the history of US-Iranian relations, but the default position, since 1979, has been that Iran and the United States are enemies. Similarly, citizens of all Western countries, not just the US, have to delve beyond the received positions on, for example, Israel and Palestine, Saudi Arabia and Egypt, to begin to make sense of how the world really is.

Q: According to your article *"Horror at Guantánamo,"* one of the terror suspects at Guantánamo is infected with the AIDS virus. Unfortunately, it is now evident that he was never involved with terrorism. That is, he is innocent. Why is America capturing innocent people outside America without proper investigations?

A: This is Abdul Hamid al-Ghizzawi, a Libyan who is married to an Afghan woman and ran a shop in Jalalabad at the time of the US-led invasion in October 2001. The US administration denies that he has been infected with AIDS, and it may be that he was told this as an act of cruelty by one of the staff at Guantánamo, but what's beyond doubt is that he has hepatitis B and tuberculosis, and that neither illness has been treated adequately, presumably because he has refused to cooperate with the interrogators by admitting that he was a terrorist.

His story is actually typical of many of the prisoners at Guantánamo, in that he was captured by bounty hunters and sold to the United States at the time when the system of bounty payments was prevalent, and that therefore it was presumed, from the moment that he was transferred to US custody, that he was a terrorist. Again, the problem is that there has been no adequate screening process to determine whether or not this is actually the case. All Arabs in US custody in Afghanistan were automatically sent to Guantánamo, and the screening in Guantánamo -- involving military tribunals -- was also inadequate, because the tribunals either relied on generic evidence that would not stand up in a court of law, or on secret evidence, which was often based on confessions made by the prisoners themselves, or by other prisoners, often under duress (or worse).

The difference between the point of view you express -- that the US is "capturing innocent people outside America without proper investigations" -- and the point of view of the US administration is that, as far as the administration is concerned, every confession, however it is derived, is valid, whereas you -- and myself, for that matter -- are appalled that the entire process stems from the presumption of guilt, rather than the presumption of innocence. Again, if people like Mr. al-Ghizzawi had been captured on a battlefield, we might be having a different conversation, but the fact is that the majority of these men -- including Mr. al-Ghizzawi -- were not, and it is therefore imperative, as it has been for over six years now, that they be allowed to challenge the basis of their detention in a meaningful manner.

Q: If that incident had happened in a poor country we would see lots of human rights organizations and the international media blaming the country. But now these same organizations are indefinitely silent. How do you explain their contradictory thinking and activism?

A: Basically, I don't agree that human rights organizations or the media have been silent. My organization, Reprieve, is just one of many Western organizations involved in human rights and the law -- including the Center for Constitutional Rights, Human Rights Watch, Amnesty International, Human Rights First, The American Civil Liberties Union and scores of legal firms in the US -- who have been challenging Guantánamo and the conduct of the "War on Terror" since the outset, and although some parts of the media -- in the States, especially -- were rather slow to pick up on the injustices that have been perpetrated over the last six years, they too -- with the exceptions of the administration's right-wing cheerleaders, of course -- have been deeply committed to discovering the truth about what has been done in their name for many years now.

Q: What are your future hopes as an author and journalist?

A: Basically to keep on exposing the truth about this most shameful of US administrations, and to stick with the story until the whole disgraceful edifice -- from Guantánamo to the secret prisons -- has been dismantled, and the United States returns to the rule of law. I hope that my book, my work as a journalist, and my work at Reprieve all contribute to the process.

April 16, 2008

22
WORLD WITHOUT TORTURE
THE RESPONSIBILITIES OF THE WEST

The CIA told Reagan that the Soviets would win the arms race, because it was a centrally planned economy that controlled investment and could allocate as many resources as necessary to the military. Reagan did not believe the CIA and appointed a committee to make the determination. The committee concluded that the Soviet economy would be unable to compete in an arms race.

- Paul Craig Roberts

DR. Paul Craig Roberts was educated at Georgia Tech, the University of Virginia, the University of California, Berkeley, and Oxford University where he was a member of Merton College. He has been the Assistant Secretary of the US Treasury in the Reagan administration, a member of the US Congressional staff, an associate editor and columnist for the Wall Street Journal, and a columnist for Business Week, the Scripps Howard News Service, and Creators Syndicate. He was also a Senior Research Fellow for the Hoover Institution at Stanford University and was appointed to the William E. Simon Chair in Political Economy at Georgetown University's Center for Strategic and International Studies. He is currently the chairman of the Institute for Political Economy and has authored or coauthored ten books and numerous articles in scholarly journals. He has testified before committees of Congress on 30 occasions. Dr. Roberts was awarded the US Treasury's Meritorious Service Award for "outstanding contributions to the formulation of US economic policy," and France's Legion of Honor as "the artisan of a renewal in economic science and policy, after half a century of state interventionism."

Q: You worked at the US treasury as Assistant Secretary during the Reagan administration, when the world economy changed towards neo-liberalism, and you are famous for being a co-founder of Reaganomics. How did this happen? What was your contribution to changing the model of world economy?

A: Reaganomics is a term the media attached to an innovation in economic theory and policy known as supply-side economics. Supply-side economics is not an ideology and it is not neo-liberalism.

I do not think that the Reagan administration changed the model of the world economy or that the administration thought of itself as neoliberal. What the Reagan administration did was to change the macroeconomic policy that had prevailed in the post-war English speaking world. That policy, known as Keynesian demand management, relied on government fiscal policy and monetary policy in order to maintain full employment and low inflation. If unemployment was the problem, government would enact a budget deficit and the central bank would expand money and credit. The monetary and fiscal stimulus would boost aggregate demand, and the increased spending would raise the level of employment. If inflation was the problem, the government would enact a budget surplus and the central bank would reduce the growth rate of money and credit.

This was how the policy was supposed to work. For example, in the early 1960s US economists understood the reduction in marginal income tax rates championed by President John F. Kennedy as a stimulus to consumer demand. Prior to Reagan, economists did not understand that fiscal policy could increase or decrease aggregate supply.

The demand management policy broke down during the Carter

presidency. Each boost to employment had to be "paid for" with a higher rate of inflation, and each attack on inflation had to be "paid for" with a higher rate of unemployment. These worsening trade-offs became known as "stagflation."

The only economists who had an answer to the problem of stagflation were the few supply-side economists of which I was one. Supply-side economics was an innovation in economic theory and in economic policy. Supply-side economists said that fiscal policy directly impacts aggregate supply. For example, a reduction in marginal tax rates (the rate of tax on additional income) changes important relative prices. It makes leisure more expensive in terms of foregone current income, and it makes current consumption more expensive in terms of foregone future income. Therefore, a reduction in marginal tax rates does not merely increase consumer demand. The lower tax rates result in an increase in labor and investment inputs, and aggregate supply increases. The demand management policy had stimulated demand, but the high marginal tax rates discouraged or made weaker the response of supply to demand. Therefore, prices rose. Supply-side economists said that the solution to stagflation was to change the policy mix: a tighter monetary policy and a looser fiscal policy. In other words, reduce the monetary stimulus and increase the supply incentives.

The policy worked, and the worsening "Phillips curve" trade-offs between employment and inflation disappeared. President Reagan had two main goals: to end stagflation and to end the Cold War. He campaigned on the supply-side policy. In order to get the policy implemented, he appointed me Assistant Secretary of the Treasury for Economic Policy. Later he associated me with his second goal by appointing me to a secret committee. Reagan thought that the Soviet economy was too decrepit to withstand the stress of a high-tech arms race. He believed that by threatening the Soviets with an arms race, he could bring them to negotiate the end of the Cold War.

The CIA told Reagan that the Soviets would win the arms race, because it was a centrally planned economy that controlled investment and could allocate as many resources as necessary to the military. Reagan did not believe the CIA and appointed a committee to make the determination. The committee concluded that the Soviet economy would be unable to compete in an arms race.

Q: The United States' image was still reeling from the Vietnam War, which ended in 1975, when President Jimmy Carter came in to power. America had learnt an expensive lesson from the loss of more than 57,000 American servicemen in the jungles of Southeast Asia. However, during Carter administration there were also tremendous conflicts from Afghanistan to Iran, Grenada to Nicaragua. It was a hot time in the Cold War. Then in 1980 Ronald Reagan won the election, and had won the Cold War by the time he left office. How was the Reagan administration different from other presidencies?

A: Reagan achieved both of his goals, and that is what makes him different from other presidents. The military conflicts during the Reagan years were minor, and, unlike the military conflicts of the George W. Bush and Obama regimes, were not conflicts on behalf of US world hegemony. Reagan said that if he was to be successful in bringing the Soviets to an agreement to end the Cold War, he had to draw the line in the sand and prevent any further communist expansion, whether in Afghanistan, Grenada, or Nicaragua. He said that if more countries fell to communism and became Soviet clients, the Soviets would be too confident to negotiate an end to the Cold War.

Q: Your book entitled, "Alienation and the Soviet Economy", has extensively examined the economic policy of the USSR and their weaknesses in planning. Could you please share with us how their weakness benefited the US to develop a neo-liberal economy and an identity as the leader of the West?

A: My book explains the Soviet economy as the outcome of an ideological attempt to remake human nature and society by substituting a planned economy for the unplanned market economy. Paradoxically, the collapse of the Soviet Union is one of the two developments (the other being the rise of the high speed Internet) that wrecked the US economy. When the Soviet Union collapsed, the American neoconservatives spoke of "the end of history," by which they meant that American capitalism was the only viable socio-economic system. The Soviet collapse caused the communists in China and socialists in India to rethink their approaches and to get on the winning side. These two Asian giants opened their vast under-utilized labor forces to western capital.

The era of jobs offshoring began. US corporations, pressed by Wall Street for higher profits, by large retailers such as WalMart, and by the cap that Congress placed on executive pay that is not performance based, moved the production of goods for US markets offshore where labor costs were a small fraction of US wages. This development caused profits to rise, but separated American consumers from the incomes associated with the goods and services that they consume. The same happened to professional service jobs, such as software engineering, Information Technology, and research and design. The ladders for upward mobility for Americans were dismantled. Wages and employment fell, medical benefits were lost, and careers disappeared.

The system by which First World corporations offshore the production of goods and services that they market in their home countries is called "globalism." Globalism is turning the US into a third world country. For the past two decades, the only jobs the US economy has been able to create are in lowly paid domestic services, such as waitresses, bartenders, and hospital orderlies. There has been no increase in real income for the bulk of the population. The gains in income and wealth are concentrated at the very top, and the distribution of income is now the worst in the developed world and worse than many Third World countries. The economy of the Reagan years is simply gone, disappeared.

Q: In more recent years, especially after 9/11, you became a critical analyst of US foreign policy. When did things start going wrong in the US and how did it happen?

A: Things began going wrong in the US when the US became "the sole superpower." American neoconservatives had a triumphal attitude and spread their attitude to the public and Congress with their propaganda. They argued that American capitalism had to be spread to the rest of the world, even if it had to be imposed by force of arms. Americans, neoconservatives proclaimed, were "the indispensable people," who had the right and the responsibility to impose their way on the world. Neoconservatives used the US Endowment for Democracy to foment "color revolutions" in former Soviet republics. The event of 9/11 provided neoconservatives with the opportunity to initiate US military invasions and "regime change" in the Middle East, Afghanistan, and North Africa.

Q: Let's start talking about our main subject – torture. I recall from our very first communication that you said you didn't have much of an idea about torture except in the context of the US and Israel. What analysis can you share, regarding torture involving the United States?

A: In the US torture is prohibited by the US Constitution and by US statutory law. It is also prohibited by the Geneva Conventions and international law. I do not know why the George W. Bush regime violated US and international law and tortured "detainees", most of whom were hapless individuals kidnapped by war lords and sold to the Americans for the bounty. It is well known among intelligence services that torture does not produce reliable information. Generally, a tortured person invents a story to tell his tormentors in order to stop the torture. Soviet dissidents accused of fantastic plots and tortured to elicit the names of their coconspirators, would give the names of dead people.

One dissident wrote that, expecting to be arrested, he memorized the names on gravestones.

In my opinion, the Bush regime, a neoconservative regime, used the hyped fear about the threat of "Muslim terrorism" to get the acquiescence of the American public, Congress and the federal courts to torture, arguing that torture was necessary in order to protect Americans from events such as 9/11.

The neoconservatives reasoned that if the executive branch could violate, with impunity, both constitutional and legal prohibitions against torture, the precedent could be expanded to habeas corpus, due process, and to free speech, free assembly, (protests) and to criticism of the government's policies, which is being redefined as "aiding and abetting terrorism."

Once law and the Constitution could be side-lined, the regime could escape war criminal accountability for its wars of naked aggression. President Obama won the presidential election, because voters expected him to stop the wars, stop the torture, and to hold the Bush regime criminals accountable.

However, Obama found the new powers convenient and held on to them and expanded them. He refused to hold the Bush regime criminals accountable. He had the illegal and unconstitutional powers asserted by the Bush regime codified in US law. And Obama asserted new powers—the right to murder American citizens of whom he was suspicious, without due process of law. What the Bush and Obama regimes have done is to turn the United States into a Gestapo-like police state. Prior to Bush/Obama it was illegal for the government to spy on Americans without cause presented to a court, which, if convinced, would provide a warrant. Now every aspect of Americans' lives are routinely watched, their movements, their emails, their internet usage, and even their purchases. Not only are air travelers subjected to intimate searches, but train and bus travelers too, and car and truck traffic on interstate highways is stopped and searched. There have been no terrorist attacks on trains, buses, or highway travel. Yet, the freedom of mobility in the US has been compromised even more than it was in the Soviet Union with the system of internal passports.

Q: What is your suggested solution to this critique? In other words how can the responsible governments correct things and lead their people towards freedom?

A: In the US, government is no longer accountable to law or to the people. Whoever is elected to the presidency or to Congress is accountable to the powerful private interest groups that provide the funds for the political campaign. Having purchased the government, the special interests expect government to serve them. The military/security complex makes billions of dollars in profits from wars, whether hot or cold. Peace is not in the interest of the military/security complex. Peace reduces the profits of the armaments industry and it reduces the power of the CIA, Homeland Security, Pentagon, FBI, and National Security Agency. In America today, peace is for sissies.

Q: Just hours after the release of the State Department's annual human rights report, you wrote an opinion saying that the US government was the second worst human rights abuser on the planet and the sole enabler of the worst abuser –Israel. If this is true, US pressure for human rights reforms in other countries seems hypocritical. Do you want the US government to stop talking to these other countries? If the US doesn't have the right to criticize human rights violence in other countries, who does?

A: To use biblical language, the US government focuses attention on the mote in Syria's or Iran's or China's eye in order to direct attention away from the beam in its own eye. It is Washington that conducted war for eight years in Iraq, killing hundreds of thousands of people on false pretenses.

It is Washington that is conducting war for eleven years in Afghanistan on false pretenses, killing an unknown, but large, number of Afghans. It is Washington that is violating the sovereignty of Pakistan and Yemen, murdering people in these countries daily on false pretenses. It was Washington that organized the overthrow of the Libyan government, leaving the country in total chaos, with untold deaths. It is Washington that is responsible for endless violence in Somalia. It is Washington that has sent US troops to four African countries as part of the new imperialist venture known as the US Africa Command. How can a government that commits massive violations of human rights in Afghanistan, Pakistan, the Middle East, Africa, and at home lecture, or speak to, any other country about human rights? The world accepts this unbelievable hypocrisy because of the success of US propaganda during the Cold War. The propaganda placed the white hat firmly on the head of the US government.

Q: You opposed the war in Afghanistan, Iraq, Libya and other ongoing conflicts in East Asia as well. We saw how torture occurred in those wars. Perhaps the most high profile and visible case of torture in recent years was the public execution of Muammar Gaddafi. Torture has become a norm, regardless of the victim's guilt or innocence. There are numerous international conventions against torture but torture still exists in many places. What are your feelings about this? Why are events moving in that direction?

A: In the 20th century, the West, which was hardly innocent, nevertheless stood for civil liberty, for law as a shield of the people instead of a weapon in the hands of the government. In Hitler's Germany and Stalin's Soviet Union, law was a weapon in the hands of the government. Today the US has caught up with Hitler and Stalin. Law in the US is a weapon in the hands of the government.

In my opinion, neoconservative triumphalism has destroyed American morality and left hubris in its place. Americans are overwhelmed by how great and good and moral and indispensable they are. American hubris raises Americans above everyone else in the world. Americans can torture, murder, invade, and still lecture the rest of the world about human rights.

Q: In one of your pieces published last April, you pointed out, "I agree that there is a lot of evil in every country and civilization. In the struggle between good and evil, religion has at times been on the side of evil. However, the notion of moral progress cannot so easily be thrown out." As you say, in many countries liberty was lost, though the notion of moral progress cannot be easily thrown out. Can you explain more about this interesting conclusion?

A: I don't know enough about the nonwestern world to answer this question with confidence. The point I was making is that the struggle between good and evil is ancient. In various historical periods evil prevails; in other periods good prevails. This means that moral concepts survive even during the periods of the prevalence of evil. As I have written, not far into the past, slavery was a fact of life, not a moral issue. Today, even the worst government would not openly legitimize slavery, although tax slavery, except for the mega-rich who control the governments, exists everywhere in the West.

The point is that we cannot give up hope that the world can be returned to a moral existence. What is discouraging is that it is no longer the West, and certainly not the US government, that is the upholder of "the rights of mankind."

Q: How can we change for the better? Where should it start if we are to achieve a torture free society?

A: In my opinion, there is no prospect for a moral and torture free world until the West is held accountable for its crimes. The war crimes tribunal in Malaysia was a beginning. The convictions of the Bush regime monsters have no legal authority, but the convictions assert morality authority. If the Malaysian war crimes tribunal is repeated in many other countries, the US and UK war criminals and their NATO (The North Atlantic Treaty Organization) puppet criminals would not be able to travel beyond their own borders. The image would be created of Western leaders hunted by the rest of the world for their criminal actions. This is the only way to re-empower morality as a force in history.

Western governments have become the antithesis of morality.

September 22, 2012

23
WHY TORTURE IS WRONG

"An interesting case is the role of guerrilla fighters in conflicts. Some places they may attain a kind of state power, that is, the state may seem rather powerless in relation to them. Nevertheless, I would say that violence from such actors is violence and crime, and if there is an unwillingness or a lack of possibility on the part of the state to deal with this, then we are talking about serious human rights violations."

- Nora Sveaass

BORN in Oslo, Norway, in December 1949, Dr. Nora Sveaass is a clinical psychologist who has been engaged in various parts of the world in relation to human rights and rehabilitation after torture. She is an internationally renowned psychologist who became a member of the Committee against Torture in the United Nations (UNCAT). Dr. Sveaass, who is currently an Associate Professor at the Department of Psychology in the University of Oslo, recently corresponded with the writer. Following is the full text of an interview in which she has explored her extensive work on torture prevention and in healing the wounds which have caused a series of conflicts in society.

Question (Q): Why is the study of psychology so important?

Answer (A) : Psychology is about human beings, their existence and co-existence with others. Psychology studies human life and action in context. The human being is a whole, and mind and body cannot be understood as separate entities or apart from each other. But it is true that psychology gives special weight to the study of how the human mind works and develops, how human behaviour can be understood, described and even explained and how human beings interact with each other. This includes the study of emotions, motivation, cognition and a lot more of course. One of the important contributions of psychology is knowledge about how human behaviour develops and how changes come about. Insight into processes and conditions for change, that is changes that happen over life span, and changes that come about as result of social processes or social events, is considered an important part of psychology.

The study of behaviour change is of course especially important in a context of therapy. I will come back to this. And all what I have mentioned must be seen as elements closely linked to each other and as part of a dynamic process. Psychology has developed a lot over the last 100 years, and today, the study of psychology and what psychology as a science has obtained in terms of knowledge and insight holds a central position in many ways. What happens in the psychological sphere in peoples' lives, whether it relates to emotions, thoughts, experiences and even mental health, may even today often be considered secondary compared to the physical body and the material world. One can often hear expressions such as "just psychological", "only mental" etc. But the psychological aspects of human life and actions represent the qualitative aspects of life. We know that a person may become extremely ill for lack of psychological stimulation, even if a lot of other basic components for survival may be present. And many people, who have experienced isolation, will say that this is the worst form of torture. That is, the body is never directly attacked with pain or suffering, but the pain that is created by lack of social, perceptual and other forms of stimuli, create not only pain then and there, but may create long-lasting suffering and trauma in the lives of those who have been exposed to this. Early research on children showed that babies could even die from what was called "anaclitic depression", that is a serious impairment in an infant's social, physical and intellectual development, due to lack of mothering, that is close emotional contact and stimulation. The knowledge that psychology establishes has important impact in the area of health, ensuring good development for children, and forms the basis I would say also for social justice and respect for human dignity and vice versa. Lack of social justice, and violations of human dignity, have serious consequences for human psychology.

Q: In the last few decades, where has the study of psychology had a major impact on the rest of the world?

A: Psychology, being the study of human beings in context, with a focus how we perceive the world, how we react in the world, how we develop in this world, how relations are established and what effect this has upon us, just has to be relevant in a lot of different areas. To be quite honest, , I can think of few areas of modern life where psychology, with knowledge and insight into the human mind and behaviour, its cognitive functions as well emotional and creative ones, is not highly relevant, or at least very interesting. And by being a science with a strong academic backing, and at the same time a practical and applied science, it represents an approach with strong impact in many ways. It will be much too much to refer to all of this here. Because we are talking about a field which over the last years has seen a tremendous development in psychological study of the brain, so-called neuropsychology. This has resulted in a far better understanding of cognitive functioning, and the strong relationship between cognition, behaviour, social and emotional functioning and health. And the strength of psychology is not only in describing the processes in the brain, but it studies the functions, how these processes in fact affect the way humans function in the world, in their bodies, and in their social world.

Psychology, given the fact that it covers such a wide array of studies, its impact is to be seen in quite different areas of society. We are talking about a science which has not only set it footprints many places but has actively contributed to , forming, changing and developing fields as diverse as corporate management and organisations, transport and security, including how can we ensure that traffic signs are perceived as easily and correctly as possible? We have psychologists in selection of personnel, from submarines to airplanes, and a lot of risk assessment, and preparation for stress. Psychology has for long been included as resources in advertisement for commercial reasons, but also in political information and propaganda. And psychology represents an important basis of knowledge and does not in itself have value direction. Therefore there is always the possibility that psychological knowledge can be used both to enhance values related to respect for human rights, and to bring them down, such as we have seen in different situations. Based on psychological knowledge techniques for interviewing has been developed, such as ways of conducting interviews, be it for jobs, for information or for diagnostic purposes.

Likewise this information has formed the bases for ways in which to interrogate as well. Good interrogation can be done according to human rights, and respectful interrogation may well be based on our knowledge of how alliances and trust are established. But psychological knowledge may also be used or misused in interrogation, where knowledge about "soft spots", what makes people break down, etc. has been used systematically to get confessions or in other ways to humiliate people. Different ways of creating pain, such as described above, including inducing severe fear, addressing aspects that create shame and humiliation and the like, have all been part of torture, and this may well seem to have been built upon insights developed within psychology. It is therefore always an important challenge to ensure that psychological knowledge is not abused in contexts that are contrary to international human rights principles, and prohibitions, such as the absolute prohibition against torture, and that nothing may ever justify the use of torture.

Psychology is also about health – about understanding regular human development and psychological illness and distress of different kind, how it develops, how it is maintained and how it can be dealt with from the point of view of therapy. In particular I want to mention the strong focus on children all we today know about the needs of children and how healthy development can be ensured, and how lack of stimulation, support, safety and active recognition can be very critical in the lives of children. But back to therapy and psychological treatment – many therapeutic approaches have developed over the years, and today there seems to be a tendency for better dialogue and communication between the different schools or traditions. But what we know about human pain and stress is also important to develop strategies for prevention, and early intervention. In particular the knowledge about effects of stress on human functioning has developed strongly the last 30 years. Active involvement in traumatic events, better ways to detect the consequences and better tools to deal with post-traumatic reactions are important. But also this rests upon early traditions in psychology, from Freud's description of sexual violence against children, to studies of shell-shock and concentration camp syndromes from the two World Wars.

It is also worth mentioning that a lot of psychologists have been engaged in peace psychology, and in conflict and conflict-resolution activities. Again, based on psychological knowledge and recent research, this area is something that needs to be highlighted even stronger, and lead to active involvement of psychologists in this area.

Q: "Restructuring meaning after uprooting and violence and Psychosocial interventions in refugee receiving and in post-conflict societies", was your PhD thesis. Can you elaborate on your findings with examples in those areas?

A: My objective was to explore ways of reconstructing lives after human rights violations and uprooting. I had worked as a therapist with refugees and victims of torture for many years and I had asked myself – what does it take from a host society to be able to, in collaboration with those who have sought protection in the country, to establish a life in exile and to re-establish a life project. This is not readily answered of course. Because this may involve a long process of rehabilitation involving psychotherapy and other forms of health care, but also because we are talking about how society can engage the newcomers and how people with refugee background can involve themselves in the new society, while at the same time dealing with the pain of the past. So part of my work was to look into therapeutic processes with refugees in Norway, in particular family therapy.

But I also included a vast material from an out-patient clinic, the Psychosocial Centre for Refugees, receiving traumatized refugees for therapy and psychosocial assistance. And the results from this study pointed in an interesting direction from my point of view, as I am very interested both in the meaning aspect of people's lives and of family and support as important conditions for recovery and development. We saw that lack of activity, that is, no work or no activity in form of training, education programs etc. , had a detrimental effect on people's health in exile, and this effect was clearly noted whether people had suffered severely or less severely prior to arrival. As to the importance of family, it seemed clear that the more exposed persons had been to violations and pain prior to exile, that is, the higher the rate of trauma-related distress in exile, the more important the presence of family seemed to be. These results strengthened my interested in having a family focus in my work with refugees, knowing that the social and emotional support that families can provide, may have a very beneficial impact on integration and recovery. But, knowing that many families struggle, the health-effects or benefits of assisting families to cope with the different hardships they face in exile seems to be a matter of priority.

But I also wanted to compare the experiences from Norway to experiences from other countries, and as the University of Oslo was collaborating with universities in Central America, I was fortunate to have a semester in Managua, Nicaragua, where I could learn about how post-conflict reconstruction was thought about and worked with in the countries where the conflict had taken place. Interviews with a large group of helpers, of different categories, but all engaged in persons subjected to and traumatized by the civil war in Nicaragua, on both sides, made it clear to me that the lack of life project, and the destruction of meaningful relationships in life, including with regard to the activity that they were good at, namely war, made life miserable and meaningless, in the eyes of many of the affected. The reconstruction of activity, relationships and meaning in life, through skills training and educational activities, and reconstruction of family relationships, seemed very important to the affected groups. Furthermore, the war-affected men and women were also offered, by some of the active NGOs in the field, so-called "moral education", that is, groups where values and norms could be discussed.

Too many had continued to live as if they were still at war, and had established a post-conflict life both with violence and drinking, and the psychosocial activities they were offered, a kind of social-therapy groups, were focusing on re-establishing the values and norms that were broken down by the war. In particular, domestic violence, sexual violence and heavy drinking were addressed, and according to many of those I interviewed both among helpers and helped ones, these interventions were regarded as highly useful and with effect in people's lives. My study was qualitative, so exact results cannot be described, but through the study, including a very rich data-material , I definitely learned a lot about the importance of recreating meaning and relationships following severe violence and violations of human rights, and how re-engaging with society again and feeling part of a collective contributes to sense of dignity and self-worth. Because armed conflicts and authoritarian and torturing regimes break down all these aspects of human living. Thus, I have often thought about war and oppression as systematic destruction of meaning. I have taken a lot of these reflections back into my work, both clinical, research and also my human rights work, such as in the UN Committee against torture.

Q: You have been working on a project known as, "Identification of vulnerable asylum seekers in Norway and EU – a comparative study". This is a very challenging subject and many countries are facing significant difficulties in regard to asylum seekers. At the same time, many asylum seekers are facing difficulties to get recognition by the authorities of their host countries. What are some of the chief concerns within this subject, and what countries are having the greatest difficulties with asylum seekers?

A: The work with asylum seekers is a very challenging one, all over Europe. The project related to identification of vulnerable asylum seekers was actually a European project, initiated as part of evaluation of and possible changes in EU's Reception directive for asylum seekers. This directive, defined by the European Council, the so-called COUNCIL DIRECTIVE 2003/9/EC of 27 January 2003, laying down minimum standards for the reception of asylum seekers, has an article 17 defining the following: "Member States shall take into account the specific situation of vulnerable persons such as minors, unaccompanied minors, disabled people, elderly people, pregnant women, single parents with minor children and persons who have been subjected to torture, rape or other serious forms of psychological, physical or sexual violence, in the national legislation implementing the provisions of Chapter II relating to material reception conditions and health care".

This said, it was important to define ways in which these vulnerable asylum seekers could be identified and provided with the care that they would need as well as protection. In Norway this has been

209

taken up and at the moment we are defining the standards by which interviewing and identification of vulnerability can be assessed. Also, the importance of finding ways of identifying and documenting torture is an important issue. Here we are working on a plan to integrate and implement the Istanbul Protocol, the UN manual for effective investigation and identification of torture and ill-treatment. The group working with this in Norway, clearly shares the viewpoint clearly expressed also by the Committee against torture in the UN, that torture experienced prior to exile must be thoroughly investigated and documented. This is important both to lay the ground for care and needed therapy and rehabilitation, but also because it may shed important light on the need for protection in an asylum country and it may represent an important document that persons may need in the context of redress, that is, compensation and justice.

Many of the asylum receiving countries today, despite council directives and other important policy documents, do not engage seriously enough in the identification of vulnerability, nor on torture and ill-treatment. We hope to be able to work with this and strengthen the work in this respect. It is important for treatment but as mentioned, also as documentation of wrong-doing.

But of course, many of the challenges today in relation to Europe and asylum seekers may also have to do with financial crises and problems related to an ever higher level of unemployment, the fear for the future etc. This is a realistic problem which cannot be concealed. But on the other hand, this is also an argument that is used to cover up for xenophobic and even racist attitudes. And this is not the first time in history this happens, so one must be very aware of the dangers involved in this.

Q: "Victims' experiences of transitional justice in Argentina and Peru" is another project that you are actively part of. Could you share some of your personal experiences while working on this project in Latin America?

A: The battle against impunity, in particular how this was initiated by human rights activists in Latin America during and after the military dictatorships, including by professionals within psychology and medicine, was a strong inspiration and an eye-opener to me.

Much of what happened in international criminal law during the 1990s can be understood in light of this strong and engaged campaign against impunity, in particular in Latin-America. The fight against impunity began during the era of the military dictatorships, and has not diminished following the adoption of amnesty laws for crimes against humanity. In Chile, Argentina, Uruguay and Peru, psychologists, doctors, and others who worked with torture survivors and families of disappeared per-sons within the framework of human rights organizations argued that impunity must be considered as a continued and on-going form of torture. Impunity for those responsible for crimes against humanity was re-garded as detrimental to any reconstruction of society and incompatible with the process of healing and moving on in life. Diana Kordon, Dario Lagos, and Lucilla Edelman from Argentina, and Paz Rojas, Elisabeth Lira, and Maria Castillo from Chile are among those who have stressed the importance of not leaving this battle to the legal field alone. The fight against amnesty laws was thus also based on arguments from a psychological and trauma-informed perspective. These professionals, who have also written extensively about the experiences, are still engaged fulltime in the fight against impunity and for justice and reparation, for the survivors and families of the disappeared, and for assistance, treatment, and follow-up of people severely traumatized some from more than 30 years ago. Inger Agger, in a recent interview with *"Torture : Asian and Global Perspectives"* (Volume 02 Number 01) also spoke about this important Nora's contribution of our Chilean and other Latin-American colleagues, and she too spoke about how our professional encounter with them have constituted very important inspiration and learning. In fact both Inger and myself have continued to work in this area since we first met with our brave friends in Latin-America, and the two of us have also had a very meaningful collaboration over the years, actively these last years with the issue of Transitional justice and the experiences of witnesses and survivors.

What our colleagues from the south have taught us has really represented important input into the fight against impunity. But in our research project (Anne-Margrethe Sønneland and myself) we wanted also to explore more in depth – what do we actually know about the effects on mental health of impunity. What does it mean to people to experience that the perpetrators and those responsible for the crimes committed against them, and here we are talking about the most serious crimes against humanity, are protected by amnesty laws and a policy of impunity, that allow them to walk freely around and are not held to account for what they have done. This may create in them, not only a deep feeling of injustice and lack of fairness, but it is fear and anxiety, and lack of trust in the society that allows this to happen. A lot has happened in relation to impunity at a global level, and today, amnesty for the crime of torture is a serious violation of the Convention against Torture.

So that is why it is so important to ask: when it finally comes to initiatives to transitional justice and transitional justice mechanisms, it is important to ask: What does it mean to the former prisoners, to the tortured ones and their families, to witness in court, to tell their story in public, often for the first time? And furthermore, what about redress, in the form of compensation and rehabilitation….. Is this something that is sought, is it wanted by the affected ones? Yes, their right to receive this is there, but how do they feel about it? These are some of the questions we are raising in our study, and we will publish our findings next year. But we see, perhaps even stronger than we had expected that courts and legal processes are important. It represents a message about accountability, that society has acknowledged the fact that the violations have taken place etc. But equally important are the reactions of society – that is recognition of what actually happened, truth-telling and social acknowledgement of pain and suffering.

Q: You have been involved in a project on Health and Human Rights which has a very comprehensive webpage. Also you are involved in developing training material to persons involved with care to women exposed to conflict and war related GBV. Could you please describe these projects, and also inform about the manual and how this will be used

A: I have often experiences that good projects aimed at assistance and support develop from the very first start each time they are required, which usually may be situation of crises and need. We wanted to put together experiences, and lessons learned in relation to psychosocial assistance and psychological help to persons exposed to war and conflict, and subjected to torture and other forms of ill-treatment. So on one hand this project is a resource data base with a lot of good practical experiences grouped together but presented in such a way that care providers, whether they are working in humanitarian crisis, such as war and conflict, or the like, or they are working with internal refugees, persons imprisoned and tortured, those who have suffered other forms of hardships and losses, given political violence and oppression, may have some input as to how to deal with and respond to such situations. In such circumstances, the problem is also that specialists and trained personnel may be far away and not available, and a lot has to be developed then and there. We hoped that communicating the experiences of others would help care givers and inspire them in their work.

At the same time we felt it was important to bridge the gap between health care professionals and human rights activists, including legal professionals in the field. To develop this website, where health care and ways of dealing with such problems are presented together with information about conventions, treaties etc. may give this extra understanding both to the human rights field and to the care and health field. Then we developed thematic pages in order to bring these aspects even closer together. Under the page called TORTURE, there is information both about conventions, methods to assess and detect, ways of assisting and providing necessary care to those exposed to this, based on a lot of experiences in the field. We include information on therapeutic principles as well as some shorter interventions. We know that this webpage has been actively used also as part of training, and we hope that our efforts with this project may be beneficial in many ways. At the moment we are developing a manual to assist those working with victims of gender based violence in conflict. We hope that after we have done completed to pilot training projects, this manual will be available on our page, and that it may prove possible to use in the work to strengthen helpers in this very serious and tragic field, of sexual violence in conflict.

Q: You are a member of the Committee against Torture, (CAT)

213

which monitors the implementation of the United Nations Convention against Torture (UNCAT). What are the some of the positive aspects you have seen since the UNCAT was first created?

A: The Convention against Torture was adopted in 1984 and entered into force in 1987. This year the 25th anniversary for the convention was celebrated in Genève at the Palais de Nation with the aim of highlighting some of the important contributions and advances that have taken place during these years. A total of 153 states have ratified the convention, meaning the states, have agreed to comply with the provisions of the convention, both in its legal system and in actual life. The state parties to the convention must bring their domestic laws in line with the requirements of the treaty. Among other things, this means that the definition of torture, as this is defined in article I, must be integrated, acts of torture must be properly defined as offences under the criminal law and penalties for such crimes must take into account the grave nature of torture. Furthermore, states must take effective, legislative, administrative, judicial or other measures, as it says in Article 2, to prevent acts of torture in any territory under its jurisdiction. This means that measures must be taken on a lot of different levels. The responsibility of the state to prevent torture also refers to the responsibility to prevent, investigate and punish acts of torture or cruel and inhuman treatment done by non-state actors as well. I consider this as one of the very important articles of the convention, and the committee has been working very specifically with this obligation. In 2009 a General comment to this article was adopted. Here state responsibility is described more in depth, and the failure to prevent, as well as the failure to investigate and punish such acts, are seen as a serious violations.

General comment No 2, in paragraph 18 states the following: "Since the failure of the State to exercise due diligence to intervene to stop, sanction and provide remedies to victims of torture facilitates and enables non-State actors to commit acts impermissible under the Convention with impunity, the State's indifference or inaction provides a form of encouragement and/or de facto permission. The Committee has applied this principle to the State parties' failure to prevent and protect victims from gender-based violence, such as rape, domestic violence, female genital mutilation, and trafficking" (Gen. comment no. 2). With this formulation, the CAT has strengthened its position with regard to different forms of violations, in particular violence against women and girls, which too often, in much too many places in the world, have been going on with impunity, and with lack of protection, compensation and assistance to those affected. I regard this point as one of the very important steps in the 25 year history of CAT, and today one will find questions, as well as expression of deep concern and clear recommendations in relation to gender based violence and violence children also in private settings, in relation to trafficking and gender mutilation, and gender discriminate laws and regulation, such as early marriage age, non-accountability in cases where rapist marries rape victim etc.

A strong focus on training in the prohibition against torture is also among the important issues worked with. Training is required not only for uniformed personnel but also doctors, psychologists, teachers etc. As part of training, a systematic training in the Istanbul protocol is among the requirements, and this is an important condition for detecting and documenting torture, as well as a strategy to prevent it.

The most recent development within the Committee against Torture and the work to prohibit torture is the focus that has been on article 14, on the obligation of states to provide redress to victims of torture, including the right to rehabilitation. In November 2012 a general comment No 3 to article 14 was adopted. This defines and clarifies the content and scope of the obligations under article 14 of the United Nations Convention against Torture and Other Cruel, Inhuman or Degrading Treatment or Punishment and seems to become a very important document in the process of ensuring that all victims of torture in fact may enjoy the rights they have under the convention, in particular to the right to compensation including rehabilitation. All victims of torture have the right to redress, which includes the right to effective remedy and to reparation. As formulated in the Basic Principles and Guidelines on the Right to a Remedy and Reparation for Victims of Gross Violations of International Human Rights Law and Serious Violations of International Humanitarian Law (UN Resolution 2005) the notion of reparation includes five forms of reparation, that is, restitution, compensation, rehabilitation, satisfaction and guarantees of non-reparation.

The General comment explicitly refers to these same forms. In the general comment the Committee affirms the importance of rehabilitation as something which must be multi-disciplinary in nature and include medical and psychological care as well as legal and social services. "The aim of rehabilitation thus refers to the restoration of function or the acquisition of new skills required by the changed circumstances of a victim in the aftermath of torture or ill-treatment. It also seeks to enable the maximum possible self-sufficiency and function for the individual concerned, and may involve adjustments to the person's physical and social environment. Rehabilitation for victims should aim to restore, as far as possible, their independence, physical, mental, social and vocational ability; and full inclusion and participation in society" (GC3). Given what one knows about the effects of torture, both the short term and long-term effects, emotionally, socially and cognitively, a holistic and integrative concept of rehabilitation is vital. We hope that this general comment will strengthen the process of ensuring not only compensation and other forms of redress, but also good therapeutic assistance and rehabilitation, in line with what we know about this from all the work that has been undertaken, and in full respect of and in full participation with the victim and his or her family.

All this said about the content of the provisions and obligations, it is important to refer to what it means to a state to ratify CAT, and how also civil society is involved in the process. In many ways this aspect is one of the central elements in the treaty body system. And during the years, the steps and structure in this process have been better and more clearly defined, so that one today has a transparency and a possibility of looking into and claim monitoring and insight that is remarkable. Ratifying means that the state has to submit reports every 4th year on compliance, that is, what has the state done to integrate and implement the requirements, both the legal ones, and implications on the ground.

The committee receives the state report (the periodic report), reports from the UN system, including the special procedures, and

216

others such as regional human rights bodies, and last but not least, the alternative information from civil society, usually national and international Non-governmental organisations. This information is vital to the committee. These alternative reports, formerly often called "shadow-reports" often point to loopholes in the practical implementation and compliance with the convention, and frequently provide concrete examples and cases. Based on this material direct questions can be raised with the states, asking them for more information, explain why things are as described by other sources and what plans the state may have to alter this. So – in this way civil society contributes importantly to the work of the committee -and the recommendations from the committee may certainly be an important basis, not only for actions by the state, but also as support to NGO-claims regarding respect for human rights.

The treaty bodies, together with an ever stronger system to monitor and overlook respect and violations of human rights, represent important developments, and it is my strong conviction that during these years of the Torture convention being in force, a number of very important monitoring and complaint mechanisms have seen the daylight, and have proved valuable in practice. This of course became even stronger with the adoption of the Optional Protocol to the convention, the OPCAT, and the establishment of the Subcommittee, which as part of its mandate, must overlook the establishments of National Preventive mechanisms in all the state parties to the convention.

Q: Torture still exists in many parts of the world. Many of those who commit torture believe that their actions are justified and that they have the support of significant portions of the general population in many countries. This has been especially true after the rise in popularity of governments "declaring war" against terrorism. What is your opinion on this?

A: The prohibition against torture is absolute. There is no justification for torture, and as it is clearly stated in article 2 of the Convention against Torture .

This is written many years before the so-called "war against terror" was launched, and emphasizes that this has been the important principle since the adoption of the convention. A state that allows torture to happen not only violates international human law but creates a room that is extremely destructive. It undermines the trust and confidence that every society must contain, and such practices open up for more violence and disrespect of human rights. What was attempted as part of the war against terror was to create the picture that better one guilty than many innocent. But there is absolutely no justification for torture. And this campaign has also been used as a way of getting rid of or pacifying opposition. A lot of human rights violations over the last years have taken place under the auspices of fighting terror. The campaigns to fight this are extremely important. In addition, it has been argued, especially from people trained in interrogation and forensic psychology that torture, in addition to be totally wrong, also brings about wrong or false intelligence.

Q: Article One of the UNCAT defines torture as: "Any act by which severe pain or suffering, whether physical or mental, is intentionally inflicted on a person for such purposes as obtaining from him or a third person, information or a confession, punishing him for an act he or a third person has committed or is suspected of having committed, or intimidating or coercing him or a third person, or for any reason based on discrimination of any kind, when such pain or suffering is inflicted by or at the instigation of or with the consent or acquiescence of a public official or other person acting in an official capacity. It does not include pain or suffering arising only from, inherent in or incidental to lawful sanctions."

Why does torture have to be instigated by or have the consent of government officials or people acting in 'official' capacities? Does this exempt torture between private individuals, rebellious groups, criminal groups, etc.? Why are governments singled out in a definition that is intended to be universal?

A: Human rights is about the relationship between state and individuals, to protect individuals from abuse of power from the state. If the state does not establish mechanisms to protect individuals, they are responsible for the results and must take action. The most important duty of states is to protect its citizens and ensure that people's rights are respected. So human rights laws deal with state vs. individuals. But – the discussion raised is a very important one because it asks about the role of non-state actors in relation to violations. The main principle here is that the state in principle should also have power over, or be able to manage violence committed by them.

An interesting case is the role of guerrilla fighters in conflicts. Some places they may attain a kind of state power, that is, the state may seem rather powerless in relation to them. Nevertheless, I would say that violence from such actors is violence and crime, and if there is an unwillingness or a lack of possibility on the part of the state to deal with this, then we are talking about serious human rights violations. An interesting example is Peru. The Shining Path was fighting the Peruvian government, in particular the military. Atrocities in very high numbers were committed on both sides. In the aftermath, the state has assumed a kind of responsibility also for those who were tortured or seriously affected by the guerrilla. They are providing them with reparation together with those that were subjected to human rights violations by the state itself. But, if people themselves have committed such crimes, for instance, participated in the guerrilla, then no reparation is given. But the victims have rights, regardless of the perpetrators.

Q: Article Two of the UNCAT differentiates between "cruel, inhuman, or degrading treatment" and "torture". What is the difference between the two and why are the defined separately? Also, is there any possibility of someone using an argument over these definitions to get away with torturing someone else? Can you give a couple of examples of when such a distinction would help protect human rights?

A: It is often referred to intent as being the difference between the two. That torture is severe pain inflicted with intent, whereas cruel, inhuman or degrading treatment or punishment (CIDT) has been looked upon as pain where the degree of intentionality is less obvious. At the same time, the term torture, or amounting to torture has also been used in situations where conditions are so serious and painful to those affected, and where the responsible one have not been capable of reducing, changing or bettering this. In such examples there has not been a clear intent to create pain, but the lack of action to reduce the pain has been so overarching that the result has been regarded by the committee as torture, or tantamount to torture. The difficulties in delineating between torture and CIDT are fully recognized. Personally I think that the most relevant text explaining the relationship between the two is paragraph 2 in CAT's General Comment no 2.

Here the following is articulated: "The obligation to prevent torture in article 2 is wide-ranging. The obligations to prevent torture and other cruel, inhuman or degrading treatment or punishment (hereinafter "ill-treatment") under article 16, paragraph 1, are indivisible, interdependent and interrelated. The obligation to prevent ill-treatment in practice overlaps with and is largely congruent with the obligation to prevent torture. Article 16, identifying the means of prevention of ill-treatment, emphasizes "in particular" the measures outlined in articles 10 to 13, but does not limit effective prevention to these articles, as the Committee has explained, for example, with respect to compensation in article 14. In practice, the definitional threshold between ill-treatment and torture is often not clear. Experience demonstrates that the conditions that give rise to ill-treatment frequently facilitate torture and therefore the measures required to prevent torture must be applied to prevent ill-treatment. Accordingly, the Committee has considered the prohibition of ill-treatment to be likewise non-derogable under the Convention and its prevention to be an effective and non-derogable measure". In other words, CIDT may lay the ground for torture, and as such must be equally prohibited and action considered to be ill-treatment, equally met with reactions similar to reactions to acts of torture.

Former special Rapporteur on Torture, Manfred Nowak, elaborated the distinction between these two concepts by pointing to differences in thresholds dependant on whether the violence happens as part of detention or out in the free. For instance, violence or force committed by police in situations for instance of riot control, may be considered as ill-treatment, whereas the same acts may be regarded as torture if committee inside prisons or places where the person is deprived of liberty and has no way out of the situation. This position was elaborated by Professor Nowak in an article in the Danish journal Torture, some years ago, and this position created an interesting discussion of course. Today there are a number of researchers and others engaged in the field who are questioning the terms and what consequences it has to separate them. It has also been argued that agreeing to acts being CIDT, may conceal acts of torture, and as such create a space for violent acts that otherwise would have come under the total prohibition. But here I would respond that this is the reason why the point referred to above from the General comment no 2 is so relevant and important.

October 9, 2013

24
I NEVER JUSTIFIED TORTURE

U.S. support of the Republic of South Vietnam was perceived by both the Kennedy and the Johnson Administrations as being politically profitable, on the one hand, and as being necessary to combat the spread of communism, on the other. Sadly, the fundamental nature of the conflict in Southeast Asia (SEA)—genuinely a civil war—was misperceived and thus the U.S. intervention in that conflict produced neither a positive domestic situation in the U.S. nor a satisfactory resolution of the civil war in SEA.

- Lawrence Wilkerson

COLONEL Lawrence Wilkerson, in the following interview with the writer, has said that he never justified torture, even while holding a key position in the Bush Jr. administration, i.e. as Chief-of-Staff, to the Secretary of State, General Colin Powel. The Bush Jr. Administration was known to have used torture against suspects under the pre-text of counter terrorism. Colonel Wilkerson volunteered to serve in the Vietnam War. Years later he was appointed Chief-of-Staff to Secretary of State Colin Powel, who was the first African American to serve in that position. Colonel Wilkerson has been outspoken on the Iraq War and the wrongdoings of the Bush administration. In particular, he has denounced the decision-making process of the Bush administration, and Vice President Dick Cheney's and Secretary of

Defense Donald Rumsfeld's parts in it. Currently Colonel Wilkerson is a Professor of Government and Public Policy at the College of William & Mary, USA. Previously, he has taught national security affairs in the Honors Program at George Washington University. Colonel Wilkerson is presently working on a book about the first George W. Bush administration.

Question (Q): Thank you for agreeing to speak with Torture Magazine Colonel Lawrence Wilkerson, Let us start this discussion with your personal experiences as an officer during the war in Vietnam, known the world over as a huge setback to the US, where thousands of soldiers lost their lives and the US lost moral highground. This month also saw the passing of Vietnamese War Hero General Vo Nguyen Giap. How do you now look back on your Vietnam experiences on a personal level and from the perspective of leadership?

Answer (A) : U.S. support of the Republic of South Vietnam was perceived by both the Kennedy and the Johnson Administrations as being politically profitable, on the one hand, and as being necessary to combat the spread of communism, on the other. Sadly, the fundamental nature of the conflict in Southeast Asia (SEA)—genuinely a civil war—was misperceived and thus the U.S. intervention in that conflict produced neither a positive domestic situation in the U.S. nor a satisfactory resolution of the civil war in SEA. Instead it produced 3.8 million Vietnamese dead and over a 100,000 U.S. casualties, including more than 58,000 dead on the battlefield. Today, the Vietnamese people have ultimately brought a resolution to the conflict—and the political solution is still a work in progress. Such results could have been achieved with far less death and destruction, and that is the tragedy of the U.S. intervention in Vietnam. On a personal level, I strongly regret having been an infinitesimal tool in that tragedy. Moreover, after much study and research, I realize how complicit in that tragedy were some of my military leadership who obscured the battlefield situation—and even lied about that situation—in their reports to Washington.

Q: Colonel Wilkerson, you teach classes on US National Security in universities in the US. However, when looking at the breadth of US military intervention since World War II, from Hiroshima and Nagasaki to Latin American coups, the bombings of Vietnam, Laos, and Cambodia, and numerous bloody wars and interventions in the middle east and Africa, some underway as we speak, what do you consider and discuss, if anything, on the issue of excess?

A: Quite a lot. We particularly study and evaluate U.S. covert operations in Iran in 1953, Guatemala in 1954, Cuba in 1961, Chile in 1970-73, Africa throughout the 1970s, and elsewhere. Moreover, we study the history of the often counterproductive activities of the CIA. We tie these past covert operations to the present day by asking questions about Egypt, Syria, Iran, and so forth. With regard to actual war, we discuss and examine every overt use of force from the Korean War to the present U.S. actions in Afghanistan. There is no question that the national security state that the U.S. has become has found waging war to be one of its raisons *d'etre*.

Q: You have described your participation in the Feb. 5, 2003 Colin Powell speech to the UN as the lowest point in your career? Would your resignation as Chief-of-Staff to the Secretary of State Colin Powell at that point have made an impact?

A: No; nor would have Colin Powell's resignation have made much of an impact. The graveyards, after all, are full of indispensable men and women. Within a week or two, we would have been replaced and the Bush Administration would have marched on.

Q: You have become a provocative and thoughtful critic of US decision-making after your tenure in the State Department. But when you were in the bubble you justified the use of torture in Abu Ghraib and other prisons. Later the same Colonel Wilkerson disclosed that many of the prisoners in Guantanamo were always known by US leadership to be innocent. What do you make of the possibilities 'integrity' within bureaucracy. And, in this light, how do you view the actions and revelations of Edward Snowden, whose first stop was here in Hong Kong?

A: You are mistaken. I never justified the use of torture nor, as far as I am aware, did my superior, Secretary of State Powell. In fact, when the abuses of Abu Ghraib came to light in early 2004, Powell charged me with helping him discover how they had come about, which I did until I left the State Department in January 2005. What I found was appalling. Partly as a result of that—and because I believe dissent is frequently the highest form of patriotism—I admire the courage of Edward Snowden to do what he did. Moreover, what he has so far revealed has not harmed real U.S. security at all, just embarrassed a great many people. More importantly, what Snowden has done so far has informed the American people of the often brutal, stupid, and even illegal actions their government is doing in their name.

Q: Is Edward Snowden a traitor? What about Chelsea Elizabeth Manning?

A: Neither is a traitor. Indeed, history may record in its long run that both are patriots. I believe it will certainly record that both men did what they did not to harm the U.S. but to help its people recover their influence on its actions.

Q: Following your term in Chief-of-Staff to Secretary of State Colin Powell you have revealed your experiences related to the war against the Iraqi people, in particular denouncing the decision-making process of the Bush Administration and the actions of Vice President Dick Cheney's and Secretary of Defense Donald Rumsfeld. But some might say you let your friend Colin Powell off the hook?

A: No, I have said that Powell was not opposed to the war, just to the timing and to the lack of international legitimacy. The timing was very bad because the U.S. had not wrapped up operations in Afghanistan. International legitimacy barely existed, particularly with traditional allies such as France and Germany bitterly opposed to the war and the second UN resolution impossible to obtain. Had the U.S. waited, there is also the chance that the existing sanctions and increasing pressure would have toppled Saddam Hussein without the need for war. We both, Powell and I, had deep concerns about the planning as well. In fact, we could detect no real planning at all. Plus, we both knew there were far too few U.S. troops involved in the invasion and its aftermath. So, we had huge concerns but were not opposed to the elimination of a tyrant who had already attacked his neighbors twice, violated 17 UN Security Council resolutions, and whose country we and the UK were still patrolling in the northern and southern No-Fly Zones.

Q: You are currently working on a book about the first George W. Bush administration. Many books on the administration by various writers have been published. How is yours going be different?

A: My book attempts to illuminate the building of the U.S. national security state from 1947 to the present. It employs as its principle character of that illumination Colin Powell, first as Chairman of the Joint Chiefs of Staff, then as Secretary of State. Here is a citation from the book's Preface:

This book attempts to illuminate that saga [the building of the national security state] and, hopefully, sheds light upon it that so far has not been shed, providing insights both positive and negative, all aimed at an understanding of where our Republic is headed. I believe that one good way to achieve such an understanding is to study the character of those at or near the helm of our republic. If Heraclitus was right—that man's character is his fate—then the character of great men (and increasingly women) is the nation's fate.

Q: National Security and Foreign Policy (and not personnel and personality-wise) do you see any marked difference in the present ruling establishment, as compared to the Bush years. From the outset, the same tactics seem to apply, from Libya to Syria.

A: Sadly, I do not see any substantive difference; in fact, I see that the Obama Administration has taken the persecution of whistleblowers, the draconian surveillance state, the use of drones, and the abuse of the war power even further than the Bush Administration did. This is another indicator that the post-WWII national security state is full-blown and altering the very nature of our republic.

Q: A human rights organization, Amnesty International recently released a noteworthy report on the US drone war in Pakistan, kill lists related to which, as we know, are sometimes directly sanctioned by US President Barack Obama. Amnesty has said the drone killings, which have resulted in the deaths of far more civilians than the US has admitted to, could be classified as war crimes. Couple this with what Human Rights Watch has revealed related to the killings of civilians in drone strikes in Yemen, and that Obama seems to have ignored his own guidelines. Your thoughts? Does this make Barack Obama a potential war criminal? (Asking the question itself is a reminder of the time there were calls for trying Bush and Cheney for war crimes.)

A: Professor Akbar Ahmed has best described what is happening in his book The Thistle and the Drone. It should be required reading for all world leaders. The drone strikes need to stop. They are counterproductive in so many ways. They need to stop.

International law has not kept up; borders are violated with impunity every month. People are killed—often innocent civilians—by, at best, the direction of a Star Chamber apparatus. I am quite confident that were it not for the sheer power of the U.S., war crimes investigations and possibly even trials would be considered, as they should have been considered with regard to torture for Cheney, Rumsfeld, and the six lawyers who supported them—David Addington, John Yoo, Jim Haynes, Doug Feith, Alberto Gonzales, and Jay Bybee.

Moreover, drone technology is spreading swiftly. Soon, not only other nations will have it but so will law enforcement agencies. It is only a matter of time before this proliferation alters the way states kill people, both internationally, and within their own borders. The rule of law lags dreadfully these technological developments. It needs to catch up. So do the ethics we should be contemplating.

Drones are not just another weapon of war; they represent the cutting edge of a new kind of warfare—inhuman, robotic, distant, and coldly calculated. The entire world needs to consider these developments and deal with them—not just the sole superpower whom everyone else fears.

Q: Despite of all international conventions signed and laws passed, torture and other inhuman practices still occur with impunity in too many countries. US is in the dock too. What is the international solution do you think, especially given that the track record and present inclinations of the most powerful nation-state?

A: The "solution" is not readily apparent to me. The world is experiencing major power and wealth shifts, huge impending transmigration, enormous challenges associated with planetary changes that will be hostile to human life, and in the meantime its greatest profit-making enterprises include drugs, human trafficking, massive arms sales to all and sundry, financial transactions that enrich the few and impoverish the many, and multinational corporate bodies in food, energy, pharmaceuticals, and media that have no other interest than their own self-preservation and profit. Time for revolution? One wonders...

November 7, 2013

25
NO ONE IS ABOVE THE LAW

"We appreciate the sacrifices that witnesses make for the sake of establishing the truth. Witnesses are in many ways an indispensable component of the proceedings. Witnesses who have the courage to come forward and tell the truth deserve our protection and praise. They deserve our utmost respect and admiration for their commitment to the pursuit of justice."

- Fatou Bensouda

IN an interview with the writer, Ms. Fatou Bensouda, the Prosecutor of the International Criminal Court (ICC), said, "We apply the law without distinction, fear or favour. We follow the mandate that has been given to us under the Rome Statute. Regrettably, often the lack of full understanding of the Court's legal framework and jurisdiction only helps to exacerbate baseless attacks against the ICC It is therefore critically important to raise awareness about the mandate and activities of the Court to counter misperceptions and to increasingly build support for the ICC".

Ms. Bensouda went on to say, "The ICC was established, among other things, to try persons accused of massive crimes in situations where their own national jurisdictions are either unwilling or genuinely unable to do so, for example, because of the powerful positions occupied by the suspects or the accused. The Rome Statute is very clear: no one is above the law".

. Before her election as the chief prosecutor of the ICC she was the Attorney General and Minister of Justice of the Republic of Gambia. Ms. Bensouda's international career as a non-government civil servant formally began at the International Criminal Tribunal for Rwanda, where she worked as a Legal Adviser and Trial Attorney before rising to the position of Senior Legal Advisor and Head of the Legal Advisory Unit. In August 2004, she was elected as Deputy Prosecutor (Prosecutions) with an overwhelming majority votes by the Assembly of State Parties of the International Criminal Court. On 1 November 2004, Ms. Bensouda was sworn into Office as Deputy Prosecutor (Prosecutions).

In December 2011, the Assembly of States Parties of the ICC announced that an informal agreement had been reached to make Fatou Bensouda the consensus choice to succeed Luis Moreno-Ocampo as Prosecutor of the ICC. She was formally elected by consensus on 12 December 2011 and her term as Prosecutor began in June 2012. In this lengthy interview, Prosecutor Bensouda elaborated the comprehensive role of the ICC and its commitments to bring the justice to the victims and their collaboration with the United Nations and its Security Council.

Please see below the full text of the interview:

Q: Let me start this interview by quoting a book written by Tom Bingham where he argued, "the core of the existing principle is, I suggest, that all persons and authorities within the state, whether public or private, should be bound by and entitled to the benefit of laws publicly made, taking effect (generally) in the future and publicly administered in the courts" (my reference: The Rule of Law', Tom Bingham, Penguin Books 2011, page 8.) How do you understand the core notion of this argument as the Prosecutor of the International Criminal Court that was created by the Rome Statute which came into force on 1 July 2002?

A: With the coming into force of the Rome Statute at the dawn of the 21st century, the treaty-based International Criminal Court

(ICC) was created as the embodiment of humanity's hope for the international rule of law, and bringing into being an international criminal justice mechanism with 'teeth,' capable of holding perpetrators of mass crimes to account for committed atrocities.

I believe in the notion that humanity must be guarded against mass crimes by an independent and impartial international legal shield – the Rome Statute, the Court's founding treaty serves this purpose by defining legal limits; the latter applies to all who fall within the jurisdiction of the ICC, and there must be legal accountability if such limits are breached. The ICC was established, among other things, to try persons accused of massive crimes in situations where their own national jurisdictions are either unwilling or genuinely unable to do so, for example, because of the powerful positions occupied by the suspects or the accused. The Rome Statute is very clear: no one is above the law.

Q. Your predecessor was Luis Moreno-Ocampo who served since 16 June 2003. Could you please elaborate the major outcome of the ICC in last few years?

A. During his nine-year tenure, former ICC Prosecutor Luis Moreno-Ocampo contributed to transforming the ICC into the global judicial institution and key player in international relations it is today. My challenge and focus, since I was sworn in as ICC Prosecutor in June 2012, has been to build on what has already been accomplished and to take the Office of the Prosecutor to the next level, in the discharge of its mandate to
end impunity, to bring justice to victims and to prevent future crimes.

The Court has now entered its second decade since the entry into force of the Rome Statute. We have reached many important milestones and acquired valuable lessons learned from the first cases and proceedings.

The Court's effectiveness and efficiency will only improve from this early experience. The ICC is no longer an ideal aspiration on paper, but a real and functioning institution whose values are being slowly but increasingly understood and appreciated. The Court is here to stay and everyone must realise that they have to adjust to this new reality: politicians, law makers, mediators, as well as warlords, have to adapt their behaviour to the new Rome Statute framework.

The past few years have been extremely busy. Currently there are 18 cases in relation to more than 25 suspects and accused persons, at various stages of the proceedings before the Court. In addition to eight situations, my Office is also conducting eight preliminary examinations on four different continents.

Much has been done but the Court is yet to demonstrate its full potential. As with all things, there's always room for improvement, but I am encouraged by our progress and our prospects for the future. I have great hopes that this institution will become increasingly relevant in this new century. This is our collective yearning and our resolve. By virtue not only of the mandate invested in me as ICC Prosecutor, but also as a matter
of personal determination reinforced by my will, this institution is resolved to bring justice to victims of massive crimes. We have to give them a voice. Victims are our daily motivation and the very raison d'être of this Court.

Q. Compared to other international organizations, the ICC is still young and many people have yet to learn about the ICC at large. May I know the difference between the ICC and other institutes which are based on justice? Why do we need the ICC?

A. The ICC is the world's first permanent international criminal court and I believe it is a crucial global institution. A first key difference is the Court's jurisdictional scope and its potential of achieving universality.

The mandates of the UN ad hoc International Criminal Tribunals (for the former Yugoslavia, and for Rwanda, respectively), the Special Court for Sierra Leone, or the Special Tribunal for Lebanon, are all limited in both time and scope, in the sense that they were created or endorsed by the United Nations Security Council as temporary judicial bodies to deal with specific atrocities occurring during the tragic conflicts in those countries.

The ICC, on the other hand, is a treaty-based international criminal court with jurisdiction to investigate and prosecute war crimes, genocide and crimes against humanity (potentially, also aggression in the future) allegedly committed on the territories or by nationals of any of its States Parties, provided these crimes occurred after July 1, 2002, the date on which its founding treaty, the Rome Statute, came into force.

Ratified to date by 122 states and growing, the Rome Statute provides a framework to protect more than two billion citizens around the world. Another unique feature of the ICC is that victims can also participate in the proceedings not simply as witnesses but in their own right as victims of mass crimes. In other words, the ICC brings to the legal fore the voice of the victims as direct parties to the proceedings in a manner that is unprecedented in international criminal courts and tribunals.

Furthermore, under the principle of complementarity, if the national authorities of a State Party do not do justice for the victims of massive crimes, then the ICC, by virtue of its mandate, can step in. Finally, the ICC seeks not only to investigate and prosecute the world's gravest crimes, but by so doing to deter the commission of such crimes in the future. In this way, under the Rome Statute legal system as established by the international community, the ICC can serve as guardian, ensuring the rule of law, while respecting the primacy of national jurisdictions and by the same token, encouraging national efforts to ensure justice and accountability for victims. By breaking the cycle of violence and revenge, justice and the law can also act as a powerful deterrent, and thereby protect future generations from becoming victims of mass atrocities.

Q. Despite positive reactions or appreciations, many criticisms have been heard about the ICC, where some leaders claim that the ICC is politically motivated and intentionally targets the leaders in the developing nations and helps the powers of the so called " west". How do you respond to these claims?

A. Any allegation of this kind is absolutely groundless and betrays a lack of understanding of the Court's legal framework and jurisdiction. The ICC is, both in law and in fact, an independent, impartial judicial institution which is bound to no one state or region, and which acts solely on the basis of the law on which is it based, its jurisdiction and the evidence before it. We should guard against politicising the Court's proceedings.

At this juncture in the Court's evolutionary history, all of our cases relate to situations in Africa. This is a fact, but this is simply a function of the Court's jurisdiction; nothing more.

Today in Africa, millions have been displaced as a result of mass crimes under our jurisdiction. Africans are being killed, raped and used as child soldiers. This we cannot ignore - the victims are African and so are the perpetrators. We are on the side of the victims. Ending impunity is important to ensuring peace, stability and prosperity for Africa and beyond. Today, 34 African States are parties to the Rome Statute, representing the Court's largest regional group.

The first country to ratify the Rome Statute was Senegal in 1999, and the latest country to do so is Côte d'Ivoire. The Court's first review conference, in 2010, was held in Kampala, Uganda, where among other things, the Kampala amendments on the crime of aggression were adopted.

So far, five African States themselves have asked the ICC to start investigations on their territories: the Democratic Republic of the Congo (DRC), Uganda, Central African Republic (CAR), Côte d'Ivoire, and Mali.

African officials at the ICC, including myself, have also been playing an important role in the development of the institution, and have been elected with the full support of African States and the African Union.

The ICC continues to have strong support from a significant number of African

States, well-known African personalities and parliamentarians, African civil society groups, African victims, and generally from the

African population. These facts, I believe, speak for themselves. Moreover, my Office is conducting preliminary examinations outside Africa including in Honduras, Korea, Afghanistan, Columbia and Georgia. As stated, we act based on the evidence and in strict conformity with our jurisdiction as set out in the Rome Statute.

In short, the ICC is a permanent independent and impartial judicial institution with just over a decade of existence. People need to be patient and not prejudge the Court.

Q. At the same time, many publications based in African countries, are criticizing your role. They claim that you are an agent of the west. I feel those who are targeting individuals as well as the institution are expecting to spoil or tarnish the reputation of the ICC. To tackle this is a challenge. Could you please let me know, how you think to maintain the reputation of the ICC, despite those who are trying to eliminate its strength?

A. Again, I think the criticism you mention is not only unfair to the Court but also unfair to the African continent, which by requesting the intervention of the ICC is effectively saying: we do not want impunity on our soil. Anti-ICC elements have worked hard to discredit the Court and lobby for nonsupport, on the basis of specious arguments and with complete disregard for the facts or the Court's legal framework. At best, it is propaganda that is being levelled against the ICC.

In fact, engagement and cooperation of individual African states with the ICC have not diminished over the years. African states have consistently helped us at each step of our activities: in opening investigations, in conducting the investigations, in pursuing and arresting individuals sought by the Court, in protecting our witnesses, and so on. These are not just words. African States receive more than 50 per cent of our requests for cooperation, and they positively respond to 85 per cent of them.

African institutions and the African people are largely responsible for building the system of international justice designed by the Rome Statute of the ICC. The experience of centuries of suffering, including by the inaction of the international community in the 1990's with regard to the genocide in Rwanda and the Congo wars, made African States lead the discussions on the Rome Statute with the goal to end impunity for those grave crimes they suffered.

Of the eight situations currently before the Court, only two (Libya and Darfur, Sudan) were referrals by the United Nations Security Council.

I reiterate that five African States themselves asked the ICC to start investigations into their territories (as I mentioned, the Rome Statute stipulates that the Court shall step in only when domestic authorities do not pursue accountability themselves. In all the cases we selected, there were no such proceedings).

The only situation that is neither a state referral nor a Security Council referral is the Kenya situation. With regards to Kenya, we should note that my predecessor decided to open investigations there in the wake of the post-election violence of 2007-2008, after a strong call from the Kenyans themselves, and also, after a strong pledge by the then leaders of Kenya to fully cooperate with the investigation and prosecution of these crimes in the country.

Doing justice is not about regional or geographic representation: where there are crimes falling within our jurisdiction that are not being addressed by national jurisdictions, then the Office of the Prosecutor will step in. It is not about focusing on Africa; it is about working for the victims, and the victims are African.

What can we do to address these misperceptions? Again, it is vital to shield the ICC from politicisation at both the national and international levels. This is a must to counter misperceptions – deliberate or not – and build support for ICC's crucial mandate. We cannot do this alone. Civil society, the media, lawyers' associations and states, to name but a few, all have a role to play.

Public awareness of the Court, its mandate and activities must be strengthened. Raising awareness is key to our universal aspiration to collectively put an end to impunity and to deter the commission of mass crimes in the future. The media can contribute to strengthening the Court and its work to ensure its important mandate of ending impunity and related activities are properly and accurately understood.

Q. I remember, in an interview that you gave to one of the television channels in Kenya during your visit, you elaborated the case against an incumbent President Kenyatta, who is allegedly responsible for severe crimes. The trial of President Kenyatta is about to start again, but at the same time there are reports of theintimidation of witnesses by the ruling party. According to the recently published article, "The standoff between Kenya and the ICC remains unresolved. Kenyatta and Ruto continue to make a show of cooperating with the court in order to avoid the issuance of arrest warrants and the ensuing pariah status now faced by Sudan's Bashir." Could you please let us know about the trial and are there possibilities to find justice for those victimized?

A. At the outset, it is important to underscore that Messrs Kenyatta and Ruto have the right to the presumption of innocence, as do all individuals who stand accused of crimes before the ICC. They are each accused on the basis of their alleged individual criminal responsibility for crimes against humanity, committed during the violence which erupted in Kenya in the wake of elections in 2007-2008. As I have stated publicly on numerous occasions, whilst our pursuit of justice for the victims of the 2007-2008 postelection violence in Kenya has faced many challenges, my Office's commitment to the victims has remained firm. We have and will continue to do all that we can to realize justice for the victims of the 2007-2008 postelection violence in Kenya. We cannot, however, discount the very serious obstacles we're faced with.

Under the Rome Statute framework, the Office of the Prosecutor has a statutory duty to protect victims and witnesses. It is a key Office priority to preserve the integrity of our cases and to protect our witnesses. Under Article 70 of the Rome Statute it is an offence to corruptly influence or intimidate a witness. I have made no secret of the fact that we have experienced witness interference on unprecedented levels in the Kenya situation, and this can be a real threat to the Court's proceedings and our goal of bringing a measure of justice for the victims of crimes.

We appreciate the sacrifices that witnesses make for the sake of establishing the truth. Witnesses are in many ways an indispensable component of the proceedings. Witnesses who have the courage to come forward and tell the truth deserve our protection and praise. They deserve our utmost respect and admiration for their commitment to the pursuit of justice. Unfortunately, we have seen witnesses in our cases being bribed, threatened and intimidated. Efforts are made to make them recant their stories, or even deny them. In October 2013, I requested the judges to issue a warrant of arrest against Mr Walter Barasa in Kenya, on suspicion of corruptly influencing or attempting to corruptly influence Prosecution witnesses.

The warrant of arrest has been issued. We are waiting for Kenya to execute this warrant and to transfer Mr Barasa to the custody of the Court in The Hague to be tried for offences against the administration of justice.

The Office of the Prosecutor will apply the full force of the law to protect our witnesses and ensure justice runs its course unimpeded.

We cannot stand idly by and allow these serious offences to undermine the Court's proceedings and credibility. It goes without saying that in this struggle, the assistance and cooperation of the Court's States Parties are crucial.

Q. Similar situations have been prevailing in many countries in Africa. What I saw is that, at the beginning many African leaders are keen to help the ICC and its protocols but later they become strongly critical of the Court, and then they start attacking the Court in the local situation. Why is this happening?

A. The difficulties are there mainly because those who allegedly commit the crimes and against whom the Court has evidence — often, heads of militia or heads of state—are protected; militias, by the army; heads of state, by the state apparatus. We are consistently and without exception guided by the evidence and the Rome Statute legal framework. These criteria alone, not any other consideration, guide the Office's actions.

We apply the law without distinction, fear or favour. We follow the mandate that has been given to us under the Rome Statute. Regrettably, often the lack of full understanding of the Court's legal framework and jurisdiction only helps to exacerbate baseless attacks against the ICC It is therefore critically important to raise awareness about the mandate and activities of the Court to counter misperceptions and to increasingly build support for the ICC.

Q. Let me quote the same article which I quoted earlier, "......the former chief prosecutor for its first nine years, Luis Moreno-Ocampo of Argentina, seemed more interested in issuing arrest warrantsthan undertaking the tough, less glamorous work of conducting rigorous criminal investigations." May I ask, will people be able see a difference from the past when they look at the present situation of the court?

A. Before I answer that, let me first point out again that the Court is created in a way that our investigations are dependent on the cooperation of States. When we deploy to the field, we need cooperation on the ground to assist us, not with collecting evidence, but with logistics or security, for example. In all cases, we must make a full assessment and be satisfied that the evidence we bring before the judges meets the requisite legal threshold for that particular stage of the proceedings.

Our investigations often take place under extremely difficult circumstances. Most of the time, we are investigating in a situation of ongoing conflict, where the security of the witnesses or our staff poses a huge challenge. As Prosecutor, I have an obligation under the Rome Statute to ensure that witnesses or people we contact are protected.

During the first nine years, the Office strategy was based on focused investigations and prosecutions. This strategy allowed the Office to achieve a number of positive results. Part of the thinking behind this approach, for example, was to reach as few witnesses as possible and necessary for the case, in order not to place the lives of individuals at peril. Once you reach the witnesses, you expose them, and your duty is to protect them.

I have just recently unveiled a new strategy with a new direction for the Office. The notion of focused investigations has been replaced by the principle of in-depth, open ended investigations.

Whereas our previous policy required a focus on those persons who according to our evidence collected were the most responsible, what I am planning to do now is broaden this approach to start with the midlevel perpetrators and then carefully move up. This does not mean that we will not go for the most responsible. We will get there if our investigations lead us there. We hope that this approach will enhance the Office's deliverables and help build stronger cases.

We also implement extremely thorough and regular case reviews to ensure that our cases are on track as well as to enable the Office to promptly react in response to developments as they arise.

The new strategy also provides for expanding and diversifying our collection and forms of evidence. Not having to predominantly depend on witness testimony has the added benefit of avoiding evidence being compromised through witness interference, and better managing the protection of persons at risk because of their interaction with the Office.

Q. The ICC receives thousands of complaints. After an initial review, 80% of the complaints have been dismissed as "manifestly outside the jurisdiction of the Court"; only 20% warranted further analysis. Do you have any procedure to redirect those complaints which are not eligible to prosecute at the ICC, to some other powerful institute?

A. My Office is responsible for determining whether a situation meets the legal criteria established by the Rome Statute to warrant investigation. For this purpose, the Office conducts a legal and factual analysis of all situations that come to its attention, based on the statutory criteria and information available. One of the ways in which a preliminary examination of a situation by the Office may be initiated is on the basis of information sent to us by individuals or groups, States, intergovernmental or non-governmental organisations: "communications." By the end of 2013, my Office had received a total of 10,470 such communications.

The Rome Statute establishes a clear legal framework for preliminary examinations, providing criteria on which to determine whether or not there is a reasonable basis to proceed with an investigation. There are no timelines provided in the Statute for a decision on a preliminary examination. Depending on the facts and circumstances of each situation, the Office may either decide to decline to initiate an investigation where the information manifestly fails to satisfy the factors set out in the Statue; to continue to collect information in order to establish sufficient factual and legal basis to render a determination; or to initiate the investigation, subject to judicial review as appropriate.

In order to promote transparency of the preliminary examination process, the Office aims to issue regular reports on its activities and provides reasoned responses for its decisions either to proceed or not proceed with investigations. The Office's actions are strictly limited to its mandate as stipulated in the Rome Statute.

Q. The ICC is based on the Rome Statute. Those who have not accepted the Rome Statute are not under the ICC jurisdiction. Unluckily, this includes many alleged criminals. The best example to my knowledge is my native country, Sri Lanka, where we faced 30 years of civil war which cost hundreds thousand lives and which ended in the middle of 2009. The International Community and other concerned parties including the UN were asking for an independent investigation which the government is reluctant to do so. What can the ICC do in this kind of situation?

A. It is the law alone, the legal framework of the Rome Statute which dictates the scope of ICC's ability to intervene. As Prosecutor of the ICC, I have jurisdiction only over crimes committed after 1 July 2002, when the Rome Statute entered into force. Equally important, as stated previously, my Office has jurisdiction only over crimes committed on the territory of a State Party to the ICC or by a national of a State Party, unless a situation is referred to my Office by the United Nations Security Council, or if the state in question were to make a declaration pursuant to Article 12.3 of the Rome Statute accepting the exercise of jurisdiction by the Court, as was the case for Côte d'Ivoire before it formally ratified the Rome Statute. Finally, as Prosecutor, I can only intervene only if the relevant national judicial authority is unable or unwilling to genuinely investigate and prosecute the alleged crimes. This is what is meant by the principle of complementarity in the Rome Statute, whereby States have primary responsibility for preventing and punishing atrocities committed in their own territories and by their own nationals. Sri Lanka is not a State Party and as such, it is a situation I cannot address, even hypothetically, in my capacity as ICC Prosecutor.

Q. Does the United Nations or its Security Country have rights of collaboration with the ICC to solve the problems faced by the people in non-member states of the ICC?

A. The extraordinary nature and importance of the ICC's relationship with the United Nations is well reflected in the fact that Article 2 of the Rome Statute expressly required that the Court be "brought into relationship with the United Nations through an agreement to be approved by the Assembly of States Parties
to this Statute and thereafter concluded by the President of the Court on its behalf."

The Negotiated Relationship Agreement between the Court and the UN concluded on 4 October 2004 provides the legal basis for the multifaceted cooperation between the two organizations in the exercise of their respective mandates. The Relationship Agreement provides that the Court and the UN shall cooperate closely, whenever appropriate, with each other and consult each other on matters of mutual interest, with a view to facilitating the effective discharge of their respective responsibilities. The many forms of cooperation between the UN and the ICC range from a regular dialogue between the officials of the two institutions aimed at identifying challenges and ways of overcoming them, including reciprocal representation at high-level meetings and proceedings; to a very practical working relationship, including exchange of information and reports, administrative and personnel arrangements: provision of services and facilities; logistical support in the field, financial matters, travel arrangements and judicial assistance, appearance of UN staff in Court to provide testimony, and supporting the activities of each other in the field.

The Court and the UN Security Council have distinct roles (the Council is a political body within the UN system, the Court is an independent judicial institution) and clear separate mandates. It is true that the Rome Statute does empower the UN Security Council to refer cases to the Court, even with respect to non-States Parties. It bears mentioning however that situations referred to the Office of the Prosecutor by the Council do not oblige the former to automatically accept the referral. In response to a UN Security Council referral, the Office will conduct its own independent assessment of whether there's a reasonable basis to proceed with an investigation and decide whether or not to proceed.

The UN Security Council and the Court do share several inter-related traits in their mandates. First of all, while the Security Council has been given the primary responsibility to maintain international peace and security, the mandate of the Court is to ensure accountability for the most serious crimes of concern to the international community as a whole; crimes which the Preamble of the Rome Statute recognizes as threatening the peace, security and well-being of the world. Secondly, both the Council and the Court have a role to play in strengthening the complementary relationship between peace and justice. From the Court's perspective, there is no dilemma or contradiction between peace and justice.

Thirdly, in addition to working on the same situations and regions, the ICC and the Council are often dealing with the same challenges, including among others, the debilitating impact of gender and sexual violence, the use of children in conflict, the impact of impunity and the lack of the rule of law on situations, and the effectiveness of peacekeeping operations.

Finally, both the Security Council and the Court have a clear preventative mandate. The Rome Statute Preamble makes clear that prevention is a shared responsibility, stating that States Parties are "determined to put an end to impunity for the perpetrators of these crimes and thus to contribute to the prevention of such crimes."

Q. Fatou Bensouda, it was privilege to have you with us and again thank you very much for your time that you gave us to discuss the ICC.

A. You are very welcome. I thank you for your interest in the work and activities of the Court.

February 10, 2014

26
THE STRUGGLE FOR JUSTICE AND FREEDOM CANNOT BE DETERMINED BY TEMPORARY SETBACKS

The call for a separate state was born after 30 years of non-violent and democratic struggle of the Tamils to live as human beings with equal rights and freedom to preserve and foster their ethnic, cultural and religious heritage in their homeland for many centuries. It is the refusal of the basic rights and freedoms of the Tamil people which pushed them to call for a separate state of Tamil Eelam. The second phase of the struggle in which the Sinhala Government and its forces treated the Tamils has strengthened their conviction that only a separate state can guarantee their rights and freedom. The defeat of the militant struggle and the post-Mullivaikal events has only strengthened the convictions of the Tamils about a separate state. The aspirations of a people to survive as a dignified people cannot be defeated or erased easily. Hence the people's struggle for justice and freedom cannot be determined by temporary defeats and losses.

- S. J. Emmanuel

REVEREND Father S. J. Emmanuel is a priest, activist and the president of the Global Tamil Forum, an umbrella organisation for Sri Lankan Tamil diaspora groups.

Father Emmanuel was born in 1934 in Jaffna, in what was then known as Ceylon. He studied in Jaffna before going to the University of Ceylon in Colombo from where he obtained a

245

Bachelor's degree in physical sciences (Mathematics & Physics) in 1958. After graduation he spent time as a teacher and a journalist before entering the priesthood. He then went to the Pontifical Urbaniana University in Rome from where he obtained a degree in philosophy and theology.

In this interview he extensively elaborates the situation in Sri Lanka from the geo-political perspectives with his personal experiences.

Q: I'm happy to be able to interview you're for the second time. Let me start by quoting what you said in 1999, on the civil war in Sri Lanka. You observed that, "Though the war is always claimed by the Sinhalese Governments as a war against the LTTE, it is crystal clear to all Tamils, especially to those still surviving in the North and east of the country, that it is directed against the Tamil people to subjugate them". The war is now over. If we view the present situation, it is blatantly evident that while the country emerged from the three decades of war in a brutal way in 2009it is unfortunately progressing now in an authoritarian direction as claimed by the UN High Commissioner for Human Rights last year. How do you view this trend that has so far not created any major discontent in Sri Lanka, leave aside the widespread disappointment overseas?

A: My earlier statement, "though the war is always claimed by the Sinhalese governments as war against the LTTE, it is crystal clear to all the Tamils, especially to those still surviving in the north and east of the country, that it directed against the Tamil people to subjugate them" has been clearly confirmed not only by the Tamils living in the North and East but also has become crystal clear to the whole world, proved especially after the May 2009 actions of the Sri Lankan Government. I made the statement because I was then a direct witness of the bombing of civilian targets like the churches of St. James in Jaffna, Saints Peter and Paul in Navali, of children in school-uniform like those in Nagarkovil etc. and also of the unjust economic blockade imposed on us Tamils for years. One of the reasons my aged mother died was because I could not carry enough medicines and foodstuff for her.

But now the attitude and actions of the Sri Lankan Government, even after declaring officially that the war against the LTTE was victoriously concluded on18th May 2009, their actions in the former war-arena, prove beyond doubt, that in the absence of an LTTE-threat/defence, the Mahinda Government has taken on a more comprehensive programme in the authoritarian direction to further subjugate the Tamils by stronger military oppression, state-aided-Sinhalisation, state-aided Buddhistisation, the raping of women by military personnel and forcible-grabbing of land from the people.

If the thousands of the Sinhalese, who visit the north to see the conquered north and the heroic actions of their sons and daughters, could also take time to talk to the people living there, reflect on their own and express some solidarity with the victims that could be considered a genuine move towards reconciliation. But what is happening?

The support given to the Rajapaksas by silence or absence of criticism or encouragement in their ongoing oppressions of the Tamils in the North, make us Tamils feel that even the Sinhala people are supporting the new forms of post Mullivaikal-war against the Tamils, namely a complete cleansing of Tamil existence in the Tamil homeland and replacing it with Sinhala Buddhist population. The Chief Minister of the elected Provincial Government has articulated the feelings of the people many times in the south too. This drives us to the conclusion that the will of the Sinhalese, not merely the extremists, but also the large majority, is to subjugate the Tamils. This exposes clearly that the war was not simply against Tiger terrorism, but an execution of a Sinhala-Buddhist hidden agenda to subjugate, if not exterminate, the Tamils in Sri Lanka.

Looking back to all the measures taken by a Sinhala majoritarian parliament and by the conduct of its military in the North and East, it was a step by step oppression and extermination of the Tamils. What is happening today on the ground is the last stage of eradicating the roots of Tamil-existence, so that in a few years' time students of history will read that Tamils once lived on that part of the island.

As one still concerned about a peaceful coexistence of peoples and religions on that island, I am surprised and saddened that the majority of the island have not yet woken up to the hidden agenda of the Rajapaksa brothers, namely, to cling on to power and wealth of the country at the expense of a peaceful coexistence of peoples and religions. So far with a very weak political opposition, there is no major discontent or opposition visible in Sri Lanka. Not even religious and civic leaders from the South have come out openly against the day to day genocidal acts of the government going on under the eyes of the elected representatives of the people in the North.

In my view, the post-independence political leaders of the majority Sinhalese have been coming to power by strengthening and riding on a Mahavamsa-mentality by which Sri Lanka is only for Sinhala Buddhists. They have whipped up anti-Tamil feelings to gain victory and once in power they could not give even the minimum reasonable rights to the Tamils. Successive governments have also favoured a system of education giving priority to the Mahavamsa mentality in their history books. What we have today is a Sinhala-Buddhist-extremism headed by the Rajapaksa regime descending fast into a national suicide. The civic and religious progressive leaders within the country have been reduced to silence or subjugation by fear. The country is ruined more by the passivity and fear of the good than by the activity and eloquence of the bad.

We can only hope against hope that:

1. the international community shake/wake us up to think realistically to come to terms with the realities on the ground as well as realities outside Sri Lanka(local politics and geopolitics);

2. the voice of the religious and civic leaders of the South, become a courageous voice to shout the saving truth: "the king is naked"; and,

3. the Buddhist leaders be liberated from a Mahavamsa vision and mission and become genuine followers of the Noble Teachings of Buddha.

Q: The government claims that it fought a war against terrorism? Your response to the media in the past was a simple,

"Absolute nonsense".

A: As a disciple of Jesus Christ and a catholic priest, I do not support or encourage any form of terrorism from any side. Unfortunately, undefined terrorism or hypothetical definitions of it to suit the states, have become a label one puts on an enemy to justify one's own anti-terrorist actions. Even super-powers have not yet defined terrorism, but have loads of security measures to combat and control it. Under cover of national security and welfare of people, they resort to one-way state-actions which are clearly terroristic. Pre-emptive actions against suspected and perceived enemies and torture of alleged victims are clearly state-terrorism.

Any action by the victims of state-oppression, using only the last resort of hit-back-violence to defend themselves or to bring injustice against them to the attention of the world, is labelled hastily as pure terrorism. No effort is made to find out why they are violent in their reactions. If a child in the family suddenly resorts to some violence, is it the remedy to punish and even kill that child? And all actions against those helpless victims are labelled as terrorism and the state's actions (state-terrorism) justified and even named unquestionable security-measures. In Sri Lanka the 1977 Prevention of Terrorism Act is very operative even five years after the war ended!

In Sri Lanka, the Tamils have experienced State-and military oppression long before the LTTE was born. The latter was born only as a response and reaction to resist state and military oppression. The majority of Sinhalese do not know the history of Sinhala military presence in the North and East from early 60s. They were initially sent to stop smuggling activities between Ceylon and India. But soon became the executive arm of fear for the discriminatory laws passed by the Sinhala-majority Parliament. I am a witness of army terror acts in the Tamil areas – firstly as a Lake House Correspondent in Mannar (1959-61) and then as a priest in Jaffna (1967-72).

I would like the majority Sinhalese to analyse the state-terrorism against the two JVP insurrections. The insurrections which were born out of deep discontent among the southern youth were brutally suppressed and thousands of Sinhala youth were killed by the state and it's military. The Governments failed to identify and remedy the discontent. They killed them. So emboldened were they by their brutal success against JVP, they went also to crush the Tamil insurgents too.

Thus the Government failed to see the LTTE as a consequence of their own state discrimination and military oppressions already going on in the Tamil areas. When the non-violent and democratic protests of the Tamils against state-discriminations were attacked by mob-violence with the connivance of the Sinhala military, and later by military-violence itself, Tamil youth most affected by discriminations and pushed to the wall without a future, responded with Tamil violence.

The spiral of state and counter-state terrorisms became a war that was brutally ended in May 2009 with the collaboration of the international community including India. But the state-terrorism continues even today in other subtle forms of military-dictatorship, rape, grabbing of lands, instilling fear into the population etc. Hence the international donors, who collaborated with finance and weapons, to crush Tamil terrorism (and acknowledged as over 20 countries by the President), have now waking up to the truth that it was not merely a war against Tamil Terrorism. But much more, it was a mass massacre of civilians too as found by the UN-Panel Report and other photographic evidence.

The majority Sinhalese for whom the Tamil problem was merely Tamil terrorism from 1983 onwards, must look at least into the last 65 years of history and ask how the Government treated the Tamils. Celebrating victories of one phase of the Tamil struggle, and eradicating the roots of Tamil existence will not bring peace on the island.

Q: A true reconciliation is when an open and transparent process is undertaken to dissect the causes of the conflict, its ramifications and finding ways to honestly respond to all the issues involved in the war including payment of reparation to the victims. It was my feeling during the military conflict that the ordinary Sinhalese, Tamils or Muslims did not support the war. But the successive governments and the movement that fought for the liberation did not understand this. The brutalities and military mechanisation overwhelmed the people for them to put their head above the parapet wall. Do you agree?

A: Yes, true reconciliation demands "an open and transparent process" into finding out the root causes of conflict and war. All the governments which came to power in the Sinhala-majority parliament, were able to bulldoze any discriminatory law against the Tamils. They were blinded by the Mahavamsa mentality and the Sinhala Buddhist nationalism which was exclusive in character. It was so embedded into the minds of the majority that even a President of the country remarked that the Tamils are like creepers and suckers of the Sinhala population. Only when they came to facing the LTTE which was clearly a result of the policies and actions of the successive governments, they woke up to a threat of violence from the other.

At least after celebrating a victory, the Government could have undertaken a sane and sincere approach towards reconciliation by following boldly the path of truth and justice. There was an iota of a chance of this politician becoming a statesman. But he messed up even his brutal victory. Without knowing the truth about the conflict and war and taking responsibility or accountability for the crimes committed against the victims, there cannot be reconciliation. Without admission of guilt there cannot be forgiveness and reconciliation. But unfortunately the Government is moving quite in the opposite direction by adding injuries to insult and making true reconciliation recede further away. Bulldozing the cemeteries of the LTTE and building military bases over them, preventing people even from mourning over their dead, asking the Tamils to sing the national anthem in Sinhalese, are acts of pouring oil into the fire. Building better roads, houses and hotels for increased Sinhala military presence and settling their families, instead of building houses for the victims of war, exposes their concern for reconciliation through rehabilitation.

You say that "The ordinary Sinhalese, Tamils and Muslims did not support the war". Yes the ordinary good people did not support the war. But they are not innocent of the war. In some way they also are the causes of war. Conflict, violence and war are all results of the so called "ordinary people" living a selfish and egoistic life, without concern for the others and the larger humanity. It is these large mass of ordinary people, by their disinterestedness and passivity help evil forces to thrive and take over leadership. Politicians and governments come to power, not so much on the intelligence and the truly patriotic giving support, but on the ignorance, disinterestedness of such people. They do not speak up their minds, do not take part in elections, and live a closed up selfish life. See to what extent the Rajapaksas are able to mislead the ordinary masses!

But who really supported the war when the conflict became a war? The war, in so far it is in consequence of oppression executed by the Sinhalese and suffered by the Tamils, is participated in different ways by each of the communities. For the majority Sinhalese, their government was using its forces fighting the "Tamil terrorists" to keep the country as a truly Sinhala Buddhist country without losing a part of the land or its power over the island. Their support was only passive, especially from the poor who sacrificed their sons joining the army and dying in the far away North in fighting "Tamil terrorists". But the major support for the war led by the government came from foreign funds and weapons won by false propaganda of the Government. Whereas for the Tamils, who were targeted as threats to the country, and war was thrust upon them by long years of state-terrorism, the Tamil youth joining the LTTE were fighting in self-defense of their homeland and people. Thus it was not a war between two states or equal forces. One side was supported by the whole world through its misunderstanding whereas the other side was fighting in self-defense using its own children and its own resources.

But the government claiming to fight Tamil-terrorism received aid and weapons and succeeded in wiping out the LTTE and thousands of civilians. Basking in the sunshine of a victory, the Government and people are refusing to render accountability to the very donors of finance and weapons for the alleged war-crimes and not caring for the victims even after four years after the war ended.

At least now, what prevents the majority people from common sense and reasoning? The majority Sinhalese still suffer from "a minority-complex ". Of being threatened by those around namely, the Tamils. Hence the need to attack – a pre-emptive attack on the imagined enemy! Power hungry politicians find the Mahavamsa chronicle to be very useful to keep the masses with them by preaching Tamil-threats to Sinhala-Buddhist existence. Why are the Rajapaksas encouraging extremist Buddhist monks to further attacks against churches and mosques? It is a shame on all the religious leaders in the South where these attacks are taking place that they have not woken up against injustices and freedom. Self-centered religions and religious leaders commit a crime by their silence in the face of injustice.

Hence true liberation for all will begin when the majority Sinhalese liberate themselves from a Mahavamsa mentality, when power hungry politicians stop whipping up false Sinhala-Buddhist nationalism and when religious leaders become courageous enough to stand up for truth and justice. I wish the rise of at least a few courageous statesmen and religious leaders to lead the Sinhala people, and see the Tamils not as opponents and threats to their race but as co-habitants and cooperators.

Q: What went wrong with the LTTE to face the defeat in the war? What are your views of the reasons for the government's "success"?

A: For both the defeat of the LTTE and for the success of the Government, there was a common reason:
   1. that the international community misunderstood the reasons behind the conflict and the war;
   2. that post-September 11th of politics of the US made a big impact – negatively for the LTTE and positively for the Sri Lanka Government.
   3. The LTTE was banned as a terror organisation and talks with Ranil-Government was derailed by the super powers moving a Washington Conference excluding the LTTE. All super-powers, including India collaborated in crushing LTTE as a pure terrorist-organisation, without any consideration for their political goal.

4. For the Sri Lankan Government unlimited finance and weapons were given by the international community including strong support from India.

Only after the end of the war it became clear to the international donors of finance and weapons:
1. that the war was not simply a war against Tamil terrorism.
2. That the Sri Lankan Government of Rajapaksa will not listen to old friends but new ones who will support a 4-brother-dictatorship on the island and overlook freedoms of the press.
3. That Sri Lanka's war against Tamil terrorism was a cover for their unwillingness to give equal dignity and rights to Tamils and to share power with them.

Hence the defeat of the LTTE and the Success of the Government have to be understood in a wider background, namely, the defeat was a military defeat, true, but the Tamil struggle will continue. Similarly, the success of the government is not the end of the story, it has to prove that they can win the hearts and minds of the surviving Tamils.

Q: The post war situation has exposed Sri Lanka as a failing state due to both legislature and the executive being all out to undermine the independence of the judiciary. Independent judiciary is a must for the much needed freedom and rule of law. In your book, "Let my people go" you have stated: "If peace is conceived as the outcome of doing justice to the truth of realities, then all genuine lovers of peace must at all cost shun untruth and injustice." Bearing this in mind, do you think, the Sri Lankan society has a better understanding of justice, freedom and their personal liberty?

A: Truth, Justice and Peace/Reconciliation are religious values preached by all religions. Any human organisation that overlooks Truth and Justice cannot enjoy peace or reconciliation. One cannot disconnect or change the order of these values. One cannot talk of Truth and Reconciliation, without addressing oneself to justice and its demands. One cannot bury the Truth of past realities and seek peace or reconciliation.

The pre-May2009 situation of war of the Government against Tamil terrorists, helped the Government to cover up or distract attention from its brotherhood-dictatorship and the amassing of wealth by the Rajapaksa clan. Masses, in their euphoria of a victory of the Mahinda and Mahavamsa Chinthanaya, overlooked the deficiencies of democracy in the Government and the building up of the Rajapaksa Empire. But the post-war situation of a victorious –government showed more of its core-corruptions. While they could bull-doze their way into the North and East without any challenge and escalate their military control, Sinhala-settlements, Buddhist temples, commit rape and disappearances with impunity, they needed to guarantee their power among the majority Sinhalese by bringing the legislature and judiciary to suit their needs. Hence the Government using Sinhala-euphoria of a victory of King-Mahinda-Dutugenunu, made serious amendments to the Constitution and handled the Judiciary too with an iron hand. The blame is not totally on the Rajapaksa-clan. What about the parliamentarians elected by the people? Love of power and corruption seemed to have their world-vision and understanding of the values of democracy. The more enlightened sections of the opposition and of the civil society, and the non-Buddhist religious leaders filled with fear –all put together could not bridle the Rajapaksa and his masses to a common-sense path.

Q: Comparative analysis of the political history of Sri Lanka will confirm that the economic revolution progressed is conflicting with the deep rooted feudal system. This conflict has helped evolving an elite class of politicians who are able to manipulate the system of governance for the few. Your take on this please?

A: After 450 years of colonialism, especially as a consequence of British colonialism, power went into the hands of the better-educated and elite. Though there were democratic parties and regular elections, though there were leftist LSSP (Lanka Sama Samaja Party) and CP (Communist Party), the masses were manipulated by the few at the centre. The first post-independence Government of the UNP was one of Colombo-based elites. But soon Mr. SWRD Bandaranaike sought people's power with the help of the Buddhist monks who were grass-root leaders. Thus the elite, this time of the SLFP, were supported by the Buddhist clergy. Getting the support of the Buddhist-clergy from the grass-roots meant accepting their narrow vision of the Mahavamsa that the island is primarily for the Sinhala Buddhists only! All successive Governments used the Mahavamsa mentality and the consequent Sinhala Buddhist extremism for their political success. Governments changed hands by whipping up false-nationalism and fears of the others – the Tamils and the Muslims!

Hence even an insurrection born out of discontent among the youth of the south was brutally put down without addressing the root causes of the discontent. Similarly the rise of the LTTE against racial discriminations has been brutally put down. What we see during the last few years is the worst form of government where a brothers-dictatorship is able to manipulate the masses.

For a change to take place in the upper rungs of power, there should be more "enlightenment" for the Buddhist leadership of the country. The Sri Lankan Buddhism, claiming to be unique, so protestantish and politicsed as to react to other Buddhist leaders of the world like Dalai Lama, has a sacred responsibility to return to the sources of Buddhist teaching, not to exaggerate the Mahavamsa chronicle to replace the Buddhist teachings, tread the path of Truth and compassion and save the island from a national suicide.

Q: Years ago in a discussion meeting with B.R. Ambedkar in Colombo, a Tamil political leader went on to explain the conflict between Sinhalaese and Tamils. Ambedkar's response was: "why Tamils can't convert their religion and become Buddhists, then the conflict will be largely over". I do not subscribe to his assertion and I am against forceful conversions.

A: I heard a few decades ago, reacting to caste-discrimination among Tamils, few hundreds in the Northern peninsula converted themselves overnight to Buddhism. But this conversion did not last long and brought no change in the attitudes of the Tamils. Hence changing religion is no solution to escape discrimination. Instead all believers, including my own, should reform their religions into accepting equality of man and his basic rights.(In my early years as priest, I had to face a hostile crowd in my church for giving equal rights to people getting married in my church!)

All religions have and teach the noble truths of love compassion and brotherhood. But the practice of religion needs courage of convictions which is lacking not only among believers but also among leaders! Religious leaders make use of human beings to enlarge their membership or following. They forget that religions are meant to serve human beings - to love one another and live peacefully.

Q: In law, religion is a basic human right and no one have the right or power to force and convert anyone. But my concern is: "Sinhala Buddhist fundamentalists" ruining the rights of the Tamils including their right to self-determination. Will Sri Lanka ever deal with the fundamentalism of the Buddhist and how this issue should be handled to bring a fairer society in Sri Lanka?

A: I have written and spoken enough as an outsider – a Tamil catholic priest – to identify Sinhala Buddhist fundamentalists as the root cause of the conflict in Sri Lanka (vide Agonies and Aspirations of the Tamil Struggle- Chapter 2). If Buddhists can proclaim and practice equality of all human beings on the island, then there is hope for a bright future. The teachings of Buddha, the enlightened One, must not be overtaken by the teachings of the Mahavamsa! Thic Nacthan – a much respected Vietnamese Buddhist monk in Paris, says "If you want peace, become peace, if you want freedom, become free" How many of our Buddhist monks have peace and freedom in their hearts? Covering their hatred for the non-Buddhists under the cover of a Mahavamsa-promoted patriotism and practicing it as Sinhala Buddhism spells a disaster for the future of this island. I will appeal to my Buddhist brothers to return to the teachings of the Enlightened Buddha as practiced in other lands where Buddhism thrives, and give up this extremist and exclusive vision based purely on the Mahavamsa chronicle written many centuries after Buddha. A return to genuine Buddhist teachings is the hope for a peaceful Sri Lanka.

Q: At the beginning of the Tamil rebellion there was sympathy and support from the right thinking Sinhalese and Muslims, but later this support base disappeared and as a result the Tamils (or even the LTTE) became isolated. This is what happened with the left wing JVP militancy in the south. We lost hundreds of thousands of youth in the counter insurgency operations that helped to create democratic dictatorships under the pretext of democracy. Is there any hope of revolutions and violent rebellions in the future?

A: Militancy is not a luxury of the powerful, but the last resort of the oppressed after having tried non-violent methods without success. I hope and pray that the oppressors- elite and communalists - who have put down violent protests by more violent and unjust ways, sooner realise their mistakes and make amends for them before the cries of the oppressed takes over them.

Militant actions, even for a just cause, have only temporary support from the people depending on how far those militant actions promote their cause or not. LTTE too had those phases. But waxing and waning of support for militant movements, do not justify the conduct of those in power as democratic. Drunk with military success they become sooner or later dictatorial.

In our context of how the Tamil rebellion was put down brutally, there was a long buildup of a hegemonic Sinhala mentality which paved the way for a dictatorial government. Rajapaksa is the result of a long pregnancy, namely, all the political leaders who rode on a Sinhala-Buddhist nationalism of hate and ethnic cleansing of the Tamils.

Q: You are the head of the Global Tamil Forum (GTF). How do you summarise GTF's activities and achievements in the post-war period in the country?

A: GTF is a post-Mullivaikal organisation, set up to coordinate the democratic and non-violent efforts of the Tamil diaspora to help the cause of liberation of the Tamils still surviving in the island of Sri Lanka. The Sri Lankan Government having labelled every Tamil as a terrorist or potential terrorist, and succeeded in getting all Tamil diaspora organisations as terrorist-organisations, saw the GTF also as the remnants of the LTTE. The Government after officially declaring the war against the LTTE as victoriously ended declared a new war against the Tamil diaspora and made propaganda against us. But we remaining non-violent, transparent, democratic and sincerely wishing well for all the peoples of Sri Lanka, have won acceptance and recognition to speak up on the international arena not only on behalf of the Tamils living both within and without Sri Lanka but also for the general welfare of a peaceful Sri Lanka..

After dedicating a good part of my priestly life for educating hundreds of priests at the Kandy Seminary as well as in the Jaffna seminary, I have not taken a leadership role against the welfare of the whole country. My collaborators in the GTF as well as Governments and international institutions with whom we work have understood us. There is nothing in the vision and mission spelt out by the GTF constitution, which spells a threat or hatred to Sri Lanka and its peoples. Our wish is that the progressive forces in the South join hands with us in our common efforts.

Q: There are several Tamil organisations in the Tamil Diaspora in addition to GTF. One of them is the Transnational Government of Tamil Eelam, which is headed by a former LTTE legal representative, Rudrakumaran. His dream is none other than establishing a separate state of Tamil Eelam in Sri Lanka. In his New Year message issued in January, he said: "Let us take necessary steps in 2014 to further isolate the Sri Lankan state in the world arena and march forward towards freedom of the Tamil Nation". Do you think separate state for the Tamils is an achievable objective considering the 30 years of failed violent warfare in Sri Lanka.

A: The call for a separate state was born after 30 years of non-violent and democratic struggle of the Tamils to live as human beings with equal rights and freedom to preserve and foster their ethnic, cultural and religious heritage in their homeland for many centuries. It is the refusal of the basic rights and freedoms of the Tamil people which pushed them to call for a separate state of Tamil Eelam. The second phase of the struggle in which the Sinhala Government and its forces treated the Tamils has strengthened their conviction that only a separate state can guarantee their rights and freedom. The defeat of the militant struggle and the post-Mullivaikal events has only strengthened the convictions of the Tamils about a separate state. The aspirations of a people to survive as a dignified people cannot be defeated or erased easily. Hence the people's struggle for justice and freedom cannot be determined by temporary defeats and losses.

The Tamil struggle to win their human dignity, rights and freedom will continue on many fronts – at home and abroad – *vis a vis* the Sri Lankan Government and *vis a vis* the international community – and by different organisations at different levels because the culprit of our oppression and destruction is primarily the Sri Lankan Government with the help and connivance and omissions of the international community. While those within the island will continue their struggle on the ground *vis a vis* the Government and its supporters, the diaspora organisations will struggle *vis a vis* the international bodies. Thus for the same goal of liberating a people to their dignity and rights as a people on the island, all Tamil organisations will stands.

Q: We now have a Chief Minister for the Northern Provincial Council, who seems to be very provocative and is providing his views on the several issues. He is strongly objecting to the idea of a separate state but asserting on devolution of power under a united Sri Lanka. Is this position acceptable to the GTF and if so will you work with him?

A: The GTF as a diaspora organisation is happily working with the TNA and its provincial government. Mr.C. V. Wigneswaran, becoming the Chief Minister of the Northern Provincial Council, was welcomed by many progressive forces in the South. Of course some among them thought that the man from Colombo with family relationship with Sinhalese will be pliable to their way of thinking. But those who knew him for a longer time knew that he was a man of principle, who spoke out his mind not as a politician, but as a promoter of justice in the society. Some Tamils were unhappy that he was not an experienced politician like Mr. Sambandan. But the unanimous choice of Mr.Wigneswaran by the TNA and the Tamil people, to lead the Provincial Council was a litmus test for the good will of the Government to cooperate with the Tamil leadership for their welfare. Mr. Wigneswaran, unlike Mr. R. Sampanthan who was second to none in making eloquent speeches in Parliament to drive home his arguments for justice to his people, is a strong human and religious being who fearlessly speaks out his convictions and knocks the nails on the head. Without losing his refined personality and giving up his convictions or hiding his intentions, he asks the right questions even from the Emperor. Hence he is not provocative as a politician, but asking questions which need only common-sense answers. Why is the military bending backwards on seeking and recruiting young Tamil women into the army? Why not a Governor without any militaristic but civic background or a Provincial Secretary who can work more with the Province than with the Centre? Why should the Tamils sing the national anthem in Sinhalese? These questions when asked in Parliament, the politicians have way of turning away. But here the Chief Minister is asking in public both the country and the international community.

To dispel the inborn fears among the majority Sinhalese that the Tamils are bent on separatism, and to start a new path to find a peaceful solution to the ethnic conflict, he chose not separatism but living and working within a united Sri Lanka with the right devolution of power. This view is also our view and we too are bending backwards to dispel fears of separatism and seeking a peaceful solution within a united Sri Lanka.

Q: The hot topic these days is the forthcoming UN resolution against Sri Lanka. This is said to be drafted by the United States – a country that contributes heavily to the annual budget of the UN. Some say the resolution passing through is a foregone conclusion. Will the resolution make any difference to Sri Lanka? If it does not what could happen next?

A: The UN and the UNHRC, consisting of 193 nations, though ranking high in keeping peace in the world, are not without weakness and corruption. After the 2nd world war these have served order and peace to a large extent. But they are not free of self-interests and hypocrisies.

The war in Sri Lanka, more than the ethnic conflict, has got internationalised because the Sri Lankan Government presented the ethnic problem as one of terrorism, consequently received international help by LTTE-ban, finance and weapons to crush terrorism. Those international bodies which collaborated with the Sri Lankan Government (over 20 countries helped us, claims Rajapaksa) are now asking a question about accountability for the help given but misused by the Government.

As long as the Government rejects international views, recommendations and offers of help from the international community, Mahinda might retain his power, but we the Sri Lankans are the poorer.

As Tamils, we know the history of those who collaborated with the Government before Mullivaikal and those who in humiliation and in repentance try to rectify past mistakes. Our struggle is led first by the Tamil people and their representatives on the ground, secondly supported by the diaspora and the Tamil Nadu and thirdly by the support given by the super-powers – India, US and Europe – for their own interests.

The final resolution of the conflict towards a peaceful Sri Lanka depends on the horse, you may take to the water, but will it drink?

Q: Certain Tamil political parties are calling for sanctions against Sri Lanka. Do you think it will help the country to find a solution to the problems if the United Nations imposes sanctions?

A: Punishment will never force anyone to do the good that is needed. Neither the UN nor any organisation of the international community can force us to think and change our ways. If any sanctions are imposed, it is the poor masses and not the Rajapaksa clan that will feel the pain. The government has been claiming that new friends will always support them and save them. But this begging to keep their present supporters happy, will be a long time burden on the future generations as well as subjugating the country to new powers.

Q: The government is still considering having South African model peace and reconciliation process. Do you think Sri Lanka is serious about it and if such a peace effort is tried could the problems be solved?

A: The Sri Lankan Government is not at all serious about peace or reconciliation, nor about learning anything useful from the South African experience. When the South African leaders offered their help to find a solution, two years ago, the Sri Lankan Government declined saying that they have learnt lessons from the Norwegian mediation and that they will seek a home-grown solution by themselves. But now with international pressure growing around it, the Sri Lankan Government had thought of a cover-up proposal, namely, to tell the world that they are seriously considering the model of South African Truth and Reconciliation Commission.

The attempt of the Sri Lankan Government to overlook the truth about the conflict and bypass justice and accountability issues by this deceptive cover-up effort to deceive the people and the world will not succeed.

Further, the TRC of South Africa was a post-political solution event, when the black majority took power and equality of races was acknowledged. But in Sri Lanka, the mood and the vision about a true reconciliation are puerile, to say the least. Whom are they trying to deceive? Development, and that too for the Rajapaksa clan and majority, whereby the Tamils are enslaved rather than empowered, cannot be a way to reconciliation. We have not even a real draft for the basics of a political solution – acknowledge the equality and human rights of all human beings on the island, take responsibility for the crimes of the past and show good will in sharing power with non-Sinhala Buddhists.

Q: It is time for us to conclude our interview. We wish you good health and success in your work. Is there anything you would like to touch on before we close?

A: God has given us a paradise island and a mix of ethnic and religious groups to live peacefully and become a model of multiethnic and multi-religious coexistence and collaboration for peace and prosperity. But extremism and fanaticism favoured by the majority and used as a vehicle for political power is ruining this paradise island. I still hope for courageous statesmen and heroic religious leaders to stand up for truth and justice to all that is happening within this small island save it from a national suicide.

The 2014 Geneva resolution is not at all against a people, but an international warning to the present government about the truth of what is happening even four years after the war and calls on the government to stop its war against the Tamils. And by other means, to stop all dictatorial and anti- minority actions and change track by cooperating with the international community in seeking accountability for the crimes committed in the past and seek a sincere way of truth and justice to peace and reconciliation.

As I conclude my interview with you, the Resolution is passed in Geneva with a clear majority agreeing and abstaining. Those who opposed the Resolution and supported Sri Lanka, made many suggestions during the draft-discussions to soften it and finally voted against it. But India sat silently on the fence till the end, gave hope to many that it will go in the way as it did for previous two resolutions, but disappointed many of us not only by abstaining but by its speech going along with Pakistan- a crisscross of self-interests!

I hope and pray that the Sri Lankan Government cooperates as much as possible with the Resolution of the UNHRC. I hope it will grasp a new chance to win credibility and respectability in the international community, bow down to the search for Truth and to the demands of Truth for justice and accountability.

March 30, 2014

EPILOGUE

DEMOCRACY AND MEDIA FREEDOM

by LAKSIRI FERNANDO

IT was just few days ago I was thinking that what keeps democracy mostly alive in any country perhaps is the free Media and the brave journalists. Otherwise, democracy would be dead as a doornail. The occasion was when the AFP raided the *Channel 7* office in Sydney and searched evidence to see whether the TV outfit paid money to the convicted drug trafficker in Bali (Indonesia), Schapelle Corby, to solicit an interview through illegal means. The raid was massive and unprecedented.

Almost all the journalists and the media outlets were up in arms against this raid and eventually the AFP had to make a studded apology. It was not that the investigation was illegal or unwarranted, but the raid was highhanded and overawe.

It is also not that the media or the journalists are all flawless. More than that, what comes to my mind is the News International phone hacking scandal and related events. These are mainly done by the media giants in cohort with businesses or the state and again the free media and the free journalists are the surest safeguards against these deviations in a democracy apart from the rule of law and the judiciary.

Situation in Sri Lanka

This is what is terribly lacking in Sri Lanka at present. In January 2009, few months before the routing of the LTTE, Lasantha Wickrematunge, the renowned Editor of the *Sunday Leader* newspaper was assassinated broad day light, and he was not the only journalist who faced the same or similar fate during that period. Nilantha Ilangamuwa, the author/editor of this useful and vivid collection of interviews with an array of renowned journalists, academics, specialists on human rights, defense matters and international law, was forced to leave the country eventually thereafter. Nilantha was not the only one to face this unfortunate predicament and leave the country for voluntary exile, 'disastrously' depriving the country of a crème of committed journalists on the spot in the country.

I use the term 'disastrously' in its true meaning because the media situation in Sri Lanka at present is quite depressing or rather oppressive, most of the journalists are being forced to trail the line of the government, willingly or unwillingly; directly or indirectly. This is nothing against their integrity or competence, but about their predicament or at times helplessness. What can counter such a situation to an extent is the advancements in information technology – websites, social media, electronic newspapers and journals etc. - however keeping in mind that the 'enemies of freedom' also use the same means and same technology and the authorities also have various ways of blocking or curtailing the flow of information and ideas through these channels.

Nilantha and his efforts have mostly been in the arena of this 'countering.' He is fortunately not alone in this venture as a Sri Lankan, and also there are and will be many in the international community and the international free media movement who would appreciate his and others' efforts in these countering and extend a helping hand in a true spirit of internationalism, freedom and democracy. This valuable Anthology of Interviews in itself is a reflection of this solidarity. I was pleasantly surprised to see the interviews given by so many Indian and Pakistani, and international experts, along with the concerned Sri Lankan academics and activists.

Importance of Freedom

It is quite fitting that this Anthology begins by the interview given by Nilantha Ilangamuwa himself to *Salem News* in April 2012 nicely captioned "Public Awakening against Injustice." It traces how he came into journalism, what were his social values transcending the ethnic divide, how he came to lock horns with the authorities, and how he ventured onto start the *Sri Lankan Guardian*, first in Sri Lanka and then abroad, after its banning inside the country. This brings me back to my departure point of this short and hurriedly written Epilogue: the importance of the free media and the necessity of brave (not adventurist) journalists for the protection and promotion of democracy in any country. Or otherwise, democracy will be dead as a doornail. May I also add 'human rights' to the agenda of democracy now?

When the Council of Europe commissioned a publication on *"Media and Democracy"* in 1998, its Secretary General, Daniel Tarschys, said the following.

> *"There can be no democracy without freedom of expression, as anyone keeps abreast of the news will know. The never-ending list of people – journalists, writers and others – who are threatened, persecuted or even killed for daring to express inconvenient or dissenting political views is a sad confirmation of this fact."*

He laid down the principle, and the connection between democracy and the freedom of the media. That was not all. Many people seem to believe that democracy or the freedom of the media is an issue only in the developing or the Third World countries. That is not the case. Having lived for considerable years in several Western countries, it is my experience that, while the conditions are far, or far-far, better than in the developing countries, there is a constant threat to democracy and/or to the freedom of the media even in these societies. Tarschys also made this point clearly:

267

"Europe may appear protected from totalitarianism of the mind, but other dangers may be present which can undermine the very foundations of our democracies. The pressure and violence to which journalists are exposed when they denounce corruption and crime, the insidious control exercised by governments anxious to silence non-conformist voices — these are painful reminders that the battle for freedom of expression is never entirely won."

The reason for this equation between the developed and the underdeveloped countries, or all countries together, perhaps is the very nature of the State as an institution, and its perennial coercive character, which has penetrated into politics or power politics in almost all countries. As a predicament of this situation, we tend to understand and interpret politics as a 'power game,' whether in the developing or the developed countries. Even in my own academic field of Political Science, politics is interpreted as a Science of Power. We are also the prisoners of this interpretation or understanding. Until our outlook/s and interpretation/s change we might not have full liberation from the existing oppressive structures and concomitant violence or violations. Thus we are not in a position to talk about 'full' media freedom or 'full' freedom of expression; and most importantly 'full' democracy. If you are not satisfied with the idealistic term 'full' in the previous sentence, you may substitute it with 'higher' to mean at least we should aspire for better conditions.

It appears that the 'progressive' media and the journalists have taken the first necessary steps in this direction or liberation in the modern era. It has been a long time and the struggle is still continuing or unfinished. I use the qualification or the adjective 'progressive' instructively, because there are always the other media and the journalists who are the defenders of the status quo, the power politics and the oppressive systems. The word 'progressive' might not be the adequate term, but what I mean is those media and those journalists who struggle for and uphold justice. Though unconsciously, they want to interpret politics in terms of justice and not in terms of power alone. Justice therefore comes or should come to the center stage.

An Overview

Throughout history, freedom of thought and expression seem to have had two main purposes or functions. First one was to ascertain the truth on a particular matter as much as possible. The second one was to achieve justice, transitional or ultimate, reasonable to all stakeholders on a given situation. In ancient times, the Buddha was an exponent of the freedom of thought and expression particularly on the first count. According to Ven. Walpola Rahula (*What the Buddha taught?*), the Buddha has said,

> *"Yes, Kalamas, it is proper that you have doubt, that you have perplexity, for a doubt has arisen in a matter which is doubtful. Now look you Kalamas, do not be led by reports, or tradition, or hearsay....And when you know for yourselves that certain things are wholesome and good, then accept them and follow them."*

Of course the Buddha has said the above in respect of religious matters and doctrines. However, it is relevant and applicable to all matters in respect of ascertaining the truth. This was also more or less the position of the Vedas, the Upanishads or the essence of the Greek philosophy in ancient times.

However, it is from the beginning of the modern era, after a long span of bigotry in the Middle Ages, that the freedom of thought and expression started to take a stronger expression with the advent of democratic revolutions in England, France and America. The same way of thinking started to spread into other continents much later. The Indian freedom struggle, for example, was an arena where the freedom of thought and expression became resurrected again for the purpose of justice in a different cultural context. The landmarks of these developments were long and arduous and what can be gleaned at here are some glimpses.

When John Locke talked about 'life, liberty and property,' he was most explicitly incorporating freedom of thought and expression within the rubric of liberty. Without freedom of thought and expression, liberty of the person does not make any sense. Locke was also a primary mover who pushed the concept as a 'natural right' and what we today understand or categorize as a 'human right.' This angle of our understanding of the freedom of thought and expression became both enlarged and concretized by the French thinkers. If we take a more cautious view of Voltaire, although it might not be correct to say that he himself said it, what is attributed to him as "I disapprove of what you say, but I will defend to the death your right to say it" captures his actual attitude towards the freedom expression.

One of the most concrete forms of this development came in the form of the First Amendment to the American Constitution in 1791. I am here not appreciating its application or practice particularly in the context of what happened in recent times to the whistleblower Edward Snowden. But the incorporation of this right in the constitution was a landmark that needs to be emphasized. Among other things, it says, the "Congress shall make no law ... abridging the freedom of speech, or of the press..." There are many constitutions in the world including Sri Lanka that theoretically uphold the freedom of thought, expression and the press. But the practice of that right or the rights would depend on the way the journalists, writers, academics, intellectual and the people exercise or assert that right.

This Anthology

The purpose of my detour was in fact to emphasize the importance of the Anthology that Nilantha has complied. This Epilogue is not at all a review or summary of the Anthology. However, it is fitting to note that it ends with the ever important interview given by Fatou Bensouda, the Chief Prosecutor of the International Criminal Court (ICC) on the title "No One is above the Law." This interview clarifies many matters and misconceptions related to the legal mandate and the work of the ICC for those who seek international justice where and when national justice is not forth coming or fails to do so in respect of what she has termed as "massive crimes."

The message of this Anthology from top to bottom is one. The matters of justice, democracy or human rights do not any longer confined to national boundaries. They seep through the national borders and cry for international solidarity and cooperation. Those who fail to understand these new vistas are doomed to fail sooner or later. This message is communicated through primarily a Sri Lankan reality on which many interviewees or authors have expressed their multifaceted opinions.

March 1, 2014
Sydney, Australia

Laksiri Fernando, *BA (Ceylon), MA (New Brunswick) and PhD (Sydney), is former Professor of Political Science and Public Policy, University of Colombo (2000-2010), and thereafter a Visiting Scholar at the University of Sydney (2011-2013). He has previously served as Secretary for Asia/Pacific of the World University Service (WUS) in Geneva (1984-1991), also in charge of WUS' human rights program, and Director of the Diplomacy Training Program (DTP), University of New South Wales, Australia (1995-97), among other positions. He has over thirty years of university teaching experience both in Sri Lanka and abroad. His teaching and research encompass the areas of human rights, labor studies, ethnic conflicts, nationalism and constitutionalism. His main specialty however is human rights with a regional focus on South and Southeast Asia. He is a regular contributor to the Sri Lankan media. His major publications include "Human Rights, Politics and States: Burma, Cambodia and Sri Lanka;" "Academic Freedom 1990;" "Police-Civil Relations for Good Governance;" "Sri Lanka's Ethnic Conflict in the Global Context" and "Political Science Approach to Human Rights." His newest publication is "Thomas More's Socialist Utopia and Ceylon (Sri Lanka)."*

ABOUT THE AUTHOR

Nilantha Ilangamuwa is a journalist, editor and the founder of the *Sri Lanka Guardian,* an online daily newspaper which has operated since 2007. He also an editor of *Torture: Asian and Global Perspectives*, a bi-monthly print magazine. Ilangamuwa writes frequently on Sri Lanka.

Previous book

Nagna Balaya (The Naked Power)
ISBN: 978-1495340215

www.ingramcontent.com/pod-product-compliance
Lightning Source LLC
Chambersburg PA
CBHW070411290526
45791CB00005B/1705